Coinage in the Low Countries (880–1500)

The Third Oxford Symposium on Coinage and Monetary History

edited by

N. J. Mayhew

BAR International Series 54

1979

B.A.R.

B.A.R., 122 Banbury Road, Oxford OX2 7BP, England

B.A.R. International Series 54, 1979: "Coinage in the Low Countries, 880-1500"

ISBN 9780860540489 paperback

ISBN 9781407348452 e-book

DOI https://doi.org/10.30861/9780860540489

A catalogue record for this book is available from the British Library

This book is available at www.barpublishing.com

CONTENTS

PREFACE

Marc Bloch once observed with some justice that 'the study of numismatics has had difficulty in emerging from the world of museum displays and curiosity shops.' The Third Oxford Symposium on Coinage and Monetary History in the Low Countries, like its two predecessors on English and Scottish medieval numismatics, was held as part of a deliberate policy to bring about such an emergence. To this end historians and numismatists were invited to join in lectures and discussions in the Coin Room at the Ashmolean and at Wolfson College over a three day weekend in September 1978. On this occasion we were concerned not so much with the details of numismatic classification as with the application of all kinds of numismatic and monetary evidence to the problems of economic and political history.

This is a large topic deliberately interpreted in its widest sense. Moreover, by 'Low Countries' we meant not merely Belgium, Luxemburg and the Netherlands, but also adjacent territories in France and Germany. So the papers which follow do not attempt a comprehensive monetary history, but rather a series of studies hopefully of interest both to numismatist and historian.

Most of the papers printed here are substantially the versions read at the Symposium. In one case we are happy to publish a much longer essay than there was time to read. In another case only a résumé of the full paper is printed. The two papers read in French are here accompanied by close English translations.

N. J. M.

LIST OF ABBREVIATIONS

ADN	Archives départementales du Nord (Lille)
ARA	Algemeen Rijksarchief (België)
ASAN	Annales de la Société Archéologique de Namur
BAR	British Archaeological Reports
BNJ	British Numismatic Journal
BSFN	Bulletin de la Société Française de Numismatique
CCR	Calendars of the Close Rolls
CEH	Cambridge Economic History
CENB	Cercle d'Etudes Numismatiques. Bulletin
CPR	Calendars of the Privy Rolls
EcHR	Economic History Review
GNB	Gazette Numismatique (Louvain)
HBN	Hamburger Beiträge zur Numismatik
Jnl. of Econ. Hist.	Journal of Economic History
Mitt. d. Bayer Num. Gesell.	Mitteilungen der Bayerischen Numismatischen Gesellschaft
PSAS	Proceedings of the Society of Antiquaries of Scotland
RBN	Revue Belge de Numismatique et de Sigillographie
RN	Revue Numismatique

LIST OF PARTICIPANTS

E. Besley, Esq.,
Research Assistant, Department of Coins and Medals, British Museum.

Professor Wim Blockmans,
Fakulteit der Sociale Wetenschappen, Erasmus Universiteit, Rotterdam.
Postbus 1738, Rotterdam.

J. D. Brand, Esq.,
(Director of the British Numismatic Society),
5 Ridley Road, Rochester, Kent, MB1 1UL.

M. Pierre Cockshaw,
(Bibliothèque Royale de Belgique),
Avenue Puccini 99, 1070 Bruxelles.

D. J. Crowther, Esq.,
Department of Coins and Medals, Sotheby Parke Bernet & Co.,
34-35 New Bond Street, London W1A 2AA.

M. Harry Dewit,
(Secrétaire-adjoint, Société royale de numismatique de Belgique),
Tervuurse Vest 21, app. 19/F, 3030 Heverlee, Belgium.

M. M. Dhenin,
Conservateur au Cabinet des Médailles, Bibliothèque Nationale,
58 rue Richelieu, 75084 Paris.

Mme. Françoise Dumas-Dubourg,
Conservateur au Cabinet des Médailles, Bibliothèque Nationale,
58 rue Richelieu, 75084 Paris.

Professor dr. H. Enno Van Gelder,
Directeur, Koninklijk Penningkabinet, Zeestraat 71b, 's-Gravenhage.

M. et Mme. Hubert Frère-Thulliez (M. Frère est Maître de Conférences aux Universités de Louvain et de Liège),
rue de la Province, 15, B-4100 Seraing.

Mr. H. W. Jacobi,
wet Ambtenaar, Koninklijk Penningkabinet, Zeestraat 71b, 's-Gravenhage.

Dr. C. M. Kraay,
Keeper of the Heberden Coin Room, Ashmolean Museum, Oxford OX1 2PH.

N. J. Mayhew, Esq.,
Assistant Keeper, Heberden Coin Room, Ashmolean Museum, Oxford OX1 2PH.

Dr. D. M. Metcalf,
Assistant Keeper, Heberden Coin Room, Ashmolean Museum, Oxford OX1 2PH.

Professor J. H. A. Munro,
Department of Political Economy, University of Toronto, 100 St. George St.,
Toronto M5S 1A1, and Associate Director of the Centre for Medieval Studies,
University of Toronto.

J. Porteous, Esq.,
52 Elgin Crescent, London W11.

Peter J. Seaby, Esq.,
B. A. Seaby Ltd., Audley House, 11 Margaret St., London W1N 8AT.

Dr. P. Spufford,
Department of History, University of Keele, Keele, Staffordshire ST5 5BG.

Mme. Marie-Rose Desmed-Thielemans,
(Chargé de cours au Seminaire d'Histoire Contemporaine, Université Libre
de Bruxelles), 171 chaussée de Drogenbos, 1180 Bruxelles.

Dr. E. Van Cauwenberghe,
Department of History, University of Leuven,
and Wilgestraat 25, 2580 Sint-Kateligne-Waver, Belgium.

Professor Dr. H. Van Der Wee,
University of Leuven and 2 Meulestraat, B-2778, Sint-Pauwels, Belgium.

M. Rene Warzeggers,
Wakkerzeelsebaan 44, 3010 Wilsele, Belgium.

D. R. Walker, Esq.,
General Editor, B.A.R., 122 Banbury Road, Oxford OX2 7BP.

M. G. Welch, Esq.,
Lecturer in Medieval Archaeology, Department of History,
University College, London.

P. Woodhead, Esq.,
(President of the British Numismatic Society), 65 Aldsworth Avenue,
Goring-by-Sea, Worthing, Sussex BN12 4XG.

COINAGE AND THE RISE OF THE FLEMISH TOWNS

D. M. Metcalf

Henri Pirenne attached considerable importance to Flanders in his analysis of European development. After centuries of agrarian self-sufficiency and regional isolation in north-western Europe during the dark ages, the stimulus to growth came initially from the revival of commerce and urban life. The Flemish towns provided Pirenne with telling illustrations of his thesis that the revival of towns after the dislocations caused by the Vikings owed almost nothing to continuity from earlier ages, but was rather the product of a new conjunction between the fortified castles of feudal princes, and the communities of long-distance merchants which grew up in the shelter of their protection. Under the joint stimulus of commerce and of an ancient woollen industry Flanders benefitted from its location at one of the nodal points of European north-south trade - an advantage which Provence and the north Italian cities similarly enjoyed, and which was to be shared by the fairs of Champagne, roughly half-way along the north-south routes. Because these regions had precociously outstripped the rest of Europe in their urban and commercial reawakening, industry followed, and they soon began to enjoy the advantages of being in the lead, in a period of sustained growth and prosperity. Flanders also enjoyed an exceptional density of population.[1]

Pirenne's thoughts on the wider significance of Flanders began to crystallize more than seventy years ago, in his articles "Villes, marchés, et marchands au moyen âge" and "Les villes flamandes avant le XIIe siècle."[2] Since then a very extensive literature has grown up in the shelter, as one might say, of his thesis. Its propositions have been elaborated unceasingly.[3] The thesis has become something of an industry in itself. Pirenne, who taught at the University of Ghent, often returned to the topic of the Flemish towns in his magisterial writings of half a century.

Weighty additions have been made to the numismatic evidence in the last twenty-five years, for example by Walter Hävernick on the general interpretation of the flow of coinage between Germany and northern and eastern Europe;[4] by Gunther Albrecht on the coinage of Lower Lotharingia and Frisia from the tenth to the early twelfth centuries;[5] by Fernand Vercauteren on early monetary circulation in Belgium;[6] by Hubert Frère on Carolingian coins minted in Belgium;[7] by Joseph Ghyssens on the coinage of Flanders in the twelfth and thirteenth centuries;[8] and by Gert Hatz on the Swedish Viking-age material.[9] These researches have not yet been as carefully integrated with the economic history of the Low Countries, and have not perhaps been as widely understood, as they deserve to be. The particular value of the Scandinavian and Baltic finds lies in the fact that they offer comparative information about monetary development in a period from which systematic evidence is otherwise not to be found. Historians have had to generalise, often, from fragmentary records, and without the benefit of the statistical series which would have helped to show whether the outlines they had sketched were in the correct proportion. Pirenne noted, for example, that coins struck by the counts of Flanders Arnould II and Baudouin IV (965-1035) have been found in Denmark, Prussia and even in Russia. This was information of a sort, but it is purely incidental in character. We are now in a position to state much more exactly what percentage the early Flemish coins make up among the finds from the Baltic regions. It is a minute fraction of one per cent. To the numismatist, consequently, the idea that Flanders enjoyed any kind of pre-eminence, or that it was in the lead in the late tenth or early eleventh centuries, would be quite astonishing, indeed one may as well say frankly incredible. Rather it seems that, because the Flemish towns have been so intensively studied, they have loomed larger, and have assumed a greater retrospective importance in our ideas about European economic development in the tenth and eleventh centuries than they deserve to do on a more balanced view.

Albrecht prepared an index of the relative intensity of minting of places in Lower Lotharingia from the late tenth to the early twelfth centuries. The revival of commerce and a growing monetary circulation eventually led to the creation of some 60-65 mints in the duchy, of which only 9 or 10, and those by no means the most important, were in Flanders. Their combined score, based on the number of finds divided by the length of time the mints were open, is about 2.5. On the same scale, Köln scores 50, that is a minting activity twenty times as intense. Tiel, Deventer, Groningen, Dokkum, and Leeuwarden together score over 70, an activity nearly thirty times as intense. It would seem that they were sharing a role as frontier mints, which in the early Carolingian period had belonged to such places as Wijk-bij-Duurstede and Maastricht. One must assume that much of the silver they minted was money coming back to Europe from the north, to purchase manufactured goods. The numbers of hoard-coins recorded by Albrecht from each mint are shown in Table 1, and the same information is presented in a map, Fig. 1. Hatz provides similar but less detailed information based exclusively on an up-to-date survey of the Swedish find-material, among which the north Frisian issues are a little less plentiful (Table 1), but which otherwise coincides quite closely with Albrecht's wider survey.

As well as the contrast between Flanders on the one hand and Cologne and the northern Netherlands on the other, there is a clear contrast between Flanders and the Meuse valley. Along the Meuse, industry (including metal-working) may have been more developed than in Flanders; and the river route-way may have helped to foster trade.

A radical criticism of the information summarized in Fig. 1 would suggest that the contrasts are not a true reflection of different intensities of mint-output, but merely show that the coins of some mints reached Scandinavia in quantity, while those from elsewhere did not. The Flemish coins, it might be argued, either stayed at home, or were carried southwards rather than eastwards, but in any case the evidence from the Viking world offers no justification for asserting that the currency of Flanders was relatively insignificant. To offer such criticism is to take a stand upon a rather extreme position. If the eastern trade could penetrate the length of the Meuse valley, and carry

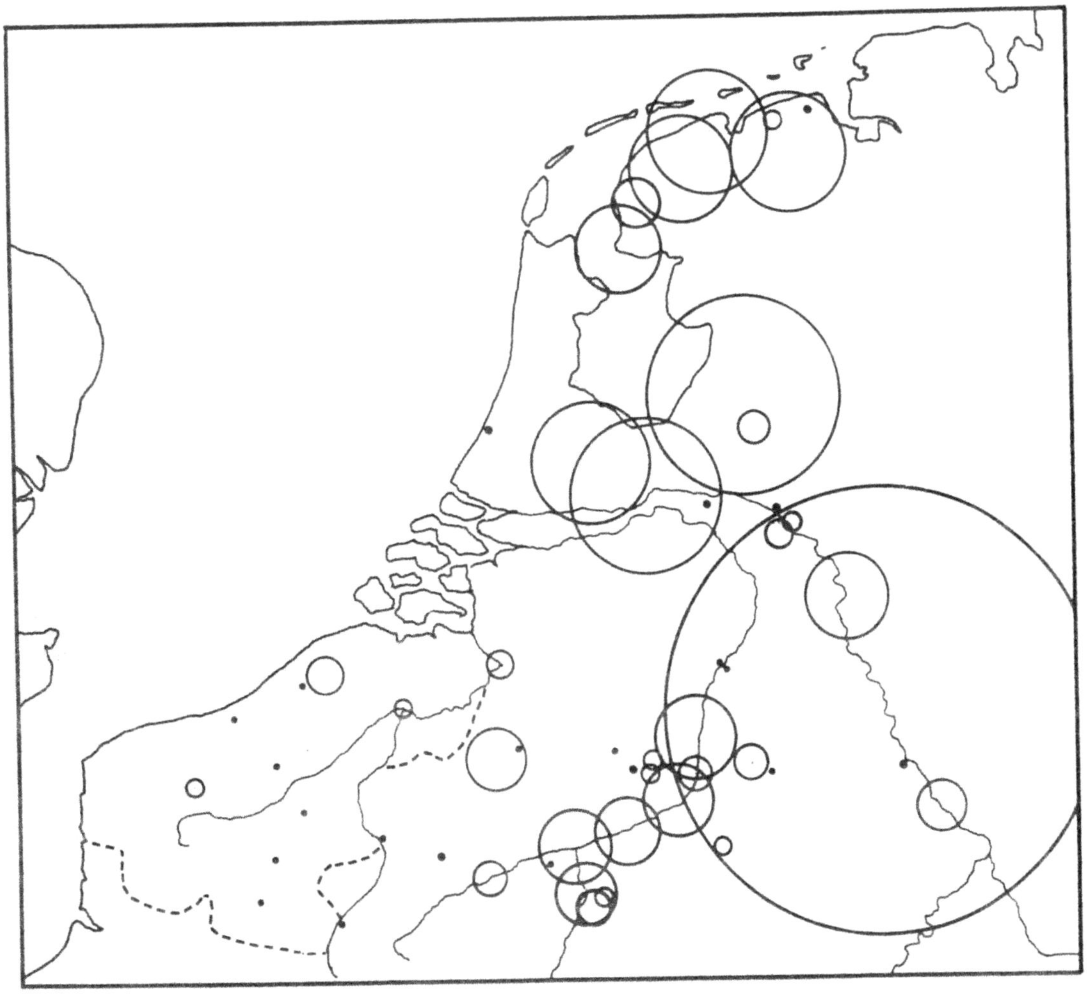

FIG. 1

its influence up the Rhine to Cologne, it is difficult to see why it should have stopped short of Bruges and Ghent so abruptly. But the criticism is in principle an important one, and it deserves to receive an answer from numismatists. Evidence exists, quite independently of the Scandinavian statistics, for the volume of mint-output: the numbers of dies used at each mint can be estimated from the frequency with which die-duplicates occur in a random selection of coins (not, for example, in a single hoard). Hatz's corpus of the Tiel mint shows that great numbers of different dies were used there. For Flanders, the work remains to be done; and, because of the careless manufacture of the coins, it will be difficult to achieve precision. But the historical interest of the result should encourage numismatists to do what they can.

Even when the deficiencies of the Scandinavian statistics have been disposed of, the comparative intensity of mint-output in different towns is, of course, not necessarily an accurate index of the towns' relative size or even of their relative commercial importance. It may also reflect the output of newly-mined silver, for example the prolific Otto-Adelheid coinage from the Harz mountains, the directions of inter-regional flows of bullion, the balance of payments, the enforcement or otherwise by the political authorities of the re-minting of foreign coins at the frontier, an economic choice to carry silver to a distant mint where it could be coined more advantageously, and so on. Nevertheless, the numismatic evidence as regards the rise of Flanders is, in a negative sense, so dramatic that it should not be ignored.

English coins in Swedish finds outnumber Flemish again, by 80 to 1. If Flanders was in the forefront of European economic development in the eleventh century, its importance is most certainly not reflected in its surviving coinage. It could be, of course, that Flanders, like France, lay too far west to receive much of the return current of silver flowing back again from Scandinavia and the Baltic, and which was evidently reminted on re-entry into western Europe. But the stimulus of long-distance trade and commerce is precisely what Pirenne claimed put Flanders ahead.

After being driven out of England in 879, a Viking army invaded Flanders, occupied the valley of the Scheldt, and devastated the whole region for some five years. Their raids continued intermittently until 892.[10] Baudouin II (883-918), having survived the Viking onslaught in the earlier part of his reign, rebuilt his castellum at Bruges, and began the work of reconstructing the region's prosperity and of expanding the territorial limits of the (already considerable) marquisate of Flanders.[11] The 890s, then, mark a new beginning. It has been widely accepted on the basis of numismatic evidence that the striking of coinage virtually ceased in Lower Lotharingia at about this date, and resumed only gradually and on a small scale after a blank period varying in length from a decade or two at some mints to a century and a half at others. Some of the Carolingian mints did not return to activity, the towns in which they were sited never having recovered from the dislocations of the Viking assault. Tournai, for example, was largely destroyed in 881, the inhabitants fled, and did not return until c. 910-11.[12]

This view of a general correspondence between monetary affairs and an economic dark age is, of course, broadly true. The Vikings were above all hungry for cash, and they did their best to extort all the moveable wealth that was to be had from Flanders. The currency of the region as it was in the years up to 879 is well illustrated by the hoards of Muizen-lez-Malines and of Zelzate.[13] It was still dominated by deniers of the "temple" type, inscribed XPISTIANA RELIGIO. All that money went in Danegeld, ransoms, pillage, and unrecovered hoards. The currency that we see in the years when Flanders was emerging from its tribulation is completely new and different.

So although there was a break in the currency, there was not an immediate end to minting. The apparatus and traditions of the earlier coinage survived the years 879-84, and were appropriated by Baudouin II. He continued to strike silver deniers of Carolingian aspect for at least a few years, for reasons that we are in no position to judge without knowing the exact dates of the coins. Were they struck for the payment of tribute, - for political and military purposes; or were the mints simply working normally, supplying merchants and other private customers who chose to call on their services? Did they continue after the final departure of the Vikings in 892? Our understanding of what happened in the tenth century has been hindered, as regards the life of the towns, by an almost complete absence of documentation, and as regards the issue and circulation of coinage, by anonymous issues which do not tell us either the date or even the ruler's name or the mint-place, and by the complete absence of hoards from Flanders. On both sides of the argument the evidence is extremely fragmentary, and our attempts to correlate x with y can therefore only be tentative.

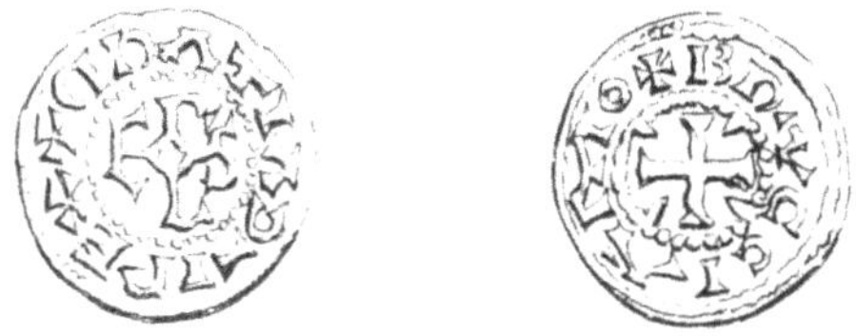

FIG. 2. Denier of the Bruges mint, of the variety which occurred in the Assebroek hoard. Obv. Karolus-monogram, GRATIA D-I REX. Rev. Cross. BRUCCIA MO.

First, the evidence of post-Carolingian continuity under Baudouin II, at Bruges and Ghent; and then at Arras. From the mint of Bruges, which Albrecht and other writers have supposed to have been inactive from at the latest 875, there are in fact numerous coins, represented for example in the Cuerdale hoard,[14] which Frère attributes to the time of Charles le Simple, and thus in effect to Baudouin II,[15] although the legal fiction may have been respected. The Assebroek hoard, found in 1858, contained 139 deniers of the mint of Bruges all of this late variety (see Fig. 2), along with 48 deniers of Arras, and 13 oboles of Quentovic and 4 of St. Denis.[16] This precious document illustrating a localized monetary circulation in northern Flanders, linked to just a few other trade centres, was carefully described by Serrure, although without the full photographic record that it would be thought to merit today. Lacking that record we cannot say how many dies were used at the Bruges mint, nor even whether the conjectured date of deposit (during the 890s or perhaps later) is exact. The relatively low weight[17] and poor alloy of the coins was noticed. Assebroek is in the suburbs of Bruges, and in that respect the hoard illustrates Pirenne's thesis rather neatly.

Similar, but increasingly blundered, coins deriving from the Bruges type of Charles le Simple and presumed to have been minted there have been found in numerous Scandinavian hoards, ranging in date from the Gerete find concealed after 991, and onwards for the next thirty or forty years. Hatz has interpreted them as a Flemish type immobilisé, dateable approximately to 930-60 or later.[18] Rather than a complete end to minting because of the severe dislocation caused by the Vikings, then, it would seem more accurate to speak of a modest continuity associated with Baudouin II and his successors at Bruges.[19] As regards the location of minting within Flanders, this is already a more political than economic explanation of the coinage. We are in no position to date the coins precisely, and therefore cannot assess the degree to which minting was sporadic. But it should eventually be possible to estimate the scale of issue of the blundered copies, from the numbers of dies that were used.

What can one say about the mint of Ghent? Like Bruges, it came into existence after 864 and, apparently, was closed by 875.[20] It is tempting to see the appearance of these two quite active mints in the years around 870 as a single phenomenon, and to link them with the figure of Baudouin I. Count Baudouin was not an independent feudal lord, but rather an administrative official of the Carolingian Empire,[21] and there is no evidence to show that he usurped the rights or exercised any unusual control over the coinage. We may nevertheless suspect that his influence lies behind the new monetary impetus at Bruges and Ghent, just as one can detect the regional influence of strong ealdormen in the royal coinage of Anglo-Saxon England.[22] Ghent may have been the main centre in Baudouin's territories,[23] or at least the equal of Bruges, but it seems to have lost its importance following the Viking occupation of the town in 879-80.[24] Few if any coins were struck after that date, but it would be rash to assert categorically that the type of Charles le Chauve did not become immobilized. Specimens of a variety with a long-armed central cross and the blundered mint-name GVVDANΛM (for Gandavum) weigh only 1.41 and 1.47 g.[25] The crux is that one similar to these occurred in the Glisy hoard, which seems to be from later than 892.[26]

Roughly contemporary with the Assebroek hoard is another from Arras, which must belong at least several years after 888 since it includes 59 coins of Eudes (888-98) from a variety of mints. The year 891, when the Vikings occupied Amiens for some months, is a possible date.[27] The southern districts, over which Baudouin II and Arnould I were later to extend their control, were not as severely affected by the Viking raids as the Scheldt valley and the north. Out of almost 500 coins, 200 are of the local mint of Arras, but numerous other Carolingian mints are represented in small quantities.

When monetary circulation was so localized, it is difficult to establish comparisons between the mints of Arras and Bruges. Hawkins listed 4 coins of Arras in the Cuerdale hoard, and 4 of Bruges, as against one each of Boulogne, St. Omer, and Cambrai.[28]

FIG. 3. Deniers of the Arras mint, dating perhaps from the early tenth century. Obv. Degenerate Eudes-monogram (ODDO). IRATIA D⊣I EX. Rev. Cross. ATREBAS CIVI.

The later history of the mint of Arras is problematic. The town was sacked at Christmas 880, when quantities of booty were taken.[29] But it was fortified between the years 885 and 890,[30] and there are coins of Eudes in neat Carolingian style which are in all probability later in date than the new defenses.[31] (To confuse the matter, they have in the past been quite erroneously attributed to Hugues Capet, c. 987-8. There is no reason to believe that he minted at Arras.[32]) There are also two blundered pieces in the name of Eudes (Fig. 3), which on the basis of their fabric and style Poey d'Avant was prepared to consider a good deal later in date than the end of the ninth century.[33] Dating on the basis of style is however tricky, and these two coins are not much more blundered - a little more, but not much - than a coin of the name of Charles from the Cuerdale hoard (thus barely into the tenth century), which has the characteristic square C in the *Karolus* monogram.[34] *Prima facie*, the sequence of issues seems to alternate between prototypes, although this is not a reading of the evidence that any numismatist will accept very happily. It certainly extends into the time of Baudouin II, and possibly even into the tenth century. The chronology of types immobilisés will as usual be be difficult to establish, but a detailed and coordinated study of dies, weights, and alloy may suggest answers. Richebé admits the possibility that Arnould I may have struck coins at Arras or at Saint-Omer[35] between 932 and 964.[36] If he did, which is on the whole improbable, the type immobilisé of Eudes is perhaps the most likely to be his. Saint-Omer, incidentally, seems to be a new mint set up after the Viking occupation of Flanders.[37] The place was fortified, apparently in the 880s, when a systematic effort was made to strengthen the coastal *burchten*, several of which at that date still sat on coastal spits, isolated from the mainland by undrained marshes.[39] The process may be compared with the creation of the Alfredian burhs in England. Later in the tenth century, each English burh was provided with a mint; this did not happen in Flanders.

If we turn now to the post-Carolingian coinages of the tenth century, it is to find that the numismatic problems are if possible even more intractable, for the coins are often unsigned, undated, and without a mint-name. As an analogous example, Liège began by striking imitations of the coins of Köln, and then modified the design by substituting the town name *Ledgia* for *Colonia*.[40] If it were not for the continuity of type and style between the two varieties, the attribution of the direct imitations would obviously be exceedingly difficult.

FIG. 4. Denier probably of the Brussels mint, *c*. 965-94. *Obv*. Cross. HLVDOVVICVS (IMP) *Rev*. S/COLONIA/A, blundered legend around.

Many Swedish hoards contain examples of another imitative coinage (see Fig. 4) copying a Köln type of Otto I and archbishop Bruno (962-5), which Hatz, following Albrecht, is inclined to give to Flanders. Baerten has, on the other hand, argued that these are the earliest coins of Brussels, minted *c*. 965 and giving way after 994 to similar coins signed BROCSA - a development exactly parallel to that at Liège.[41] Their average weight is 0.75-0.80 g.[42]

There are other less plentiful anonymous coinages from the end of the tenth century and later, which from their style have been tentatively identified as Flemish.[43]

From Arras there are coins in the name of Lothaire of France (954-86), who took advantage of the minority of Arnould II to take control of Artois in 964.[44] They are of reduced module and weight, and may be assigned to Rothard, bishop of Cambrai and Arras from 980.[45] They give the appearance of a sporadic attempt to regularize the coinage.

Equally sporadic are the so-called "grands deniers" of St. Omer, showing English influence. They imitate Æthelred II's *Crux* type (991-7), and name a moneyer Rumold (the name is not copied from English coins).[46] Unless the *Crux* design was created independently, the Artesian coins cannot be earlier than the 990s.[47]

Three imitative coins in the Fécamp hoard, of coarse manufacture and low weight, are probably from the region of Arras and the 970s. They have been tentatively attributed as the earliest (revived) coinage of the counts of Boulogne.[48]

FIG. 5. Deniers of Baudouin IV or V. The obv. normally reads BALDVINI MAR. The rev. legends are: 1. BRVGIA...; 2. SCI DONATII BRV; 3. GANT CIVIT...; 4 and 5 BONVS DENARI.

That brings us to the end of the tenth century, and to the varied coins naming Baudouin as marquis of Flanders (Fig. 5). They appear in hoards from about 1016 onwards,[49] and they may have been introduced - although it is by no means certain - before the creation of the county of Flanders in 1006. They have traditionally been attributed to Baudouin IV, perhaps with that in mind; but the title of marquis continued to be used throughout most of the eleventh century,[50] and one cannot therefore easily exclude the possibility that the issue of the coins extended into the time of Baudouin V (1037-67). Haeck, who has proposed a scheme of classification for the varieties, has said as much, and has suggested that coins of lighter weight, and also some of the coins reading BONUS DENARIUS, again of light weight, belong to Baudouin V. They occur in Swedish hoards of the 1040s to the 1060s.[51] One would still like to see a full photographic record of the evidence, which presents delicate problems of interpretation. Hatz records the coins of Baudouin in ones and twos in some sixty Swedish hoards, to a total of 130 specimens. A thorough study of the dies represented among these 130 coins plus the relatively few in collections in western Europe would advance our understanding of the monetary history of eleventh-century Flanders more securely than any other project one can envisage, as the survival of numismatic evidence seems in general to have been excessively thin. Later issues, up to c. 1125, reached Sweden in smaller quantities; there are fewer than 40 specimens, from only a dozen hoards, while coins of Baudouin IV and V remain the latest Flemish issues in numerous hoards from the very end of the eleventh century or the early twelfth. Since these hoards contain later coins from other German mints, it seems probable that there was actually a decline in minting in Flanders, or at least in northern Flanders, as the eleventh century progressed. This should not surprise us. It is in harmony with a wider monetary pattern, which can be observed, for example, in a dwindling stock of currency in England.

The Swedish coins are not yet published in detail in the Corpus. The Polish finds, however, give us another sample of Baudouin's issues from some

14 hoards.[52] They show that, alongside a few coins of Bruges, Bruges-St. Donatianus, and Ghent, the majority of the specimens name no mint, but are inscribed BONUS DENARIUS. One suspects that they all belong fairly close together geographically. Richebé's attribution of one of them to Arras is rather implausible, and his mention of Alost is unsupported.[53] A coin of Bergues-Saint-Winnoc that was dated by Albrecht to before c. 1040 and attributed to an abbot Rainhold who is first mentioned in 1052,[54] is reported by Haeck as occurring already in the Djuped hoard (c. 1026). It might, one suspects, be an anonymous coin of an earlier date whose legend RAINOLIDUS ET echoes the name of Rumoldus at St. Omer. More plausibly, coins have been attributed to abbot Oddobold at Ghent in the period c. 1020-35.[55] Recovery at Ghent is further documented by the finding of a Rainoldus coin there.

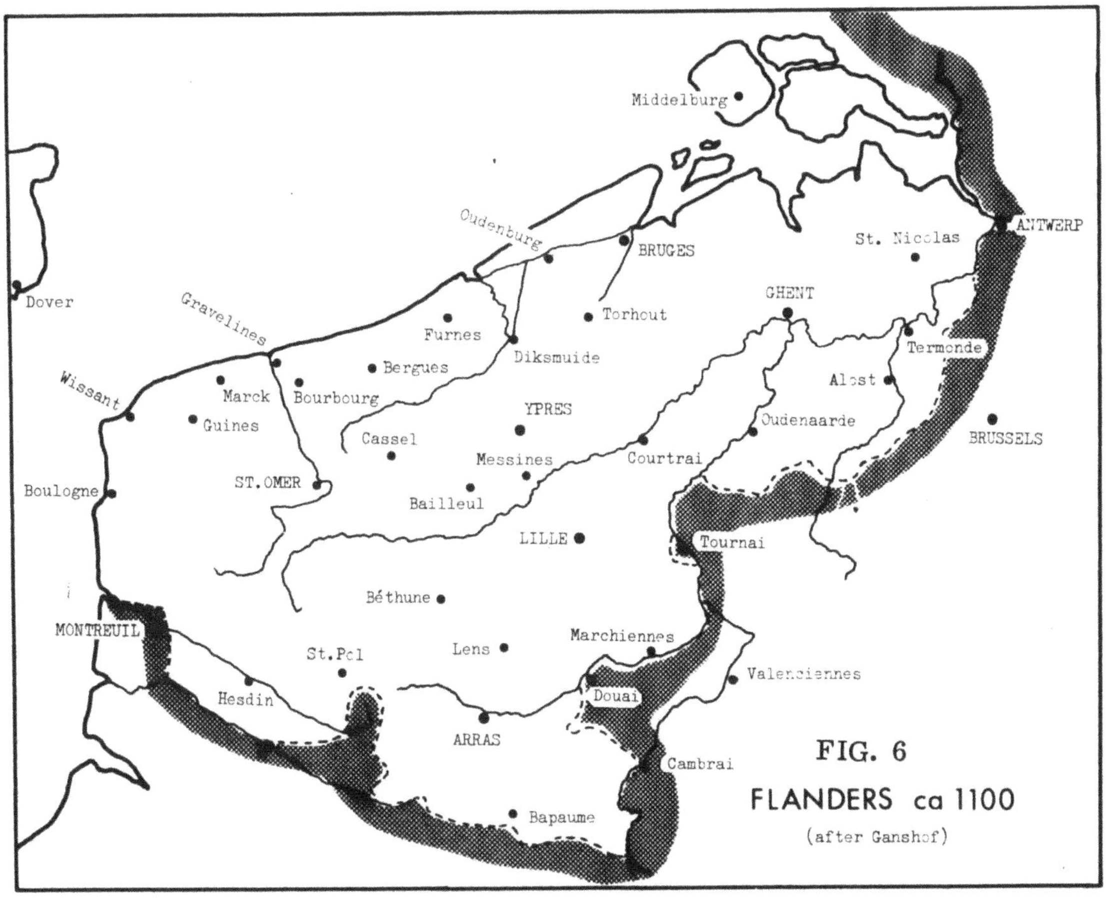

FIG. 6

FLANDERS ca 1100

(after Ganshof)

Allowing for these numerous uncertainties, the tendency of the evidence is fairly clear, and it should be made more certain by a die-study of the surviving coins of the Baudouins. Anticipating its results, it is already fairly safe to say that mint-activity does not in the least mirror the urban and commercial development of Flanders at this time, for it was in the middle of the eleventh century that there began to occur revolutionary economic and social changes, namely the migration of the cloth industry from the Flemish countryside to the towns, where it became a full-time occupation for those engaged in it. There followed the development of an export trade with careful quality control.[56] The documentary evidence for urban growth in the tenth century is unfortunately almost as tenuous as the numismatic information. But there are good reasons to accept that already by the end of the tenth century there were thriving towns in the coastlands of Flanders, namely Bruges, Bergues-Saint-Winnoc, St. Omer, Wissant, and Montreuil, and also in the south, at Ghent, Oudenaarde, Tournai, Valenciennes, Cambrai and Arras (Fig. 6). In the zone between, by contrast, towns were lacking.[57] Very few of the towns had mints, a contrast with England at the same date, where they were about 75 mints.

In seeking to assign a date to the origins of industrial development, there is a risk that one may merely identify the date from which documentation begins to survive. There are, obviously, no statistical series which might give an objective measurement of changes in the population of the towns, or of cloth production or export. Much of the evidence is of institutional change, as new structures were created, after a certain delay, to correspond more exactly with changed social realities. Thus for example the power and influence of the merchants was reflected by the gilds which grew up during the eleventh century.[58]

In the middle of the century, the international character of the cloth trade found expression in the creation of the Flemish fairs, and here the political initiative seems to have preceded the economic response. They were set up under the protection of the count and on his domain lands, to form a commercial axis which would cement the unity of Flanders. Each fair lasted a month, and merchants could go from one to the next up and down through Flanders. At Torhout, for example, the fair began on the feast of St. John, at Ypres on the Saturday before the Ascension, at Lille on the day after the Assumption, and at Messines a month before All Saints' Day. Lille, Ypres and Messines grew to importance because of their fairs; they are mentioned as places for the first time under Baudouin V (1037-67).[59] He and Robert le Frison did much to create the Flemish *Wirtschaftswunder* of their day, and to put Flanders alongside England, Normandy, and Capetian France, as a group of progressive states. In all four, the effects of the eleventh-century economic revival led to the development of more efficient systems for the collection and disbursement of revenue. In Flanders this particular initiative can be dated to 1089, when Robert II appointed the provost of St. Donatian's, Bruges to be his chancellor and *susceptor et exactor de omnibus reditibus principatus Flandrie*.[60]

FIG. 7 Denier of the Ypres mint. *Obv*. Blundered legend and inscription. *Rev*. Cross. MONETA IPRENSIS.

Of the four towns with fairs (the Bruges fair was a later creation), Lille had a mint almost from the moment the fair was established,[61] but its earliest coins seem to be excessively scarce. Much the same is true of Ypres, of which a single coin (Fig. 7) occurred in the Liesborn hoard of 1111 or a little later.[62]

One cannot be quite certain that this is a just appreciation, for the few surviving coins of Robert le Frison and Robert de Jérusalem (Fig. 8) mostly bear no clear mint-signature. Nevertheless it seems very probable that the majority of the Flemish issues of their time were struck at St. Omer, and at Arras, where the counts held their brilliant court; and one variety actually carries the legend VEDASTVS, which no doubt refers it to the Abbey of St. Vaast at Arras.[63] The neat style, small size, and characteristic lettering of the coins are reminiscent of some English pennies of Henry I. One would guess that, like his earlier issues, they were struck in very restricted

FIG. 8 Deniers of Robert le Frison, of the mint of St. Vaast at Arras, and of Robert II de Jérusalem, of uncertain mints. 1. Obv. Cross. ROTBERTI. Rev. Helmeted head r. VEDASTVS; 2. Obv. Seated figure holding palm-branch and sword. MONETA ROBERTI COMITIS. Rev Cross with two heads and two hands in angles. HIEROSOLIMITANI; 3. Obv. Helmeted bust holding sword; palm-branch. Blundered legend. Rev. Cross. Blundered legend.

quantities, and that there was something not far short of a silver famine in the early twelfth century.

The localised and sluggish monetary circulation of the eleventh century, illustrated by hoards such as Betekom or Thionville, both from c. 1040, and Wierum, from c. 1056,[64] gave way rather later in the twelfth century, helped perhaps by the traffic of the fairs, to a greater velocity of circulation, and to a currency under firmer political control. The age of the Viking trade coin, in Hävernick's phrase,[65] was superseded by the age of the regional penny. From 1092/3 onwards we find references to Flandrensis moneta.[66] At the same time there was a conflicting tendency for various feudal and ecclesiastical authorities in the south and east of Flanders to usurp the right of coinage - at Lens, Saint-Pol, Béthune, Saint-Bertin, Saint-Omer.[67]

So far as one can judge from limited evidence, the so-called mailles of the late eleventh and early twelfth century were on a weight-standard of between 0.5 and 0.6 g,[68] tending to fall lower at Saint-Omer.[69] Some sort of monetary reform was undertaken during the reign of Thierry d'Alsace, probably (as Ghyssens has argued)[70] as a response to the creation of the denier parisis, c. 1137/41. The characteristic small deniers of Flanders which were introduced at that time formed the currency of the county until the late thirteenth century, and for most of that period they were cut at 408 to the mark, and thus weighed 0.45-0.46 g.[71]

The hoards of Saint-Omer and Beveren allow us to recognise an early phase, running from 1137/41 to c. 1180.[72] There are two main questions which the monetary historian will wish to ask of these early petits deniers. First, on what scale was the currency; and secondly, does the geographical distribution of minting within Flanders offer any clues to the character of monetary affairs? The first question calls for an estimation of the numbers of dies used, based on statistical sampling of die-duplicates, - which remains to be undertaken. The second is hampered by the uncertain mint-attribution of most of the coins. Those by the moneyer Simon, which dominate the early hoards, have for long been attributed to Arras.[73] Richebé however questions this, and argues that Philippe d'Alsace confirmed to Simon the farm of various mints.[74] It is at first sight surprising that Arras should mint the bulk of the Flemish coinage, while there were no issues from Bruges or Ghent, and virtually none from Lille, the more so as there are some coins from Ypres, Saint-Omer and Amiens, and others in relatively tiny quantities, the mint-names clearly inscribed on them, from Arras, Béthune, Saint-Venant, Lens, Aire, Bergues-Saint-Winnoc, and Orchies, together with a number of unattributed types some of which may belong to mints such as Oudenaarde, Termonde, and Cassel.[75] We have no firm idea where the coins of these minor mints fall, within the period c. 1140-80: a large hoard from c. 1150-60 is very much a desideratum. Meanwhile, all we can say is that the middle of the twelfth century, roughly, saw a proliferation of minting, and a growing emphasis on the municipal character of the coinage. In light of the economic history of Flanders, one cannot but feel that this is (in the words of Winston Churchill) "too little, and too late."

Should one say, then, that towns were able to develop in Flanders in the tenth and eleventh centuries with no special stimulus or support from a monetary régime? Certainly, there is no obvious correlation between a plentiful coinage and precocious urban growth. Minting activity seems, on a broad view, to be more a reflection of the regional accumulation of silver stocks resulting from a favourable balance of trade. Flanders evidently did not run a persistent balance of payments surplus. This assessment, based on the numismatic evidence, may need to be modified in two respects. First, the silver stocks of a region were not necessarily maintained wholly in coin. There is evidence for the use of silver bars, and these may have been of importance in the commercial centres. The absence of any archaeological finds, or of mixed hoards of coins and bars, is negative evidence, and should be treated with caution.

Secondly, it may be that one should expect commercial, but not industrial, activity to find a reflection in the currency. The Flemish economic growth of the tenth to twelfth centuries was based on the surplus production of wool in the salt-grass areas of the coastlands, and on cheap labour in the rising urban centres; but this expansion was organized (and financed) from centres which had become industrialized at an earlier date. To some extent, therefore, we ought perhaps to recognize a connexion between economic development within Flanders, and monetary growth elsewhere: the surplus wealth generated in Flanders was transferred to the "entrepreneurial" areas of (1) Ile-de-France/ Arras; and (2) Köln and other cities of the Lower Rhine and Meuse.[76]

When the Flemish towns grew to importance, they benefitted from the relatively late development of an institutional infra-structure in the region, in the sense that they were not constrained by the persistence of earlier patterns of urban organisation. In the event, this gave them the considerable economic advantage of being well-adapted to profit from new paths of European economic development.[77]

From the middle of the twelfth century, then, - to return to the coins - for the next hundred years or more each town, essentially, had its own design of denier, immediately recognizable by simple pictorial types - a warrior at Bruges, a helmeted head at Ghent, a lily at Lille, a shield with a lion at Ypres, and other armorial devices at some of the smaller mints (Fig. 9). The hoards show that, although all these issues mingled together freely throughout Flanders, monetary circulation was quite localized, in the sense that the local mint often accounted for twice or three times its proper share. The Flemish currency was thus very different, for example, from that of England, where uniformity of type was allied with a complete mixing of the issues of different mints.

FIG. 9 Deniers of Bruges, Ghent, Lille, Ypres, Dixmude, and Courtrai from the thirteenth century.

The coinage of Brabant followed a very similar pattern of administrative development in the twelfth and thirteenth centuries to that of Flanders, but the two currencies did not intermingle, for the sufficient reason that they were on different weight-standards.

The evidence of the coins alone has tempted numismatists to suppose that the petits deniers were municipal issues. This unhistorical view is quite without foundation: the money was the count's money. The college of municipal magistrates, the Echevins de Flandre, had an obvious interest in the quality and reliability of the currency, and they were accorded a certain role in the assaying and in the proclamation of the coins,[78] but it amounted to very little more than the functions performed in London by a jury in the Trial of the Pyx. Tourneur has discussed the terms under which, in the twelfth century, the coinage was farmed in Ponthieu, Brabant and Flanders. In the thirteenth century, the Flemish counts bowed to the economic interests of the towns only to the extent that they undertook not to alter the coinage without consent.[79]

The second phase of the small deniers of Flanders extends from c. 1180 to c. 1220, and is thus contemporary with the Short Cross coinage of Classes I-VI, when the English currency enters upon a hundred years of sustained growth. There seem to have been five major mints, namely Lille, Ghent, Alost, Ypres and Bruges, probably in that order, which together accounted for about 90 per cent of the total coinage. Arras no longer figures in the list, as it was lost to Flanders in 1191. The Lille hoard[80] which seems to have more than its share of coins of Ypres, may be erratic. Naster has studied the numbers of dies represented among a group of 135 coins of Alost, almost all from the Lille hoard.[81] There were 31 different obverse dies, and 44 different reverse dies. This suggests that there may originally have been about 35 obverse dies and 50 reverse dies. These coins of Alost accounted for c. 5-7% of the Lille hoard, which implies that the second phase of the Flemish petits deniers may have amounted to at least 750-1000 reverse dies. The average output of a reverse die is conjectural. At 10,000 it would lead us to a total coinage of the order of 10 million deniers. At 20,000 (which would be technically possible), the figure would be 20 millions. Even on the higher estimate, it seems clear that the Flemish currency was a mere fraction of the size of the English. But, as has been said, the Lille hoard may be erratic, and these tentative figures, which are dependent on the proportion of Alost coins in it, may therefore need to be fundamentally revised when other hoards of the second period are available for comparison.

Later (third- and fourth-period) hoards, although they do not offer an ideal statistical basis because many of them are incompletely recorded, nevertheless reveal a similar ranking order among the leading mints, with Lille predominant, and striking far more silver than Ypres. Ghent generally runs in second place, Alost mints strongly, and Bruges is nowhere. This rather curious pattern does not match the economic realities of the cloth industry and the export trade in the thirteenth century. Bruges was already a major city, rivalling London in size. It was a commercial centre, and was to become a highly important money market.[82] Yet its mint-output was obviously tiny in relation to that of London.

If we compare the ranking of the towns according to the value of goods sold in Genoa in 1197 (about which we happen to have detailed information),[83] Ypres takes a far higher place in terms of its cloth output than it does for its mint output; and Alost is absent;

Montreuil	1427	Amiens	111
Ypres	1004	Cambrai	95
Arras	921	Valenciennes	72
Tournai	575	Rheims	30
Lille	332	St. Omer	22
England	258	Chalons	22
Provins	240	Beauvais	17
Ghent	135		

The relative activity of mints in the middle ages depended very largely on the custom that merchants brought to them. If, as seems to have been the case, only Flemish coins had official standing in Flanders (with the exception of coins of Duisburg and Aachen, which were allowed to circulate by an agreement of 1173), the pattern might perhaps be explained in terms of bullion flows. For merchants arriving by way of Brussels, for example, and needing to convert their money into Flemish coin, Alost would be the first mint-town on their journey. It is true that Alost lay in imperial Flanders, and that the count could strike coinage there without infringing the prerogatives of the French king, and this was no doubt a good reason for the creation of the mint. But, unless we assume that bullion was artificially transported there in preference to the other mints striking petits deniers, the scale of activity at Alost points to a role as a "point of entry" mint. Similarly in the south-west of Flanders, those arriving from Champagne would first reach Lille, not Ypres. There was in all probability a net outflow of silver to Britain in the Short Cross period; evidently little demand was made upon the coastal mints to recoin English or Scottish silver.

On the same hypothesis, before the loss of Arras it may have been the main mint of Flanders because it was the point of entry for merchants coming from the south, and Lille may have been left without much business. This would at least explain the dramatic geographical shift in the late twelfth century in the proportions of bullion coined.[84]

Given the trading links between Flanders and England, it seems almost inevitable that the volume of the Flemish issues should have increased during the first half of the thirteenth century. The hoards reveal a currency in the early thirteenth century, in which hardly any of the late twelfth-century issues survive, and documents mentioning the old and the new money of Flanders point to some kind of renewal shortly before 1208 (cf. the English reform of 1205).[85] In the second half of the century there were further renewals, possibly at dates close to 1247 and 1259.[86]

NOTES

1. H. Pirenne, Medieval Cities, their Origins and the Revival of Trade, 3rd edn. 1939; id. Histoire économique et sociale du moyen âge, 1969.

2. In Revue Historique LXVII (1898) and in Annales de l'Est et du Nord I (1905) respectively.

3. A. F. Havighurst (ed.), The Pirenne Thesis: Analysis, Criticism, Revision, 1969.

4. W. Hävernick, "Epochen der deutschen Geldgeschichte im frühen Mittelalter", Hamburger Beiträge zur Numismatik IX/X (1955/56), 5-10.

5. G. Albrecht, Das Münzwesen im niederlothringischen und friesischen Raum, 1959.

6. F. Vercauteren, "Monnaie et circulation monétaire en Belgique et dans le nord de la France du VIe au XIe siècle", Moneta e scambi nell'alto medioevo (Settimane di Studio, VIII) Spoleto, 1961, 279-311.

7. H. Frère, Le denier carolingien, spécialement en Belgique (Numismatica Lovaniensia, I), 1977; id., "Les noms de lieux sur les monnaies carolingiennes de 'Belgique' ", Revue Belge de Numismatique CXXIII (1977), 133-48.

8. J. Ghyssens, Les petits deniers de Flandre des XIIe et XIIIe siècles, 1971.

9. G. Hatz, Handel und Verkehr zwischen dem Deutschen Reich und Schweden in der Späten Wikingzeit, 1974.

10. A detailed account and discussion of the invasions will be found in A. d'Haenens, Les invasions normandes en Belgique au IXe siècle, 1967. See also F. Vercauteren, "La formation des principautés de Liège, Flandre, Brabant, et Hainaut (IXe - XIe siècles)", in L'Europe aux IXe - XIe siècles. Aux origines des Etats nationaux (ed. T. Manteuffel and A. Gieysztor), 1968, pp. 31-41.

11. The creation of the marquisate by Charles the Bald for his son-in-law was by no means a half-hearted gesture. The marquisate (from 866) included Waas, Ghent, Courtrai, Tournai, Caribant, Mélentois, and la Pévèle. See L. Vanderkindere, La formation territoriale des principautés belges au moyen âge, 1902, vol. I, p. 38.

12. M. Hoc, "Un denier carolingien inédit de Tournai", BSFN 1966, 12-13. Quentovic disappeared, to be replaced by Wissant. On Cassel, Lens, and various other mints, see Frère, op.cit.

13. H. Roosens, "Trouvaille de monnaies carolingiennes à Muizen-lez-Malines (1906)", RBN XCVI (1950), 203-8; P. Naster, "Trouvaille de monnaies carolongiennes à Zelzate (1949)", ibid., 208-24. But Frère reports (in a letter of 5 November) that the hoard is post-892.

14. R. H. M. Dolley and K. F. Morrisson, The Carolingian Coins in the British Museum, 1966, no. 102.

15. Frère, op. cit., no. 2, adopts the attribution. The type has hitherto been given to Charles le Chauve.

16. E. Gariel, Les monnaies royales de France sous la race carolingienne, Strasbourg 1883-4, vol. I, pp. 132f. There were said to be 5-600 coins but only 204 were described; the rest were probably melted down. Of the 139 coins of Bruges, only 5 read BRUCCAMO, the rest BRVCCIAMO. All had the 4 spikes in the quarters of the reverse (as did one of the oboles of Quentovic). They were characterized by a square C in the Karolus monogram and by their rather low weight and poor metal. The coins of Arras read ATREBASCIV. See also C. A. Serrure, "Karolingische munten gevonden te Assebrouck", Vaderlandsch Museum voor Nederduitsche Letterkunde, Oudheid en Geschiedenis III (1860), 417-21. The hoard was found in the locality Rike-Velden.

17. J. Lafaurie, "Deux trésors monétaires carolingiens: Saumeray (Eure-et-Loire); Rennes (Ille-et-Vilaine)", RN[6] VII (1965), 262-305 argues that Charles le Simple reduced the weight of the denier between 880 and 920, from 184 to the pound, through 216, to 240 (or 230, 270 and 300 to the 15-ounce pound).

18. The tables in Hatz, op. cit., refer to these coins when they indicate issues of Flanders, 930-60. They occur, for example, in the hoards of Gerete, Lännäs, Glemminge, Lilla Haltarve, Digeråkra, Hallsarve, Binge, Igelösa, Näs, Stockholm, and Österryftes. The type is illustrated in E. Bahrfeldt, Der Silberfund von Leissower Mühle, 1896, 230, 231-5. I am indebted to Dr. Hatz for a detailed explanation of the view represented in his book. Much of the interest of the hoard-evidence lies in comparing the numbers of specimens of this type with that dated 962-5, and with the earliest coins of Liège.

19. On the early history of Bruges, see M. Verkest, Bruges, 1952; A. E. Verhulst, "Les origins et l'histoire ancienne de la ville de Bruges", Le Moyen Age XV (1960), 37-63.

20. Frère, op. cit., 51-2.

21. F. L. Ganshof, La Flandre sous les premiers Comtes, 2 ed., 1944, p. 15; F. Vercauteren, op. cit. (note 10 above).

22. This has been argued by Dr. Pauline Stafford, in a lecture to the British Numismatic Society, June 1978.

23. Ganshof, loc. cit.

24. On the early history of Ghent, see H. van Werveke, "Formation et développement de la ville de Gand", Revue du Nord XXV (1939), 208ff. A. Verhulst, "Die Frühgeschichte der Stadt Gent", Die Stadt in der Europaischen Geschichte. Festscheift Edith Ennen (ed. W. Besch et al.), 1972, 108-37.

25. Frère, op. cit., nos. 4b and 4k, from the same reverse die.

26. On the Glisy hoard, see the original account by E. Gariel, in Annuaire de Numismatique II (1867), 349-58, remarking inter alia on the rough workmanship and in one case poor alloy (85.7%) of the coins of the Palace mint, which he regarded therefore as a type immobilisé dating from the reign of Louis II or even Louis III. See also Gariel, Monnaies royales, I, 95ff. Frère reports a coin of Eudes which dates the hoard.

27. The hoard is described in detail in Gariel, op.cit., I, 107ff. On the inadequacies of Morrison and Grunthal's summary of the same, see the reviews by J. Lafaurie in RN 1967, 294 and by P. Grierson in NC 1969, 348. For the suggested date of concealment, see J. Lafaurie, 'Les trouvailles de monnaies mérovingiennes et carolingiennes d'Amiens', BSFN 1969, 404-7.

28. E. Hawkins, 'An account of coins and treasure found in Cuerdale,' NC V (1842-3), 1-48 and 53-104, at p. 57 lists four coins of Bruges, not one as in Hardy's list published in R.H.M. Dolley and K. F. Morrison, 'Finds of Carolingian coins from Great Britain and Ireland', BNJ XXXII (1963), 75-87.

29. D'Haenens, op.cit., 48.

30. Ibid., 117. J. Lestocquoy ventures to date the fortification more precisely to 883-7, in Etudes d'histoire urbaine, 1966, 129, on which see d'Haenens.

31. M. Prou, Les monnaies carolingiennes, 1896, no. 222.

32. A. Dieudonné, Monnaies féodales françaises (Manuel de numismatique française, IV), 1936, p. 77.

33. F. Poey d'Avant, Monnaies féodales de France, nos. 6739-40.

34. Dolley and Morrison, op.cit. (note 14), no. 106.

35. Fougères and Conbrouse, no. 116 is a blundered coin reading S¯CIΛIID¯TM¯NT. Its attribution to Saint-Omer should be regarded as extremely tentative.

36. C. Richebé, Les monnaies féodales d'Artois du Xe au début du XIVe siècle, 1963, p. 36.

37. Manfred van Rey, 'Die Münzprägung Karls des Kahlen und die westfränkische Königslandschaft', in Die Stadt in der Europaischen Geschichte. Festschrift Edith Ennen (ed. W. Besch et al.), 1972, pp. 153-84, lists two coins of St. Omer in the Compiègne hoard (concealed before c. 890?). They are, however, two oboles of distinctly uncertain attribution (Gariel, vol. I, XVII, 85-6), one of which reads ?SITVI. Sithiu is the name of the hill on which the monastery of Saint-Bertin was built—to become the nucleus of Saint Omer. There is no reason to believe that the name Sithiu was used for the place.

38. Lestocquoy, op.cit.

39. H. van Werveke, De oudste burchten aan de vlaamse en de zeeuwse kust. F. Lentacker, 'Débats entre historiens et géographes à propos de l'évolution de la plaine maritime flamande au cours du haut moyen âge', Revue du Nord XLII (1960), 407-8.

40. Albrecht, op.cit., p. 38.

41. Ibid., p. 84, as an "unidentified mint in western Lower Lotharingia", = Hävernick 53-4. Again I am indebted to Dr. Gert Hatz for his advice. Cf. J. Baerten, 'La plus ancienne monnaie de Bruxelles (vers 965)', Cercle d'Etudes Numismatiques, Bulletin II (1965), 1-2.

42. There are 27 specimens in the Digeråkra hoard, for which see Corpus nummorum saeculorum IX-XI qui in Suecia reperti sunt, I, 2.

43. Albrecht, op.cit., 84-5. Note P. Berghaus, 'Monnaies du XIe siècle trouvées à Domburg', Cercle d'Etudes Numismatique. Bulletin, 1974 recording specimens of Havernick 32, Dbg. 1160, and Salmo 93:49.

44. F. Dumas-Dubourg, Le trésor de Fécamp, 1971, pp. 124-6.

45. Ibid., cf. Poey d'Avant, op.cit., 6738. Dolley and Morrisson, no. 286 (0.72 g).

46. A. Dieudonné, Monnaies féodales françaises (Manuel de numismatique française, IV), 1936, pp. 76f and fig. 35. Richebé, op.cit., no. 2 (1.20 g). In addition to the references cited, see Bahrfeldt, op.cit. (note 18).

47. An earlier date was once suggested on the basis of the incorrect reconstruction of the legend as ARNOLDV. Albrecht gives the earliest hoard-context (Leissow/Lisówek) as c. 1015.

48. Dumas, op.cit., pp. 127ff.

49. Hatz, op.cit.

50. Vanderkindere, op.cit., vol. I, p. 43.

51. A. A. Haeck, 'Les monnaies de Baudouin IV (989-1036) et de Baudouin V (1036-1067), comtes de Flandre', Cercle d'Etudes Numismatique. Bulletin, II (1965), 24-5.

52. They are published in the five volumes of the Polskie Skarby Wczesnośredniowieczne, = Polskie Badania Archeologiczne, vols. I, IV, X, XII (with general index), and XIII. The relevant hoards include those from Dobra (Bruges), Grojec, Łask, Maniów, Mgowo (St. Donatian), Mierzeszyn, Niederlandin (Ghent), Sokolniki, Uznam-Wyspa, and Vossberg.

53. Richebé, op.cit., pp. 36-8.

54. Albrecht, op.cit., pp. 65-6. Haeck, op.cit., observes that the type is linked with those in the name of Baudouin IV by its weight.

55. C. Turnwald, 'Zwei neu bestimmte Denare von Gent', HBN XVII (1963), 495-501.

56. H. van Werveke, 'Industrial growth in the middle ages. The cloth industry in Flanders', Economic History Review[2] VI (1953-4), 237-45.

57. J. Dhondt, 'Développement urbain et initiative comtale en Flandre au XIe siècle', Revue du Nord XXX (1948), 133-56.

58. H. Laurent, Un grand commerce d'exportation au moyen âge. La draperie des Pays-Bas en France et dans les pays méditerranéens, (XIIe - XIVe siècle), 1935.

59. Dhondt, op.cit.

60. B. Lyon and A. Verhulst, Medieval Finance, A Comparison of Financial Institutions in Northwestern Europe, 1967; A. Verhulst and M. Gysseling, Le Compte Général de 1887...et les institutions financières du comté de Flandre au XIIe siècle, 1962.

61. Albrecht, op.cit., p. 53; Dhondt, op.cit., gives the first mention of Lille as 1054.

62. Albrecht, op.cit., p. 56.

63. Richebé, op.cit., pp. 38-44, 75-86.

64. For an inventory of German finds, see Hatz, op.cit., pp. 127-35.

65. W. Hävernick, 'Epochen der deutschen Geldgeschichte im frühen Mittelalter', HBN IX/X (1955/56), 5-10.

66. C. Wyffels, 'Contribution à l'histoire monétaire de Flandre au XIIIe siècle', Revue belge de philologie et histoire XLV (1967), 1113-41, at p. 1124.

67. Richebé, op.cit.

68. Ghyssens, op.cit. (note 8), p. 13, note 3, where the median value is 0.55 g.

69. Richebé, op.cit., cat. nos. 24-6.

70. Ghyssens, op.cit., p. 12.

71. Wyffels, op.cit., pp. 1120-3.

72. Ghyssens, op.cit., pp. 56-7.

73. R. Serrure, 'Les mailles du monétaire Simon sont battues à Arras'. Bulletin mensuel de numismatique III (1883-4), 57.

74. Richebé, op.cit., p. 50.

75. Ghyssens, pp. 63-90.

76. I am much indebted to Professor Herman Van der Wee, who discussed this interpretation with me during and after the Symposium.

77. Again, this hypothesis was suggested by Professor Van der Wee.

78. V. Tourneur, 'Le monnayage dans les villes de Flandre et de Brabant au XIIe et XIIIe siècles', Académie royale de Belgique, Bulletin de la classe des lettres et des sciences morales et politiques 5. XXVI (1940), 34-48.

79. Ibid.

80. Ghyssens, op.cit., pp. 95-6.

81. P. Naster, 'Les deniers d'Arnot émis à Alost', Revue Belge de Numismatique XCVIII (1952), 41-55.

82. R. de Roover, Money, Banking and Credit in Medieval Bruges.

83. R. L. Reynolds, 'The market for nothern textiles in Genoa, 1179-1200', Revue belge de philologie et histore VIII (1929), 831-51, at pp. 846-7.

84. We know that there was a corporation of moneyers at Arras, and that there were also money changers established there. - Richebé, op.cit., p. 48.

85. Ghyssens, op.cit., p. 91. But there are similar references in the years 1199-1202 - Wyffels, op.cit., p. 1123.

86. Ghyssens, op.cit., p. 141.

After this paper was read M. Frère commented on the reference to G. Albrecht's work (see note 5), and listed the following hoards which either escaped Albrecht or have been published since he wrote.

Chatelet (Belgium) GNB, 1910, p. 114
Silenrieux (Belgium) ibid.
Mirwart (Belgium) RBN 104, 1958, p. 95
Sion (Valais, Switzerland) RBN 1850, p. 448
Namur—19th century finds in the Meuse, ASAN passim

A number of other hoards are mentioned in various papers in

HBN: Unghanse, Broungs, Gandarve (Gotland, Sweden)
Vichmjask (U.S.S.R.), Daugmale (Latvia)
Schidlitz (Poland), etc.

M. Frère also urged caution when consulting Albrecht's chapters on Louvain, Brussels, Cambrai, Léau, Tongres and the dukes of Lower Lotharingia since old attributions were not always brought up to date.

Table 1. Finds of coins from Lower Lotharingian and Frisian mints

Column A gives the number of specimens recorded by Albrecht, plus the imitative pieces he records. Column H gives the corresponding sub-totals from Hatz's survey of the Swedish material, and the numbers in the left-hand column are his section numbers. The mints included in each section are listed at pp. 208-9. Coins of doubtful attribution have been included. The symbol > signifies "at least".

		A	H
8	Lower Lotharingia, dukes	96	122
9	Western Lower Lotharingia [mostly Brussels ?]	149	88
10	Bruges	21	
	Ghent	3	
	St. Omer	17+1	
	St. Vaast-Arras	6	
	Lille	-	
	Ypres	1	
	Ghistelles	-	
	Bergues-St-Winnoc	3	
	Lens	4	
	Uncertain mint [mostly Bruges/Ghent]	>84+8	430
11	Cambrai	1	
	Câteau-Cambrésis	-	0
12	Tournai	4	
	Mons	13	
	Thuin	46+11	72
13	Brussels [cf. 9]	101+7	
	Nivelles [but 50 are from one hoard]	(65)	
	Antwerp	>39	
	Löwen	3	
	Léau (Leeuw)	6	322
14	Namur	>278	
	Dinant	197	
	Bouillon	22	320
15	Liège	>262	246
16	Huy	213+1	201
17	Maastricht	360+1	450
18	Fosses	6	
	Ciney	19	
	Tongern ? [but 52 are from one hoard]	(75)	
	Münsterbilsen	24	
	Visé	48	
	Saint-Trond	10	
	Celles	47	
	Thorn	2	
	Wessem	4	
	Stavelot (Stablo)	19	
	Aachen	48	
	Kornelimünster	2	260
19	Köln	9801 +> 877	
	Bonn	13	
	Neuss	-	
	Xanten	25+10	
	Rees [from only 4 hoards]	(41)	9255
20	Remagen	127+2	175
21	Duisburg	384+4	483
22	Emmerich ?	2	
	Berg	-	51
23	Utrecht	737	
	Utrecht district	23	429
24	Deventer	1979 +18	1767
25	Groningen	699	256
26	Tiel	>1231	
	Tiel district	5	1258
27	Vlaardingen	-	
	Rijnsburg	4	

Table 1 (contd.)		A	H
	Nijmegen	9	
	Zwolle	-	
	Zütphen (76 from one hoard]	(125)	143
28	Frisia, imperial	26	64
29	Frisia, counts:		
	Staveren	255	
	Bolsward	> 74	
	Leeuwarden	373	
	Dokkum	533	
	Winsum	22	
	Garrelsweer	12	
	Emnigheim	20	
	Uncertain	689	432

COMPARAISON ENTRE L'EVOLUTION POLITIQUE, ECONOMIQUE ET MONETAIRE DU NORD DE LA FRANCE AU XIIè SIECLE

Francoise Dumas

Quelle est la valeur de la monnaie comme témoin de l'évolution politique et économique? c'est une question que l'on peut se poser pour toutes les époques. Mais le déroulement des faits politiques et le développement économique du nord du royaume au XIIè siècle sont assez bien connus pour qu'on puisse les comparer avec ce que nous savons de la monnaie à la même époque.

La principauté flamande connut un essor rapide dans lequel on peut distinguer plusieurs étapes.

Dans un premier temps au Xè siècle le comte Arnoul le Grand (918-965) respecta l'Escaut qui séparait la Flandre de la Lotharingie, mais étendit son territoire de la Canche jusqu'à la Somme à la faveur de luttes menées contre le comte de Vermandois, le marquis de Normandie et le duc des Francs. Cette expansion fut ralentie par deux minorités et il se constitua au sud plusieurs comtés: le comté de Boulogne tourné vers la mer, celui de Ternois ou de Saint-Pol, celui de Guines pris sur le comté de Boulogne, celui de Hesdin pris sur le Ternois.

La barrière méridionale formée par ces petits comtés et la puissante Normandie provoquèrent une extension vers l'est en Lotharingie. La minorité d'Henri IV, roi de Germanie, facilita la création d'une Flandre impériale (1056). De ce fait, le comté, à cheval sur le royaume et sur l'empire, devint beaucoup plus indépendant.

Une nouvelle tentative encore plus hardie échoua: l'union de la Flandre et du Hainaut sous Arnoul III, fils du comte de Flandre et de la veuve du comte de Hainaut. Arnoul, chassé de Flandre par Robert le Frison (1071-1093) ne conserva que le Hainaut, inféodé à l'éveque de Liège.

Si nous nous tournons vers le sud et examinons la situation du point de vue du roi, nous constatons qu'au cours du XIè siècle et plus encore au début du XIIè, les capétiens ont cherché à faire reconnaitre leur autorité par les seigneurs du nord du royaume et même à accroitre leur domaine. Il est bien connu que Robert Ier, fils d'Hugue Capet après avoir répudié sa femme Suzanne veuve d'Arnoul III de Flandre garda Montreuil. A Soissons, Beauvais, Senlis, les officiers ou les prélats étaient des fidèles qui apposaient leurs seings sur les diplomes royaux.[1] Philippe Ier (1060-1108) fit onze voyages en Picardie (Amiens, Noyon, Laon, Montreuil); il intervint à Soissons entre les habitants et la clergé (1093); il recouvra la seigneurie de Corbie donnée par Henri Ier à sa soeur lors de son mariage avec Baudoin V de Flandre, maria son frère Hugues avec la fille du comte de Vermandois qui tenait en outre de sa mère les comtés de Valois, Montdidier et Amiens.

Louis VI (1108-1137) aussi intervint à diverses reprises en faveur du comté épiscopal de Beauvais, de la ville épiscopale de Noyon, du comté de Vermandois à qui il rendit Péronne enlevé à Ebles de Rouci, de l'éveque d'Amiens. En 1132, les alliances de paix entre Corbie et Amiens furent renouvelées devant le roi.

Durant le règne de Louis VI, la Flandre connut de graves difficultés; le comte Charles le Bon fut assassiné en 1127; Guillaume Cliton, soutenu par le roi de France ne fut reconnuqu'après avoir concédé des chartes à presque toutes les grandes villes et commit la faute de s'appuyer sur la noblesse. Du coup, les villes se rallièrent à Thierry d'Alsace qui respecta leurs privilèges. Avec le nouveau comte s'installa pour plus de 60 ans un pouvoir rendu plus fort encore par les énormes ressources financières que procurent les tonlieux alimentés par les courants commerciaux qui se développent à ce moment là.

Dans le seconde moitié du XIIè siècle, le domaine comtal s'étendit à nouveau, particulièrement vers le sud. Le comte rattacha à son domaine Hesdin (v 1151), Lillers (1151), Lens (1160), Alost (1165). Le fils cadet de Thierry, Mathieu, épousa l'héritière du comté de Boulogne, Seule la puissance de Saint-Pol se maintient. Plus au sud, l'emprise de la dynastie flamande s'affirma d'une autre façon. Philippe d'Alsace, fils de Thierry, avait épousé en 1156, Elisabeth de Vermandois qui hérita de son frère, quelques années plus tard en 1163, les comtés de Vermandois, Amiens, Valois et Montdidier. Voici donc le comte de Flandre installé en Picardie, dans cette région que les capétiens surveillaient dâutant plus attentivement qu'elle était plus riche en hommes et en ressources (En 1194, la Picardie fournit le quart d'une prisée de sergents, 2000 h sur 8000 h). Elle fournit également le quart des recettes des prévotés alors que les terres ne représentent que 6% du domaine). (cf. R. Fossier.)

En principe les relations du roi et du comte étaient bonnes et Louis VII en mourant (1180) confia la tutelle du nouveau roi Philippe (Auguste) à Philippe d'Alsace. Le comte de Flandre fit épouser au roi sa nièce Isabelle de Hainaut, fille de Marguerite de Flandre et de Baudoin V comte de Hainaut puis marquis de de Namur, héritier présomptif de Flandre depuis 1177. Il promit en dot à sa nièce le sud de son comté, les territoires qui formeront l'Artois: Arras, Bapaume, Hesdin, Lens, Aire, Ardres, Lillers, Richebourg, Saint-Omer. Cependant lorsque mourut sans enfant Isabelle de Vermandois, comtesse de Flandre (1183) et que son mari, Philippe d'Alsace s'accorda avec sa belle-soeur Aliénor de Vermandois pour garder une partie de l'héritage de sa femme, Philippe Auguste intervint pour défendre les droits d'Aliénor qui n'avait pas d'enfant. En 1185, par le traité de Boves, le roi garda les comtés d'Amiens et de Montdidier, les chatellenies de Roye et Thourotte en compensation des droits de rachat et de propriété de Péronne, Saint-Quentin et Ham dont le comte de Flandre avait la jouissance. Le roi avance donc dans les vallées de l'Oise et de la Somme.

Lorsque Philippe d'Alsace mourut en 1191, à Saint-Jean-d'Acre, Philippe Auguste s'entendit avec Aliènor à laquelle il céda d'abord Péronne et Saint-Quentin qu'il échangea ensuite contre d'autres seigneuries. En 1213 à la mort d'Aliénor, le roi de France réunit à son domaine le Vermandois et le Valois, (il complèta son emprise par d'autres acquisitions: Clermont-en-Beauvaisis, Beaumont-sur-Oise).

Plus au nord, Philippe Auguste occupa pour son fils la dot d'Isabelle de Hainaut: Arras, Aire, St-Omer, Hesdin et Lens, les comtés vassaux de Guines, Boulogne, Saint-Pol, Béthune et Lillers. Il dut céder la partie septentrionale de ces territoires en 1200, il les reprit en 1212 lorsque la jeune comtesse Jeanne épousa Ferrand de Portugal. La victoire de Bouvines rendit cette cession définitive (1214);le roi confisqua un temps le comté de Boulogne sur Renaud de Dammartin, le Ponthieu sur Simon. Ce n'est plus le comté de Flandre qui s'étend vers le sud mais au contraire le roi de France qui s' installe solidement dans le nord de son royaume. L'Artois forma l'apanage de Robert, frère de Louis IX en 1226 et devint un comté en 1237, suzerain du comté de Boulogne. Il y eut donc durant le XIIè siècle un "mouvement de va-et-vient" très net qui se termina par la victoire du roi sur le comte de Flandre.

Les luttes politiques que je viens de retracer ne sont pas sans fondement économique. La Picardie par les produits du sol, la Flandre par l'industrie et le commerce étaient des régions riches qui jouaient un rôle de premier plan. L'une et l'autre ont eu un élan démographique important qui a amené la conquête de sols vierges par défrichements et aussi par assèchements. En Flandre les princes de la maison d'Alsace ont été assez puissants pour mener une véritable politique économique. Ils ont entrepris des assèchements dont les terres leur revenaient fournissant des patures à coté des cultures. Il ont aménagé par des digues et des canaux les ports qui existaient déjà tel, Saint-Omer et fondé des villes nouvelles: Gravelines (1163), Calais, (1163-73), Dunkerque (1180), L'écoulement des eaux en a été facilité et donc les liaisons commerciales avec l'intérieur. Les liaisons par terre sont facilitées aussi, grâce à l'amélioration de l'attelage (chevaux ferrés, collier d'épaule, nouveau chariot) et à de nouvelles routes (Cologne-Bruges par le Brabant par exemple). Une partie de la population rurale est employée dans les villes, en particulier dans l'industrie textile qui devient urbaine. L'activité marchande se développe. Des foires successives se tiennent en Flandre tout au long de l'année. Les marchands voyageurs se groupent en des associations ou gildes au XIè siècle en Hainaut, en Flandre et à Montreuil. Les voyages se font en direction de l'Angleterre dès 1024-1036. Au XIè siècle également le tonlieu de Saint-Vaast d'Arras atteste le passage de fromages anglais, de laines, de draps, de plantes tinctoriales. La translation de Sainte Lewine qui raconte la quête des reliques par un moine de Bergues fait connaitre aussi la rencontre de ce moine avec des marchands flamands dans le Sussex. Au milieu du XIIè siècle les marchands de Saint-Omer ont leur maison à Londres. Les échanges ont lieu aussi avec l'Est: les draps d'Ypres se trouvent à Novgorod au XIIè siècle; Gand est tournée vers l'Empire; Arras, elle est tournée vers le Sud.

La ville qui occupe la première place dans ce développement économique c'est Arras dont l'activité semble etre très importante et dont le dynamisme commercial est très grand: en 1127 elle jouit d'un tarif préférentiel au péage de Bapaume, sur la route du sud. Dix ans plus tard des marchands se trouvent aux foires de Champagne alors à leurs débuts; les échanges portent sur des tissus flammands et des produits exotiques. Puis ils vont jusqu'à Gênes où ils exportent leurs produits et ceux d'autres centres.

On les trouve aussi à Saint-Gilles-du-Gard, à Marseille. Parallèlement à cet accroissement d'activité, la population urbaine acquiert ses premières libertés (1102). La ville importante (20 000 h environ) est formée de deux ensembles: Arras cité épiscopale où l'éveque siège à nouveau depuis la fin du XIè (1094, le siège est détaché de Cambrai) et Arras ville autour de l'abbaye de Saint-Vaast. Elle est ceinte d'une grande muraille de pierre, comporte deux grandes places avant 1090. Les constructions vont bon train. La cathé- Notre Dame construite en style roman en 1030 est reconstruite en style gothique entre 1160 et 1183.

D'autres centres textiles se développent aussi: Ypres, Dixmude, Abbeville, mais la draperie qui déclinera au XIIIè siècle n'est pas le seul revenu commercial: produits alimentaires: le vin, le blé, le poisson jouent leur rôle (Saint-Omer surtout).

Enfin et surtout la finance prime. Ce qui est important et caractéristique de ces villes du sud de la Flandre c'est qu'un certain nombre de bourgeois jouissent de capitaux dont l'origine serait à chercher dans les revenus fonciers augmentés de ceux du commerce.[2] Ces capitaux leur donnent une liberté d'action remarquable. Guillaume Cade, de Saint-Omer fait des opérations à terme comme des achats massifs à l'avance de laine, de troupeaux, en Angleterre.[3] Mais ce sont surtout des bailleurs de fonds. Le même Guillaume Cade a avancé au moins 5000 livres à Henri II. A Arras, les Crespin qui négocient surtout le vin font des avances aux comtes, aux villes, aux abbayes. En février 1223 ils prêtent 1040 l.p. à Gui de Chatillon, comte de St Pol; en juillet c'est 9000 l.p.; en 1225, c'est 2050 l.p. à la comtesse du Flandre. Ils vont jusque'à prêter 20 000 l.p. en une fois soit la moitié des revenus du comte de Flandre.

Naturellement les seigneurs dont nous venons de parler profitent eux aussi directement, et non par l'intermédiaire de prêts, de cette activité d'échanges. Si le passage au royaume du sud du comté de Flandre fut marqué de luttes âpres c'est qu'il s'agissait de points de trafic marchand: Bapaume, Péronne, etc. On connait, pour la Flandre, le compte général de 1187 qui porte sur la partie ancienne du domaine comtal. Il est intéressant pour le montant des sommes qu'il fait connaitre mais aussi par l'emploi très généralisé du numéraire dont il témoigne. Tous les revenus même touchés en nature sont convertis en numéraire sauf ce qui est immédiatement redistribué.[4]

Ce numéraire, on est conscient depuis un certain nombre d'années qu'il a pénétré les campagnes. Il est utilisé dans le cadre de la seigneurie foncière, issue de la villa carolingienne. Les corvées dues au seigneur pour permettre l'exploitation de la réserve sont achetées ou bien la réserve est affermée; les droits sur les tenures sont eux aussi payés en numéraire (Cens, droits de succession). Il est utilisé aussi dans le cadre de la seigneurie banale où le seigneur est passé de l'exercice de la protection et de la justice à l'exploitation économique (usage des fours, moulins, viviers, pressoirs, droits de tonlieux péages...). L'exploitation des droits seigneuriaux provoque en réaction la formation de communautés rurales à l'échelle du village, de la paroisse, ou de la seigneurie; les communautés dirigées par un maire et des échevins ont des pouvoirs administratifs et judiciaires et peuvent aussi etre frappées d'amendes collectives.

L'argent parait donc circuler dans cette France du Nord à tous les niveaux.

Il est temps de se demander ce que l'on retrouve de cette situation politique et économique en examinant les monnaies, leur évolution typologique et intrinsèque, leur circulation.

Le Monnayage royal

Les Capétiens sont partis de très peu puisque la seule monnaie portant le nom du roi Hugues Capet est celle de l'éveque Hervé de Beauvais. Cependant la monnaie royale apparut très tot à Montreuil, sous Philipps Ier et s'y maintint sans interruption jusqu'à Philippe Auguste. Frappée à Paris dès Robert le Pieux, fils d'Hugues Capet, elle s'implanta progressivement au nord de la Seine à Senlis et Pontoise sous Louis VI, à Compiègne sous Louis VII de façon épisodique. Dans la seconde moitié du XIIè siècle, à la suite d'un accord avec l'éveque de Laon en 1158, le nom de Louis VII puis celui de Philippe Auguste figurent sur les monnaies épiscopales.

Il n'y a aucune unité typologique entre ces monnaies; les monnaies royales ne sont que des monnaies locales; il en est de même pour le reste du domaine (Etampes, Orléans, ...). Cependant, un mouvement se dessine qui privilégie la monnaie de Paris; le parisis. Par exemple à Beauvais en 1179 un cens de 5 sous beauvais est transformé en cens de 6 sous parisis.[5] Les conditions de fabrication de ces monnaies sont mal connues. A. Dieudonné a montré qu'elles subirent plusieurs affaiblissements sous Philippe Ier, sous Louis VI (1108-1137) qui dut s'engager auprès des gens de Compiègne en 1120 à ne pas descendre au-dessous du demi de fin puis sous Philippe Auguste. La monnaie aurait été 8è puis 7è sous Philippe Ier (666/1000 puis 583/1000), 6è sous Louis VI (500/1000) et sous Louis VII, 5è sous Philippe Auguste (395/1000). Le poids d'argent fin serait passé par les étapes suivantes: 0.92 g; 0.78 (Philippe Ier); 0.63 (Louis VI); 0.48 (Louis VII),[6] si l'on considère que l'on connait 5 types de parisis sous Philippe Ier, autant sous Louis VI et Louis VII, qu'à Montreuil le type a changé 5 fois sous Louis VI; 2 fois, sous Louis VII, que divers accords font état d'une possibilité d'affaiblissement en 1164, en 1185, il est probable que les mutations ont été encore plus nombreuses.

Le monnayage seigneurial en Picardie

Est depuis plus ou moins longtemps aux mains de diverses puissances bien établies.

L'abbaye de Corbie fut l'une des premières à s'adjuger un monnayage indépendant. A la fin du XIè siècle en 1080, la monnaie est au meme titre et poids que celle d'Amiens (7è, 583/1000).

Le monnayage d'Amiens est anonyme (PAX CIVIBVS TVIS) jusqu'à ce que Philippe d'Alsace, par sa femme ait mis la main sur le comté.

Le comté de Vermandois a un atelier monétaire à Saint-Quentin où l'on fabrique au XIIè siècle des deniers au type du Saint-Quentin assis avec au revers, le mot MARTIR barrant le champ. Signalons encore la monnaie épiscopale de Noyon dont l'existence est attestée dans la seconde moitié du XIè et au XIIè siècle.

En Ponthieu, les comtes monnaient à Abbeville depuis le XIè siècle.

A Boulogne enfin les relations des comtés avec l'Angleterre se manifestent par l'emploi de certains types originaux et de gravure délicate; l'alliance du comte avec la maison de Flandre apparait dans le choix d'un type à l'A dans le champ qui se rapproche du type amiénois de Philippe d'Alsace: PAX puis A entre deux fleurs de lis.

En Ternois les Candavène, comtes de Saint-Pol, monnaient au XIIè siècle, peut-etre dès la fin du XIè, selon 2 types dont l'un n'est pas sans rappeler le parisis.

Il n'y a pas entre ces monnaies de lien typologique marqué, tout au plus une préférence pour les motifs fleuronnés à Boulogne, Ponthieu et Saint-Pol.

Le monnayage seigneurial en Flandre a commencé à la fin du Xè siècle. Au XIIè siècle, il est attesté à Arras, Saint-Omer ou il est le fait du comte, de Saint-Bertin et peut-être de la commune, à Aire, Bergues, Lille, Orchies, Ypres, Dixmude et peut-être Bruges, Courtrai, Gand (émissions plus tardives). Les ateliers monétaires sont situés, d'après le compte de 1187,[7] aux endroits des recettes les plus importantes sauf à Furnes au nord, Lécluse, Bapaume, Hesdin et Lillers au sud. Il est étonnant qu'on n'ait pas monnayé àFurnes et je me demande s'il n'y aurait pas lieu de reconsidérer le classement de petits deniers de Flandre si complexe à cause des difficultés d'interprétation des légendes en raison de l'anonymat ou de la ferme. Dans la partie méridionale du comté, on pourrait chercher une explication dans la ferme accordée par le comte à un monétaire Simon qui inscrit son nom sur les monnaies plutôt que celui de l'atelier (les monnaies de Simon pourraient provenir, outre Arras ou Amiens, de Lécluse, Bapaume, Hesdin ou Lillers). En Flandre l'apparence de la monnaie a subi une évolution particulière. Le poids d'argent fin y a diminué, mais plutot que de compenser cette diminution de l'argent et de maintenir le poids en ajoutant du cuivre, on a maintenu le titre et donc diminué le poids et le module. Le denier de Flandre connut ainsi des amenuisements successifs dont les étapes ont été déterminées récemment par J. Ghyssens.[8]

Au début du XIIè siècle, le denier de bon argent pesant 0.60 g est l'équivalent sous une forme différente de celui de Louis VI.

Une réduction a lieu entre 1137 et 1141 àl'époque de la création du parisis du type FRA/NCO en boustrophédon. Les pièces seraient les 3/4 ou les 4/5 des précédentes. Cette émission dure jusque dans les années 1180. Avant 1187, une nouvelle réduction est effectuée dont le compte de 1187 se fait l'écho en distinguant des deniers forts qui se trouvent dans un rapport de 9 à 10 avec de nouveaux deniers. La monnaie flammande serait restée stable ensuite durant un siècle. Cependant les tableaux comparatifs des trésors monétaires dressés par J. Ghyssens montrent que les deniers des diverses périodes qu'il a déterminées ne se mélangent pas sauf pour le passage de la 1ère à la 2ème aux environs de 1180 (ce qui recoupe la donnée du compte de 1187) et dans une moindre mesure par le passage de la 2è à la 3è(3p/400 dans le trésor de Bèrelles); il y aurait donc eu des refontes systématiques et probablement des mutations dans les premières années et au milieu du XIIIè siècle.

Parallèlement à ce monnayage flamand existent un monnayage à Lens avant que Thierry d'Alsace ne s'empare du comté, un monnayage à Béthune dans la seconde moitié du XIIè siècle, un monnayage à Tournai dont les deniers avaient cours à la fin du XIIè pour la moitié des deniers flamands en 1187 ou 1202 (d'après J. Ghyssens). Le système monétaire flamand typologiquement original mais intrinsèquement équivalent à la monnaie royale est étendu vers le sud après que Philippe d'Alsace, par sa femme, ait assuré son autorité sur l'Amiénois. Le denier amiénois est ainsi rattaché à une autre aire de circulation: il pénétrait jusqu'à Pontoise; on le trouve désormais dans le nord du comté de Flandre (Beveren) et dans un fief de l'éveque de Cambrai (Saint-Aybert). Cette mesure ne touche d'ailleurs que l'Amiénois. Dans les autres possessions d'Isabelle en Vermandois, à Péronne, à Crépy, le grand denier est maintenu.[9]

Cette remarquable tentative d'extension de la zone du petit denier flamand est arrêtée net par Philippe Auguste, le premier souverain qui ait mené une politique monétaire systématique, vers le nord de la Seine d'abord, vers la Loire ensuite.[10] Après son intervention dans la succession d'Isabelle de Vermandois le roi garde Amiens, Montdidier et Roye. Au même moment il oblige l'abbé de Corbie, enclave dans l'Amiénois à suspendre sa fabrication tout en lui délivrant une charte de non-préjudice.[11] Il est donc probable que le roi a éliminé le petit denier flamand et l'a remplacé par le parisis. Le petit denier qui disparait à ce moment là a sans doute été refondu et transformé en parisis ce que l'équivalence du poids d'argent rendait facile. En tout cas les rôles sont renversés, c'est le parisis qui progresse vers le nord et non le petit denier flamand vers le sud.

Une seconde initiative encore plus importante est prise par le roi après la mort de Philippe d'Alsace. Philippe Auguste non content d'avoir ramené l'Amiénois vers le système royal y rattache maintenant "l'Artois". Il décide de la création d'un grand denier assez fortement allié à Arras. Ce denier sera fait selon le type parisis qui est ainsi privilégié par rapport aux autres monnaies royales, et est étendu à Montreuil (qui abandonne de ce fait le type de l'église) à Péronne et à Saint-Omer (que le roi dut céder à nouveau au comte de Flandre entre 1200 et 1212). Cette unification marque le renouveau de la monnaie royale qui connait un type commun à une partie du royaume pour la première fois depuis l'époque carolingienne (au sud de la Loire la fabrication cesse à Etampes et Orléans).

Le succès du parisis se traduit tout d'abord par des imitations dues à Aliénor de Vermandois à Saint-Quentin, à Mathieu d'Alsace à Crépy, à Guillaume de Pontieu à Abbeville, à Renaud de Dammartin à Boulogne. Seuls les seigneurs de Béthune maintiennent un monnayage de type flamand.

Ainsi au début du XIIIè siècle, dans les Pays-Bas français peu de monnaies subsistent en dehors de la monnaie royale et de la monnaie flamande. Ces monnaies sont en général plus faibles que le parisis quelles ne concurrencent pas: la monnaie de Noyon est dans un rapport de 3 pour 2; celle de Tournai et celle de Laon (accord de 1158) de 2 pour 1.[12] L'artésien ou monnaie de Flandre et le parisis sont équivalents au milieu du XIIè (1259); il en est sans doute de même au début du XIIIè siècle.

Les autres monnaies seigneuriales s'effacent au moins pour un temps: Celle du Vermandois réuni au domaine royal à la mort d'Aliénor, celle du Comté de Boulogne confisqué sur Renaud de Dammartin en 1212; celles des cités épiscopales de Beauvais, Laon et Noyon disparaissent après Philippe Auguste. Saint-Pol et Ponthieu ne semblent pas monnayer à cette époque mais ils reprennent leur monnayage durant la seconde moitié du XIIIè siècle.

Bref le parisis royal a supplanté puis étouffé au nord de la Seine la prolifération des monnaies seigneuriales.

La circulation monétaire s'en trouve assainie.

Quelle est cette circulation et que nous apprend-elle?

A considérer les trésors monétaire il y a dans le Nord du royaume deux aires de circulation nettement distincte.

Durant le règne de Louis VII les monnaies picardes circulent d'abord dans la région où celles sont émises (la Boisselle, Picardie ?) où se trouvent également des monnaies de Laon, de Champagne (Meaux, Troyes, Provins). Les monnaies picardes se retrouvent vers le sud (Pontoise), l'est (Champagne, Thourotte, trésors de la vallée de la Meuse) où elles ont entrainés par les pièces de Verdun, (Transinne, Ciney, Fischbach).[13]

Aucune de ces monnaies ne se trouve en Flandre.

Aprés le milieu du XIIè siècle, elles ne dépassent pas le Ponthieu ou un fief de l'éveque de Cambrai. Le seul exemple de deniers de petit module trouvés en Picardie (La Bouteille, Aisne) concerne des pièces de Douai, Tournai, Valenciennes.

La Flandre par contre est ouverte aux pièces de Hainaut, d'Anvers, aux monnaies anglaises et surtout aux monnaies impériales. Le témoignage des trésors recoupe ici celui des textes et l'on peut mettre en parallèle la convention passée entre Philippe d'Alsace et Frédéric Barberousse en 1173 par laquelle le comte de Flandre, en contre partie de privilèges accordés aux marchands flamands, donne libre cours dans ses états aux monnaies frappées par l'empereur à Duisbourg (deniers) et à Aix (oboles) et à celles de l'archevêque de Cologne. Deux trésors composés uniquement de monnaies germaniques ont été découverts l'un à Huy (5500) l'autre à Bruxelles (400); un 3ème trésor, celui de Beveren est formé pour un quart de monnaies impériales. Les deniers de Cologne couraient les 3 pour 10 deniers de Flandre.

La présence des pièces impériales se justifie par cette équivalence. Elles faisaient office de multiple des deniers flamands. L'on voit ici s'ébaucher un système monétaire complexe adapté à des échanges de plus grande envergure. On peut s'interroger d'ailleurs sur la durée de ce phénomène car les monnaies impériales ne sont pas mentionnées dans le compte de 1187. Avaient-elles encore cours quinze ans après l'accord? Seules les monnaies d'Anvers, doubles de celles de Flandre et les monnaies de Douai, moitié du denier flamand, apparaissent en 1187. A la fin du XIIè, et au XIIIè siècle, apparait un nouveau système de multiples basé sur l'esterlin, dont la monnaie de compte se fait l'écho très tôt, les trésor monétaires surtout dans la 2è moitié du XIIIème.

Le rattachement de la monnaie d'Amiens au système flamand n'a pas eu apparemment pour résultat d'élargir l'aire de circulation du petit denier. Par contre, la création d'un parisis en Artois a eu des conséquences plus nettes.

Ce parisis artésien et ses imitations pénètrent très avant dans le reste du royaume. Cependant il s'agit la plupart du temps d'un, 2 ou 3 exemplaires et lorsqu'il y en a plus ils représentent de toutes façons, une très faible proportion des monnaies thésaurisées: 7% à Lusignan, 3.5% à Saint-Jean-Brévelay, 1.3% à St-Clair-sur-Elle, 8% à Pagny-sur-Moselle, 1.5% à Corcelles-Frémoy. Les 4 trésors qui comprennent beaucoup de parisis sont ceux de Compiègne (début XIIIè; 314 ex), Gisors (milieu XIIIè; 69% dont Arras 42%, Chappes (2è moitié XIIIè; 66% dont Arras 43%) d'origine bretonne (dernier quart XIIIè: 21% dont Arras 10%).[13]

Les trésors de parisis attestent l'activité de l'atelier d'Arras presque toujours mieux représenté que celui de Paris quelques soient le nombre d'exemplaires et le lieu d'enfouissement.

Le parisis parvient même en petite quantité en Flandre. Deux trésors l'un du 2è quart de XIIIè siècle l'autre de la seconde moitié, contenaient des parisis et des monnaies de Champagne en proportion égale ou inférieure à 10% du total (Bérelles, Pulderbos); la proportion est plus importante à Saint-Omer rendu au roi (30%). Pour important qu'il soit,ce témoignage sur la circulation de l'artésien puis du parisis artésien est curieusement incomplet puisqu'il ne témoigne d'aucune ouverture sur les foires de Champagne.

Somme toute, le témoignage des trésors monétaires se montre partiel, intéressant dans certains cas: les grands deniers d'Amiens au XIIIè s, la convention entre l'empereur et le comte de Flandre. Pour diverses raisons, en particulier la ferme de plusieurs ateliers au monétaire Simon, la circulation monétaire rend mal compte de l'extraordinaire développement de l'Artois au XIIè s, de sa puissance au XIIIè et surtout des relations internationales que pratiquait la partie la plus riche de sa population.

C'est donc sur une note restrictive que je terminerai cet exposé. Dans le cas qui nous intéresse aujourd'hui, l'évolution monétaire a suivi fidèlement l'évolution politique, essentiellement sans doute parceque le roi de France avait un dessein politique qu'il a mis en oeuvre. Par ailleurs, les liens entre le développement économique et le monnayage sont évidents mais on ne peut se fier à celui-ci pour déterminer les orientations de celui-là. La monnaie ne joue pas un role prééminent dans les échanges qui dépassent l'échelle régionale. La nécessité de la création d'une monnaie plus importante se fait jour. Dans un premier temps, l'esterlin suffira; dans un second temps la création d'une espèce nouvelle, d'une valeur nettement plus élevée s'avérera nécessaire: le gros.

Mais ceci est une autre histoire

Amiens Saint-Quentin Noyon

Ponthieu Boulogne Saint-Pol

Petits Deniers Flamands

Aire Lille Saint-Omer Béthune

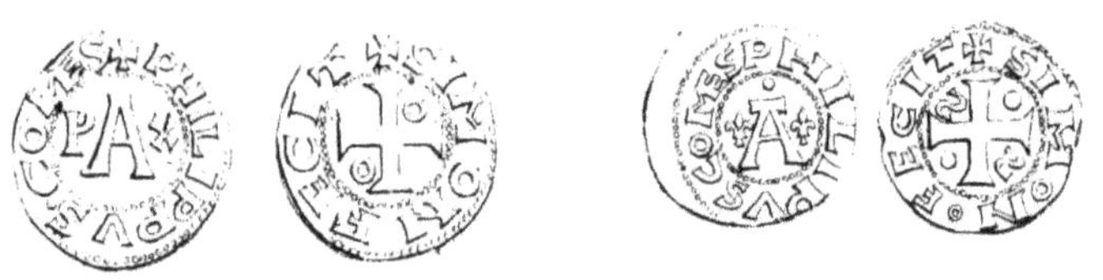

Monetaire Simon

Saint Quentin Crepy

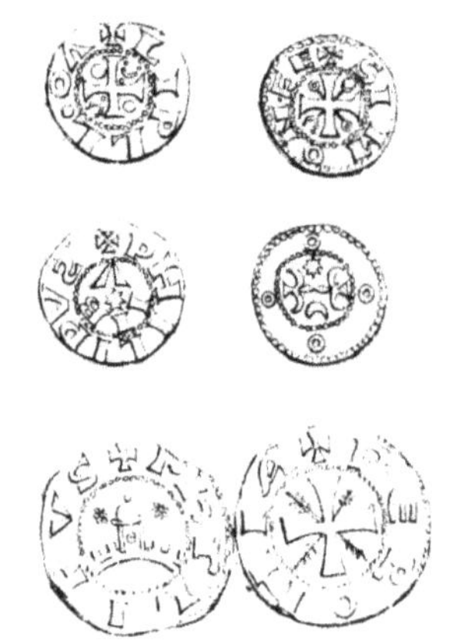

Monetaire Simon

Amiens

Peronne

Monnaies de Philippe d'Alsace

Paris

Philippe Auguste

Arras

Imitations du Parisis

Ponthieu Boulogne Vermandois

COMPARISONS BETWEEN THE POLITICAL, THE ECONOMIC AND THE MONETARY EVOLUTION OF THE NORTH OF FRANCE IN THE TWELFTH CENTURY

Françoise Dumas

Of what value is coinage as a witness of political and economic evolution? This is a question that one can ask of all periods. But the unfolding of political events and the economic development in the north of the French kingdom in the twelfth century are sufficiently well understood to allow us to compare them with what we know about the coinage at the same period.

* * *

Flanders enjoyed a rapid growth, in which one can distinguish several stages. In an early period, in the tenth century, count Arnoul le grand (918-65) respected the Escaut, which separated Flanders from Lotharingia, but he extended his territory from the Canche as far as the Somme, as a result of contests with the count of Vermandois, the marquis of Normandy, and the duke of the Franks. This expansion was slowed down by two minorities and several counties were set up in the south: the county of Boulogne, (facing the sea); that of Ternois or Saint-Pol; Guines carved out of the county of Boulogne; and Hesdin, taken from Ternois.

The barrier in the south formed by these small counties, and a powerful Normandy, led to expansion towards the east, into Lotharingia. The minority of king Henry IV of Germany made the creation of an "imperial Flanders" easier (1056). As a result, the county, with one foot in the French kingdom and one in the Empire, became much more independent.

A new and still bolder attempt failed, namely the union of Flanders and Hainaut under Arnoul III, son of the count of Flanders and the widow of the count of Hainaut. Arnoul, driven out of Flanders by Robert the Frisian (1071-93), kept only Hainaut enfeoffed to the bishop of Liège.

If we turn to the south, and examine the situation from the point of view of the king, we see that in the course of the eleventh century and even more at the beginning of the twelfth, the Capetiens sought to secure recognition of their authority by the feudal lords in the north of the kingdom, and even to enlarge their domain. It is well known that Robert I, the son of Hugues Capet, after having repudiated his wife Suzanne, widow of Arnoul II of Flanders, kept Montreuil. At Soissons, Beauvais, and Senlis, the officers or prelates were loyal subjects, who affixed their seals to royal diplomas.[1] Philippe I (1060-1108) made eleven journeys into Picardy (Amiens, Noyon, Laon, Montreuil).

He intervened at Soissons between the inhabitants and the clergy (1093). He recovered the lordship of Corbie given by Henri I to his sister on her marriage with Baudouin V of Flanders, and married his brother Hugues to the daughter of the count of Vermandois, who also held from her mother the counties of Valois, Montdidier, and Amiens.

Louis VI (1108-37) also intervened on several occasions on behalf of the episcopal county of Beauvais, the episcopal city of Noyon, the county of Vermandois to which he returned Péronne taken from Ebles de Rouci, and on behalf of the bishop of Amiens. In 1132, the peace treaties between Corbie and Amiens were renewed, in the presence of the king.

During the reign of Louis VI, Flanders experienced serious difficulties. Count Charles the Good was assassinated in 1127. Guillaume Cliton, supported by the king of France, was recognized only after having granted charters to almost all the main towns, and made the mistake of relying on the nobility. Thereupon, the towns gave their support to Thierry d'Alsace, who respected their privileges. With the new count there began a period of more than sixty years of strong government, made stronger still by the massive financial resources deriving from the customs, fed by the commercial currents which developed at that time.

In the second half of the twelfth century, the count's domain grew again, particularly towards the south. The count joined Hesdin (c. 1151), Lillers (1151), Lens (1160), and Alost (1165) to his territory. Thierry's younger son Mathieu married the heiress of the county of Boulogne. Only Saint-Pol maintained its power. Further south, the ascendancy of the Flemish dynasty was asserted in a different way. Philippe d'Alsace, Thierry's son, had in 1156 married Elisabeth of Vermandois, who inherited from her brother, a few years later, in 1163, the counties of Vermandois, Amiens, Valois, and Montdidier. So we see the county of Flanders encroaching upon Picardy—a region that the Capetians watched over the more attentively because it was rich in population and resources. (In 1194, Picardy supplied a quarter of a force of sergeants, 2,000 out of 8,000 men. It also suppied a quarter of the receipts of the provostships, although the lands represented only 6% of the domaine.)

The relations between the king and the count were in principle good, and on his death (in 1180) Louis VII entrusted the guardianship of the new king Philippe (Auguste) to Philippe d'Alsace. The count of Flanders arranged for the king to marry his niece Isabelle de Hainaut, daughter of Marguerite de Flandre and Baudouin V, count of Hainaut, later marquis of Namur, the heir presumptive of Flanders from 1177. As a dowry Philippe promised his niece the south of his county, the territories which were to form Artois, namely Arras, Bapaume, Hesdin, Lens, Aire, Ardres, Lillers, Richebourg, and Saint-Omer. However, on the death without issue of Isabelle de Vermandois, countess of Flanders (1183), her husband Philippe d'Alsace came to an agreement with his sister-in-law Aliénor de Vermandois to keep a part of his wife's inheritance; Philippe Auguste then intervened to protect the rights of Aliénor, who had no children. In 1185, by the treaty of Bôves, the king kept the counties of Amiens and Montdidier, and the chatellenies of Roye and Thourotte in compensation for the rights of redemption of and title to Péronne, Saint-Quentin, and Ham, which the count of Flanders enjoyed. The king thus made headway in the valleys of the Oise and the Somme.

When Philippe d'Alsace died at Acre in 1191, Philippe Auguste came to an arrangement with Aliénor, to whom he first ceded Péronne and Saint-Quentin, and then exchanged them for other lordships. In 1213, on the death of Aliénor, the French king recovered Vermandois and Valois into his domain (and he completed his ascendancy by other acquisitions: Clermont-en-Beauvaisis, and Beaumont-sur-Oise). Further north, Philippe-Auguste occupied on his son's behalf the dowry of Isabelle de Hainaut: Arras, Aire, St. Omer, Hesdin, and Lens, and the vassal counties of Guines, Boulogne, Saint-Pol, Béthune, and Lillers. He had to give up the northern part of these territories in 1200, but he took control of them again in 1212 when the young countess Jeanne married Ferrand de Portugal. The victory of Bouvines made this transfer definitive (1214). The king confiscated for a time the county of Boulogne from Renaud de Dammartin, and Ponthieu from Simon. It was no longer the count of Flanders who was expanding his interest southwards, but on the contrary the king of France who was taking a firm grip in the north of his kingdom. Artois formed the appanage of Robert, the brother of Louis IX, 1226, and it became a county in 1237, paramount over the county of Boulogne. There was therefore during the twelfth century a clear-cut ebb and flow, which ended in the victory of the king over the count of Flanders.

The political struggles which have just been outlined were not without an economic basis. Picardy by the produce of its soil, and Flanders by its industry and commerce, were rich regions of the first importance. In both, there was a strong demographic upturn, which led to the conquest of virgin lands by reclamation and also by drainage schemes. In Flanders, the princes of the house of Alsace were powerful enough to carry out a genuine economic policy. They undertook drainage schemes, which brought land into their hands, and provided pasture in proximity to cultivated ground. They provided dykes and canals to improve the ports which already existed, such as Saint-Omer, and founded new towns: Gravelines (1163), Calais (1163/73), Dunkerque (1180). The flow of the waterways was improved, and thereby the commercial links with the interior were made easier. So were contacts by land, thanks to improvements in harnessing (the use of horse-shoes, the shoulder-collar and new types of cart) and to the opening of new routes (Cologne-Bruges via Brabant, for example).

Part of the rural population found employment in the towns, in particular in the textile industry, which became urban. Mercantile activity developed. Successive fairs were held in Flanders throughout the course of the year. Travelling merchants formed themselves into associations or guilds in the eleventh century, in Hainaut, in Flanders, and at Montreuil. Journeys to England were made from as early as 1024-36. Also in the eleventh century, the customs records of Saint-Vaast d'Arras prove the movement of English cheeses, of wool, of cloths, of vegetable dye-stuffs. The translation of Saint Lewine, which tells of the search for relics by a monk of Bergues shows him meeting with Flemish merchants in Sussex. In the middle of the twelfth century, the merchants of St. Omer had their own house in London. Exchanges also took place with the East: the cloths of Ypres are found at Novgorod in the twelfth century; Ghent looked towards the Empire. Arras, however, looked south.

The town which occupies the leading place in this economic development is Arras, of which the activity seems to be very important, and the commercial dynamism very great: in 1127 it enjoyed a preferential tarrif at the toll of Bapaume, on the route southwards. Ten years later, its merchants were to be found at the Champagne fairs, which were then just beginning. The transactions involved Flemish cloths and oriental luxury goods. Then they went as far as Genoa where they exported their products and those of other centres. They were found also at Saint-Gilles-du-Gard and at Marseilles. In parallel with this growth of activity, the urban population acquired its first liberties (1102). The town, which was already of some importance, with about 20,000 people, comprised two groupings: Arras, the episcopal city, where a bishop again resided from the end of the eleventh century (in 1094, the see was separated from Cambrai), and Arras, the town around the abbey of Saint-Vaast. It was surrounded by a great stone wall, and contained two large squares before 1090. Building went on apace. The cathedral of Notre-Dame, built in the Romanesque style in 1030, was rebuilt in the Gothic style between 1160 and 1183.

Other centres for textiles developed as well: Ypres, Dixmude, Abbeville. But the cloth industry, which was to decline in the thirteenth century, was not the only source of commercial revenue: foodstuffs, wine, grain, fish, played their part (especially at Saint-Omer). Finally, and most of all, finance took the lead. What is important and characteristic about these towns in the South of Flanders is that some of the citizens enjoyed capital resources, of which the origin should be sought in income from landed property, augmented by revenues from commerce.[2] Their capital gave them a remarkable freedom of action. Guillaume Cade of Saint-Omer made forward deals, for example, enormous forward purchases of wool from flocks in England.[3] But they were above all money lenders. The same Guillaume Cade lent at least £5,000 to Henry II. At Arras the Crespin family, who dealt especially in wine, made loans to the counts, to towns, to abbeys: in February 1223 they lent 1040 livres parisis to Guy de Chatillon, count of St. Pol. In July of the same year they lent 9000, and in 1225, 2,050 livres parisis to the countess of Flanders. They even lent 20,000 livres parisis on a single occasion—that is, half as much as the revenues of the count of Flanders.

Naturally the feudal lords whom we have just mentioned also profited directly, and not just through the medium of loans from their commercial activity. If the transfer of the frontier zone in the south of Flanders to the French kingdom was marked by bitter struggles, it was because focal points of mercantile traffic were involved: Bapaume and Péronne, for example. For Flanders we have the compte général of 1187, which deals with the old part of the count's domain. It is of interest for the total sums of money which it reveals, and also for the very general use of coin, of which it provides evidence. All the revenues, even when they are collected in kind, are converted into money, except for those which are immediately redistributed. As regards the coinage, we have been aware for some years that it spread into the countryside. It was used within the framework of the manorial estate, which evolved from the Carolingian villa. The customary labour owed to the lord to permit the exploitation of the demesne was bought out, or else the demesne was farmed; tenancies were also paid for in cash (quit-rents, and heriots). Coin was also used within the framework of the communal lordships where the lord progressed from the exercise of protection and justice to economic exploitation (the use of bakeries, mills, fish-ponds, and wine-presses; rights of custom and toll). The exploitation of seigniorial rights provoked, by reaction, the formation of rural communities, on the scale of the village, the parish, or the lordship. The communities, directed by a mayor and magistrates, had administrative and judicial powers, and collective fines could also be imposed on them.

Money seems therefore to have circulated in northern France at all social levels.

We must now ask how this political and economic situation is reflected in the currency, by looking at the evolution of types, changes in intrinsic value, and the circulation of the coinage.

* * *

The royal coinage

The Capetians started out with very little: the only coin bearing the name of king Hugues Capet is that of bishop Hervé of Beauvais. But royal coinage very soon appeared at Montreuil, under Philippe I, and its issue was maintained there without interruption until the reign of Philippe Auguste. It was struck at Paris from the time of Robert le Pieux, the son of Hugues Capet; and it was introduced progressively north of the Seine, at Senlis and Pontoise under Louis VI, and at Compiègne under Louis VII, in a piecemeal way. In the second half of the twelfth century, following an agreement with the bishop of Laon in 1158, the name of Louis VII, and subsequently that of Philippe Auguste, appeared on the episcopal coins. There is no typological unity among these coins: the royal coinage is nothing but local coinages. The same is true for the rest of the domain (Etampes, Orléans, etc.). However, a shift can be discerned whereby the money of Paris, the denier parisis, acquired a privileged status. At Beauvais, for example, in 1179, a tax of 5 shillings in the money of Beauvais, 5 sous beauvaisis, was transformed into a payment of 6 sous parisis.[6] The conditions under which these coins were minted are not at all well known. Dieudonné has shown that they underwent several debasements, first under Philippe I, then under Louis VI (1108-37), who had to agree with the people of Compiègne in 1120 not to reduce the alloy below 50%, and again under Philippe Auguste. The coinage seems to have been 8d, and later 7d fine under Philippe I (67%, then 58%), 6d under Louis VI and Louis VII (50%), and 5d under Philippe Auguste (39.5%). The weight of fine silver in a denier will thus have gone from 0.92g to 0.78 g under Philippe I, to 0.63 g (Louis VI), and 0.48 g (Louis VII).[6] Considering that we know of five varieties of parisis under Philippe I and a similar number under Louis VI and VII; and that at Montreuil the type was changed five times under Louis VI and twice under Louis VII; and that various agreements envisage a possible debasement in 1164 and another in 1185, it is probable that the alterations in the alloy were even more numerous.

The seigniorial coinage in Picardy

Various authorities had already, for shorter or longer periods, firmly established their own coins. The abbey of Corbie was one of the first to appropriate an independent coinage. At the end of the eleventh century, in 1080, the issues were of the same alloy and weight as those of Amiens (7d. fine, or 58%).

The coinage of Amiens was anonymous (PAX CIVIBVS TVIS), up to the time when Philippe d'Alsace, through his wife, took control of the county.

The county of Vermandois had a mint at Saint-Quentin where in the twelfth century deniers were struck with, as their obverse type, Saint Quentin seated, and, on the reverse, the word MARTIR placed as a bar across the field. Mention should also be made of the episcopal coinage of Noyon, the existence of which is attested in the second half of the eleventh and in the twelfth century.

In Ponthieu, the counts struck coinage at Abbeville from the eleventh century onwards.

At Boulogne, the relations of the counts with England are shown by the use of certain original and delicately-engraved types; the alliance of the count with the house of Flanders is seen in the choice of a design with an A in the field, which is comparable with the type of Philippe d'Alsace at Amiens, namely the word PAX, and subsequently an A, between two fleurs-de-lis.

In Ternois the Candavène family, counts of Saint-Pol, minted in the twelfth century, and perhaps at the end of the eleventh, using two types, of which one is not without some similarities to the denier parisis.

Among these various coinages, there is no pronounced typological similarity, at most a preference for designs using fleurs, at Boulogne, Ponthieu, and Saint-Pol.

The seigniorial coinage in Flanders began at the end of the tenth century. In the twelfth century, it is attested at Arras, at Saint-Omer (where it is struck by the count, by Saint-Bertin, and perhaps also by the Commune), at Aire, Bergues, Lille, Orchies, Ypres, Dixmude, and perhaps Bruges, Courtrais, and Ghent (later issues). The mints were located in the places where, according to the compte of 1187,[7] receipts were greatest, except at Furnes in the north, and L'écluse, Bapaume, Hesdin, and Lillers in the south. It is surprising that there was no mint at Furnes, and I wonder whether it would not be in order to reconsider the classification of the small deniers of Flanders, which is a complex problem because of the difficulty of interpreting abbreviated legends or anonymous types, and because of the leasing of mint-rights. In the southern part of the county, one might look for an explanation in the lease granted by the count to a moneyer Simon, who put his own name on the coins rather than that of the mint. (The coins of Simon could come, apart from Arras or Amiens, from L'écluse, Bapaume, Hesdin, or Lillers.) In Flanders the physical appearance of the coins evolved in a particular way. The weight of fine silver in each coin dwindled, but rather than compensate for this reduction in silver contents by adding copper and thus maintaining the weight, the fineness was maintained, and therefore the weight and module were decreased. The denier of Flanders was thus subject to successive reductions, the stages of which have recently been determined by J. Ghyssens.[8]

At the beginning of the twelfth century, the denier of good silver, with a weight of 0.60 g, is the equivalent under a different form of that of Louis VI.

A reduction occurred at a date between 1137 and 1141 at the time when the denier parisis was created, with FRA/NCO in boustrophedon as its type. The new coins would seem to have been three-quarters to four-fifths of the value of those they replaced. This issue lasted until the 1180s. Before 1187, a new reduction was made, which the compte of 1187 reveals when it distinguishes denier forts, 9 of which are equal to 10 of the nouveaux deniers. Thereafter the Flemish coinage seems to have been stable for a century. The statistical tables of hoards drawn up by J. Ghyssens show, however, that the coins of the various periods that he recognized did not mingle, except during the transition from the first to the second period, in the years around 1180 (which tallies with the information from the compte of 1187), and to a lesser extent during the transition from his second to his third period, as in the Bérelles hoard. There would seem, therefore, to have been systematic recoinages, and probably devaluations, at the beginning and in the middle of the thirteenth century.

In parallel with this Flemish coinage, there was a coinage at Lens before Thierry d'Alsace took control of the county, a coinage at Béthune in the second half of the twelfth century, and a coinage at Tournai, of which mint the deniers circulated at the end of the twelfth century in 1187 or 1202 (following Ghyssens) at half the value of the Flemish deniers. The Flemish monetary system, which was original in its types, but intrinsically equivalent to the royal coinage, gained an extension towards the south after Philippe d'Alsace, through his wife, had established his authority over the region of Amiénois. The denier amiénois was thus attached to another area of circulation: it penetrated as far as Pontoise, and was to be found thereafter in the north of the county of Flanders (Beveren), and in a fief of the bishop of Cambrai (Saint-Aybert). This arrangement, however, affected only Amiénois. In Isabelle's other possessions, in Vermandois, at Péronne and at Crépy, the large denier was retained.[9]

This remarkable attempt to extend the zone of the small denier of Flanders was halted abruptly by Philippe Auguste, the first ruler to conduct a systematic monetary policy, at first northwards of the Seine, and later at the Loire.[10] After his intervention in the succession of Isabelle de Vermandois, the king kept Amiens, Montdidier, and Roye. At the same time he obliged the abbey of Corbie, which was an enclave in Amiénois, to suspend its mint-activity while at the same time giving it a deed of non-prejudice.[11] It is probable, therefore, that the king eliminated the small denier of Flanders and replaced it with the parisis. The small deniers which disappeared from circulation at that moment were no doubt melted down and transformed into deniers parisis—a task made easy by the equivalence in silver contents. In any case, the roles were reversed, and it was the parisis which made progress towards the north, and not the small denier of Flanders towards the south.

A second and still more important initiative was taken by the king after the death of Philippe d'Alsace. Philippe Auguste, not satisfied with having brought Amiénois into the royal system, now added Artois to it. He decided on the creation of a large denier with a considerable degree of alloy at Arras. This denier was to be made in accordance with the parisis type, which was thus privileged in relation to the other royal coinages. It was extended to Montreuil (which gave up thereby its design with a church), to Péronne, and to Saint-Omer (which the king had to cede once again to the count of Flanders, between 1200 and 1212). This unification marked the renewal of the royal coinage, which now had a common design in a part of the kingdom, for the first time since the Carolingian age. (South of the Loire, minting ceased at Etampes and Orléans.) The success of the parisis resulted directly in imitations produced by Aliénor de Vermandois at Saint-Quentin, by Mathieu d'Alsace at Crépy, by Guillaume de Ponthieu at Abbeville, and by Renaud de Dammartin at Boulogne. Only the lords of Béthune maintained a coinage of the Flemish type.

Thus at the beginning of the thirteenth century, there remained few coinages in the French Low Countries other than the royal coinage and the Flemish coinage. These few were in general of lower value than the parisis, with which they did not compete: the coinage of Noyon was in a relationship of 3 to 2; that of Tournai and that of Laon (an agreement of 1158) of 2 to 1.[12] The denier artésien i.e. the coinage of Flanders and the parisis were equivalent in the middle of the thirteenth century (1259); and the same was doubtless true at the beginning of the thirteenth century.

The other seignorial coinages were suppressed at least for a time: that of Vermandois, reunited to the royal domain at the death of Aliénor, that of the county of Boulogne confiscated from Renaud de Dammartin in 1212; those of the episcopal cities of Beauvais, Laon and Noyon disappeared after Philippe Auguste's reign. Saint-Pol and Ponthieu seem not to have struck at this time, but they resumed minting in the second half of the thirteenth century.

In short, the royal parisis supplanted and then suppressed the proliferation of seignorial coinages north of the Seine.

Monetary circulation was thus put on a sounder and healthier footing.

<u>What was this circulation, and what does it teach us?</u>

From the point of view of the hoards, there were in the north of the kingdom two clearly distinct areas of circulation.

During the reign of Louis VII the coins of Picardy circulated at first in the region where they were issued (Boisselle, Picardy (?)), where there were also to be found coins of Laon, and of Champagne (Meaux, Troyes, and Provins). The coins of Picardy are found again towards the south (Pontoise), and the east (Champagne, Thourotte, and hoards from the Meuse valley where they were carried along by the coins of Verdun —Transinne, Ciney, Fischbach).[13] None of these coinages is found in Flanders. After the middle of the twelfth century, they go no further than Ponthieu or a fief of the bishop of Cambrai. The only case of deniers of small module found in Picardy (La Bouteille, Aisne) involves coins of Douai, Tournai, and Valenciennes.

Flanders on the other hand was open to the coins of Hainaut and Antwerp, to the English coins, and above all to imperial coins. The evidence of the hoards is in agreement here with the texts, and one can adduce the convention agreed between Philippe d'Alsace and Frederick Barbarossa in 1173 by which the count of Flanders, in response to privileges accorded to Flemish merchants, granted free circulation in his territories to the coins struck by the emperor at Duisberg (deniers) and at Aachen (oboles), and to the issues of the archbishop of Cologne. Two hoards made up exclusively of German coins have been discovered, one at Huy (5,500), and the other at Brussels (400); a third hoard, from Beveren, includes a quarter of imperial coins. The deniers of Cologne were current at 3 for 10 deniers of Flanders. The presence of imperial coins is justified by this exchange-rate. They served as multiples of Flemish deniers. We see the rough sketch for a complex monetary system adapted to transactions of wider scope. It may be questioned, however, how long this phenomenon lasted, for imperial coins are not mentioned in the compte of 1187. Were they still in circulation fifteen years after the agreement? Only the coins of Antwerp, which matched those of Flanders, and the coins of Douai, worth half the Flemish denier, are mentioned in 1187. At the end of the twelfth and in the thirteenth century, there appears a new system of multiples based on the sterling. The money of account reflects the use of sterling at a very early stage, but the hoards do so especially in the second half of the thirteenth century.

The link between the coinage of Amiens and the Flemish system did not, apparently, result in an enlargement of the area of circulation of the small denier. On the other hand, the creation of a denier parisis in Artois had clearer consequences.

This parisis of Artois, and its imitations, penetrated very deeply into the rest of the kingdom. But for most of the time it is a matter of one, 2, or 3 specimens, and when there are more they represent in any case a very minor proportion of the coins hoarded: 7% at Lusignan, 3.5% at Saint-Jean-Brévelay, 1.3% at Saint-Clair-sur-Elle, 8% at Pagny-sur-Moselle, 1.5% at Corcelles--Frémoy. The four hoards which contain numerous parisis are those of Compiègne (beginning of the XIIIth century: 314 specimens), Gisors mid-XIIIth century (69%, of which Arras contributes 42%), Chappes (second half of the XIIIth century: 66% of which Arras contributes 43%), and a hoard from Brittany (last quarter of the XIIIth century: 21%, of which Arras contributes 10%).[14]

The hoards of deniers parisis demonstrate the activity of the mint of Arras, which is almost always better represented than that of Paris, whatever the total number of coins or the place of concealment.

The parisis even reached Flanders in small quantities. Two hoards, one from the second quarter of the thirteenth century, and the other from the second half of the century, contained parisis and coins of Champagne in proportions equal to or less than 10% of the total (Bérelles, Pulderbos). The proportion is greater at Saint-Omer, which had been given back to the king (30%). Important as this evidence is regarding the circulation of the denier artésien, and then the parisis artésien, it is curiously incomplete since it has nothing to say about any access to the fairs of Champagne,

All told, the evidence of the hoards seems to be incomplete, and of particular value only for certain topics: the large deniers of Amiens in the twelfth century; the convention between the emperor and the count of Flanders. For various reasons, in particular the lease of several mints to the moneyer Simon, the circulating medium gives a poor account of the extraordinary development of Artois in the twelfth century, of its power in the thirteenth century, and above all of the international contacts of the richest sector of the population.

It is on a restrictive note, therefore, that I end this survey. In the example that we have looked at today, monetary evolution faithfully followed political evolution, essentially, no doubt, because the French king had a political plan, which he put into action. On the other hand, while the links between economic development and minting are plain to see, one cannot rely on the latter to determine the directions of the former. Coinage did not play a pre-eminent role in transactions which went beyond the scale of the region. The necessity to create a more important coin emerged. In an early stage, the sterling sufficed. At a later stage, the creation of a new domination, of a distinctly higher value, was to prove necessary: the gros.

But that is another story.

OUVRAGES A CONSULTER

F. L. Ganshof. La Flandre, dans F. Lot et R. Fawtier, Histoire des Institutions francaises au Moyen Age, I, Paris, 1957.

H. Platelle, dans Histoire des Pays-Bas francais. Toulouse 1972.

R. Fossier, dans Histoire de la Picardie, Toulouse, 1974.

J. Lafaurie. Les Monnaies des rois de France, I, Paris, 1951.

F. Poey d'Avant. Monnaies féodales de France. Paris, 1858-1862.

A. Blanchet et A. Dieudonné, Manuel de Numismatique francaise, IV, Paris, 1936.

C. Richebé. Les Monnaies féodales d'Artois. Paris, 1963.

P. Crinon. La Monnaie de Reims au Moyen Age VI-XIVes. Thèse pour le doctorat de 3e cycle. Paris-Nancy, 1978, dactyl.

Trouvailles Monétaires Portées sur la Carte

1. Avesnes (Nord): E. Tordeux. Mémoire de la Société d'émulation de Cambrai, 1833, 203-211.
2. Beaugency (Loiret): RN, 1836, 250. (Non porté sur la carte.)
3. Bérelles (Nord): R.B.N., 1924, 206-209. Ghyssens, 130-131.
4. Beveren-Waas (Belgique): RBN, 1892, 211-214-Ghyssens, 56.
5. Bretagne: RN, 1976, 171-185. (Non porté sur la carte.)
6. Bruxelles (Belgique): RBN, 1872, 295.
7. Chappes (Allier): RN, 1964, 162.
8. Charleroi (Belgique): RBN, 1948, 87-93; 1858, 362-373. Ghyssens 97.

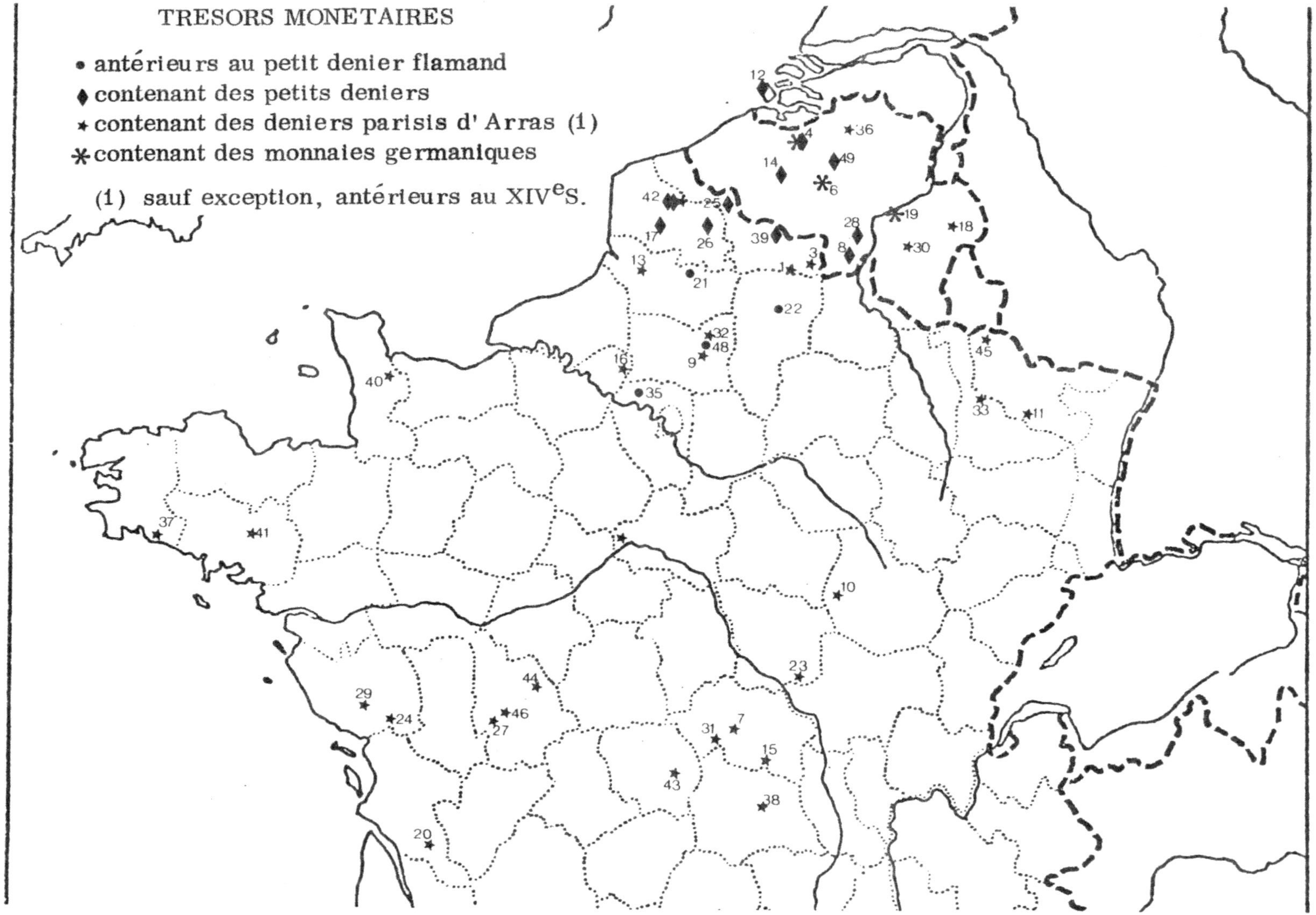
TRESORS MONETAIRES
• antérieurs au petit denier flamand
♦ contenant des petits deniers
⋆ contenant des deniers parisis d'Arras (1)
✻ contenant des monnaies germaniques
(1) sauf exception, antérieurs au XIVe S.

9. Compiègne (Oise): M. Hémery. Bulletin de la société historique de Compiègne, 1925.

10. Corcelles--Frêmoy (Cote d'Or): RN, 1962, 237.

11. Dieuze (Moselle): RN, 1843, 185.

12. Dombourg (Pays-Bas): R. Macaré, Dissertation sur les monnaies trouvées à Dombourg, 1856.

13. Epagne (Somme): A. Van Robais. Notes d'archéologie, d'histoire et de numismatique. Abbeville, 1877-1883.

14. Erwetegem (Belgique): RBN, 1880, 216.

15. Gannat (Allier): RN, 1839, 67, 152, 216.

16. Gisors (Eure): BNJ, 1972, 22-43.

17. Grammont (Pas-de-Calais): L. Deschamps de Pas. Bull. historique de la société des Antiquaires de Morinie, 1879, 281. Ghyssens 96-97.

18. Grand-Halleux (Belgique): G. Piot Notice sur un dépot de monnaies... Ac. royale de Belgique. Mémoires XXI.

19. Huy (Belgique): Bulletin mensuel de Num., 1883, 145.

20. Jonzac (Charente-Maritime): ASFN, 1878, 232.

21. La Boisselle (Somme): ASFN, 1877, 184. RN, 1916, 294.

22. La Bouteille (Aisne): Bulletin de Num., 1893, 74.

23. La Nocle-Mauclaix (Nièvre): BSFN, 1959, 332.

24. Le Poiré-sur-Velluire (Vendée): Bulletin de Num., 1897, 21.

25. Lille (Nord): Ghyssens, 95-6).

26. Lillers (Pas-de-Calais): Mém. de la Société des Antiquaires de Morinie, 1850, 592.

27. Lusignan (Vienne): RN, 1848, 399.

28. Marcinelle (Belgique): CENB, 1975, 3-7.

29. Mareuil (Vendée): RN, 1844, 374.

30. Mohiville (Belgique): Bulletin mensuel de Num., 1883, 10.

31. Néris-les-Bains (Allier): Bulletin de Num., 1891, 184.

32. Noyon (Oise): RN 1841, 36.

33. Pagny-sur-Moselle (Meurthe et Moselle): RN, 1844, 464.

34. Picardie: RN, 1842, 69. (non porte sur la carte)

35. Pontoise (Val d'Oise): ASFN, 16, 275.

36. Pulderbosch-Zoersel (Belgique): RBN, 1910, 405.

37. Riec-sur-Belon (Finistère): Courrier numismatique, 1925, 53.

38. Riom (Puy-de-Dome): RN, 1842, 460.

39. Saint-Aybert (Nord): RBN, 1853, 17.

40. Saint-Clair-sur-Elle: RN, 1908, 499-521.

41. Saint-Jean-de-Brévelay: RN, 1867, 135.

42. Saint-Omer (Pas-de-Calais): RN 1839, 236; RN 1923, 227; Bulletin de la société des Antiquaires de Morinie, 1852-56, 49.

43. Saint-Pardoux-les-Cards (Creuse): RN, 1868, 232.

44. Sénillé (Vienne): BSFN, 1951, 3.

45. Sierck (Moselle): Mélanges de Numismat, 1878-1882, 240.

46. Smarves (Vienne): RBN, 1873, 229-230.

47. Somme: Bulletin de la Société des Antiquaires de Picardie, 12, 275.

48. Thourotte (Oise): Bulletin mensuel de Numismatique, 1882, 163, 1883, 148.

49. Willebroeck (Belgique): RBN, 1849, 87. La plupart de ces trouvailles ont été repertoriées par C. Richebé (op.cit. supra).

NOTES

1. J. F. Lemarignier, Le Gouvernement royal aux premiers temps capétiens 987-1108, Paris, 1965.

2. Bigwood, Les Financiers d'Arras. Revue belge de philologie et d'histoire, 1924, pp. 770-1.

3. G. Fourquin, Histoire économique de l'Occident médieval, Paris, 1969, p. 259.

4. A. Verhulst et M. Gyseling, Le compte général de 1187...et les institions financières de la Flandre au XIIe siècle, Bruxelles, 1962.

5. P. Guilhiermoz et A. Dieudonné, Chronologie des documents monétaires de la numismatique royale..., R.N., 1929, p. 213, 26.

6. A. Blanchet et A. Dieudonné, Manuel de Numismatique francaise, II, Paris, 1916, p. 203 et 219.

7. A. Verhulst et M. Gysseling, op.cit.

8. J. Ghyssens, Les Petits deniers de Flandre des XIIe et XIIIe siècles. Bruxelles, 1971 (Cercle d'études numismatiques, Travaux, 5).

9. Le droit s'apparente à celui de l'esterlin (St-Quentin), du denier germanique (Péronne) du parisis (Crépy).

10. Il a accordé des chartes de communes à différentes villes: Saint-Quentin (1195), Roye (1197), Crépy (1215) en s'engageant à ne changer la monnaie qu'à certaines conditions. En fait, il s'est gardé d'y monnayer, ce qui était une habile façon de résoudre le problème de ses engagements. P. Guilhiermoz et A. Dieudonné, op.cit., p. 214, 32, 33, 42.

11. Ibid., p. 213, 29.

12. M. Prou, _RN_, 1894, pp. 525-26; 1897, pp. 229-230.

13. _Trésors monétaires à predominance française trouvés en Belgique_, Bruxelles, 1967. (Cercle d'études numismatiques. Travaux 4). Cf. _infra_ P. Crinon.

14. 21% à Beaugency (fin XIIIe) mais seulement 1 monnaie de St Omer.

SOME COINS OF STEPHEN AND EUSTACE AND RELATED ISSUES OF WESTERN FLANDERS

P. J. Seaby

The 'York group' of twelfth-century pennies, of which some 75 specimens are known at the present day, presents intriguing problems of attribution.[1] There are eight main types—the 'WIS' variants of Stephen's first issue, the Flag type, the Lozenge-sceptre coins, the Two-figure type (Stephen and Matilda), the Rodbert horseman pennies, the Bishop Henry coins, and the two main types of Eustace (the Standing Knight pennies and the Lion coins). It is clear that they are associated issues, because of their use of common ornamentation and on typological grounds.

The coins have been recorded only from English finds. There are two single finds: a WIS variant from Peterborough (Cambs.) and a Flag cut halfpenny from the 1977 excavations at Warn on the Tees (Cleveland). One Flag penny is known to have come from the partially recorded 1802 Winterslow (Wilts.) hoard. Three coins, and possibly a number more, come from a late 17th century hoard found at Cattal, near Wetherby (Yorks.). It is only the Flag penny from Winterslow that is known to have occurred in association with other English coins of Stephen and this was a hoard from the latest years of Stephen's reign (*c*. 1150-53).

Some of the Eustace 'Knight' coins display the inscription EBORACI (followed by the additional letters ED.TS or TDEFL) and, not unreasonably, the whole ornamented group of coins has been attributed to the mint of York for this reason. However, not one coin of the group has the conventional 'moneyer-copulative-mint' formula, invariably used on English coinage at this period, and this is a major obstacle to attributing them to a regular English mint.

The coins are generally lighter in weight but of better quality silver than the run of Stephen's coins (although they have been checked only against Stephen's early coinage), but within the ornamented group the Flag coins with Stephen's name and the Knight coins of Eustace can be divided into heavy and light issues.

The lettering employed on the ornamented group has certain characteristics *not* present on other English coins of the period: a rounded E on some coins, a chevron-barred A an omega ω and an uncial U

If one examines the contemporary (or near contemporary) coinage of western Flanders, including Stephen's counties of Boulogne and Lens, the associated county of St. Pol, the seigniory of Bethune, and the neighbouring mint at St. Omer it is noted that ornaments are employed that also appear on the 'York Group' coins: in particular (1) the shield charged with 3 or 6 roundels (a device later found on the armorial bearings of the counts of Boulogne); (2) a curved ornament, shaped like an ox-shoe with six nail holes, found on coins of Lens, St. Omer and an uncertain mint, and (3) a circular ornament with central hole and eight smaller depressions set in a circle.

The accompanying two sheets of illustrations depict some of the early Flemish petits deniers or deniers artesiens which show either the St. Omer mint signature S O ΩE, or its abbreviated forms SΩ, Sω or S O. It seems possible that the SΩ or Sω was adopted as a punning device (jeux de mots); the first two syllables of "omega" approximating to the sound of 'Omer'. The SΩ (or Sω), or variants such as S O, are frequently arranged to appear twice, in opposing quarters of the reverse. That these same letters, arranged in opposing quarters, also appear on some of the Flag type pennies of Stephen and on some of the Standing knight coins of Eustace would be remarkable if there were not some kind of link between them and the mint of St. Omer. Perhaps a die-cutter from St. Omer mint was responsible for producing the dies.

No coins of Stephen are known from the mint of Boulogne, though there are deniers attributed to his father-in-law, Count Eustace III, and to Stephen's sons Eustace IV and William. If the argument that certain Stephen and certain Eustace ornamented coins were somehow connected with St. Omer can be sustained, then one wonders whether Stephen moved his mint from Boulogne (and possibly also from Lens) to St. Omer, a major centre of the Flemish woollen industry situated beyond the normal boundaries of the county of Boulogne. So far as we know, however, St. Omer never owed allegiance to Stephen or Eustace.

Various questions arise:

1. If some of the ornamented 'York Group' coins can be connected with St. Omer, can <u>all</u> the coins of the group be so linked, despite the word EBORACI found on certain coins of Eustace?

2. Are the Eustace Knight and Lion types correctly attributed to Eustace Fitzjohn rather than to Eustace of Bologne?

3. Can the Rodbertus horseman type, currently attributed to Robert de Stuteville, a minor Yorkshire baron, be regarded as a coinage of Robert V le Roux, lord of Bethune and protector of the abbey of St. Vaast at Arras and the abbey of St. Bertin at St. Omer.

4. Who is the Bishop Henry of whom two coins are known?

5. For what purpose could coins of 'penny' denomination have been struck by a Flemish mint-master? For purchasing English wool or possibly for paying Flemish mercenaries employed in England? Was there a formal link between the wool merchants of York and St. Omer at this period?

NOTE

1. Discussed by the writer in a paper read to the British Numismatic Society in September 1977, entitled, 'The anomalous "York Group" coins of Stephen's reign'; this article is offered as a summary and postscript.

M.217p

M.224a

H.64

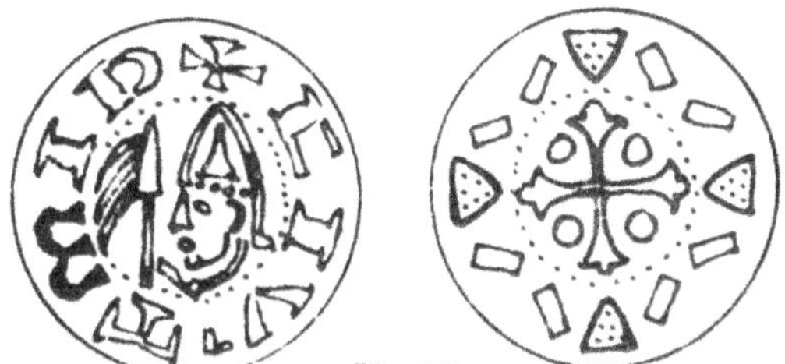

H.62

H.71

H.56

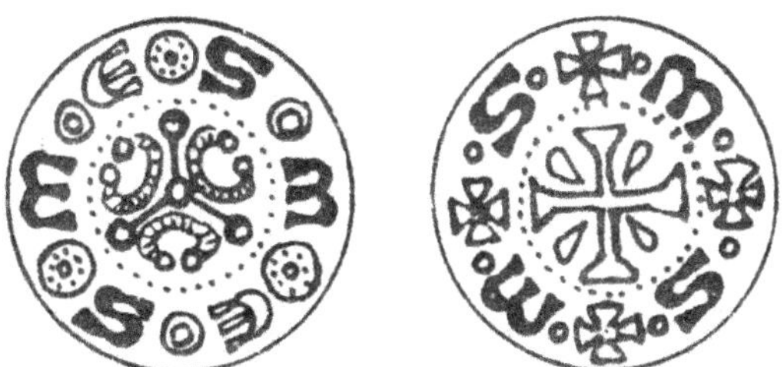

H.100

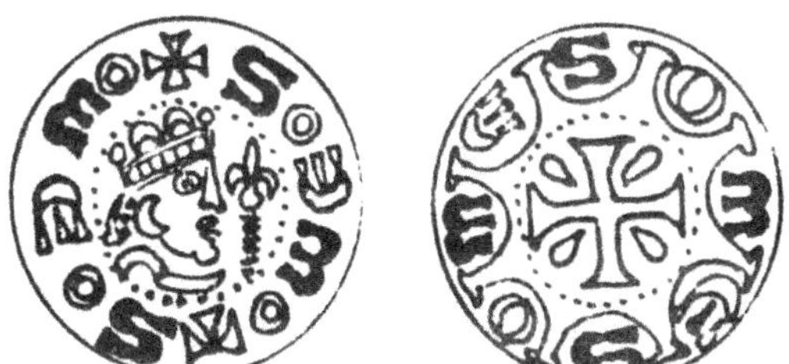

H.K

H.72

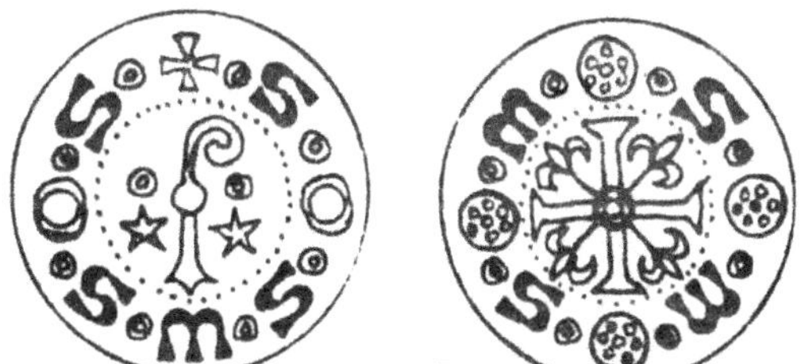

H.87

Some 12th Century coins of Flanders, and England.

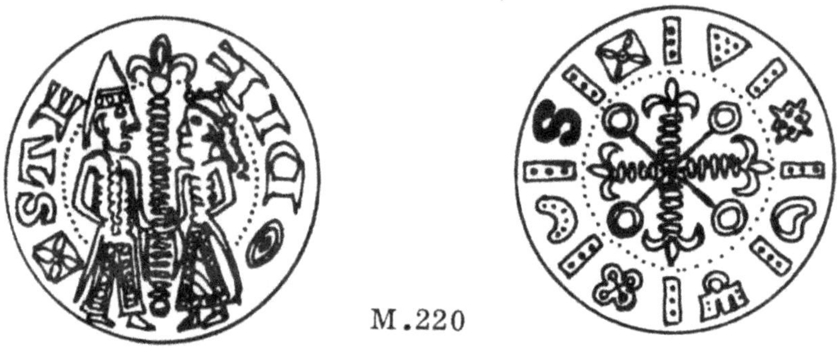

M.220

H.108

H.69

R.38

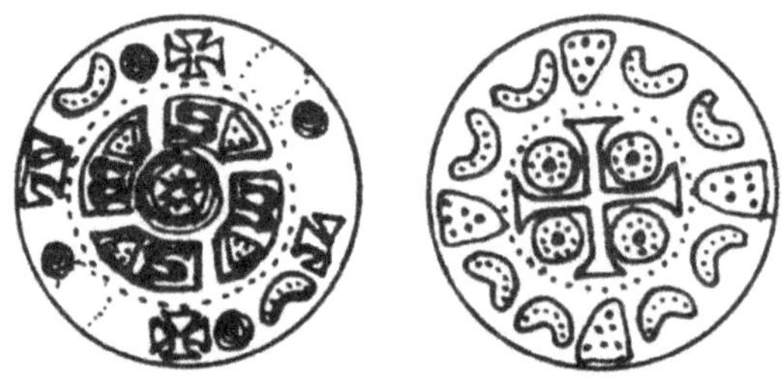

Coll. Vernier

R.36

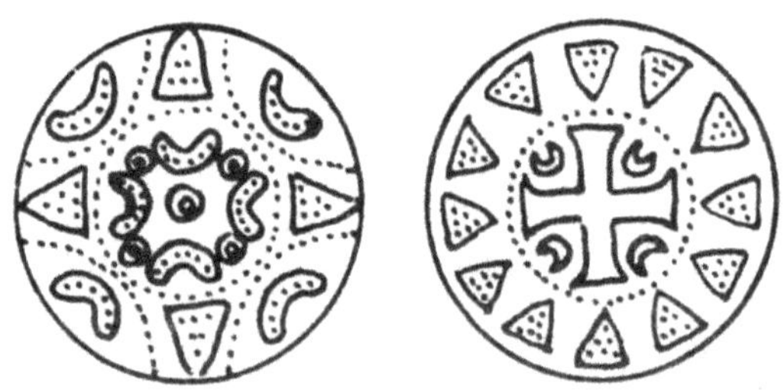

Coll. Vernier

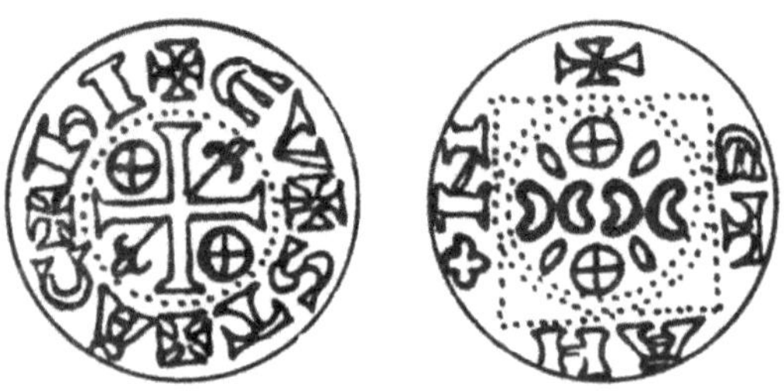

R.37var.

P.d'A.6615

Some 12th Century coins of Flanders, and England.

KEY TO THE PLATES

M217p	Stephen 'flag' penny
M224a	Eustace 'standing knight' penny
H.64	St. Omer
H.62	Uncertain (St. Omer?)
H.71	St. Omer
H.56	St. Omer
H.100	St. Omer
H.K	St. Omer
H.72	St. Omer
H.87	St. Omer
M.220	Stephen 'two figure' penny
H.108	St. Omer
H.69	St. Omer
R.38	Lens(?)
Coll. Vernier	St. Omer
R.36	Lens
Coll. Vernier	Lens(?)
R.37 var	Lens
P.d'A	Boulogne

The illustrations are diagrammatic and are not to scale and the letters S, Sm and Sω have been shaded for emphasis.

ABBREVIATIONS

M = R. P. Mack, SCBI 20: R. P. Mack collection, 1973.

H = A. Haeck, De Munten van de Graven van Flaanderen, Brussels 1973.

R = C. Richebe, Les monnaies féodales d'Artois du Xe au debut du XIVe siecle, Paris 1963.

P. d'A = F. Poey d'Avant, Monnaies féodales de France, Paris 1858-62.

THE CIRCULATION AND IMITATION OF STERLINGS IN THE LOW COUNTRIES

N. J. Mayhew

Although my title, and the terms of the Symposium, restrict this enquiry to the Low Countries, I make no apologies for the fact that at times we will have to review the evidence from France, Germany and Scandinavia as well. Also it is necessary to establish a clear picture of the English output of sterlings. The English Short Cross coinage was an enormous issue compared with anything which had gone before. During the years for which Short Cross figures survive, London and Canterbury struck some £667,000 or 160 million pennies, at an annual average of £33,000 or 8 million pence.[1] These years correspond to the issues known to numismatists as Classes VII and VIII (1218-47).[2] Yet even before the 1220s the evidence of the hoards[3] indicates that the annual figures of production were running at high levels, certainly since John's huge coinage of c. 1205, (Class V 1205-10, Class IV 1210-17) and possibly since the last years of Henry II's reign. This is perhaps not the place to explore the relationship between prices and money supply in England, but it is in passing worth noting that the monetary explosion of the Short Cross coinage does coincide with a period of acute inflation c. 1180-1220; before this argument can be taken much further, much work needs to be done on pinpointing the precise chronology of the growth in output.

More immediately relevant to the present enquiry is the question: How much of the huge English Short Cross coinage found its way to Europe? We cannot really put a figure on this, but it is clear that, compared with the overall size of the Short Cross coinage and the quantities of Long Cross and Edwardian sterlings which later circulated in Europe, the Short Cross presence was very modest. In order to establish where Short Cross sterlings circulated in northern[4] Europe we must turn to the hoards. I have found no hoards containing Short Cross coins from the Low Countries. In due course some hoards with Short Cross coins may come to light—or I may have missed some already known. There is for example documentary evidence of a rent in Utrecht in 1208 expressed in sterling.[5] There must be other examples. In general I imagine sterlings were more likely to occur in the northern and eastern parts of the Low Countries than in the southern and western regions.[6] However, it seems clear finds and documents mentioning Short Cross sterling in the Low Countries will always be out-numbered by the evidence for the circulation of sterlings in France and Germany in the first part of the thirteenth century. The expansion of the English money supply ante-dates the arrival of English coin in the Low Countries by some fifty years, yet but for the sale of English wool in the Low Countries, that expansion could not have occurred.

The evidence from France has recently been summarised by Yvon,[7] while sterlings in Germany have been studied by Berghaus.[8] In France most hoards containing Short Cross can be dated before 1205 and occur in regions whose links with England may fairly be described as political and military rather than economic. Gascony and French-Flanders do not provide Short Cross provenances, and after the loss of Normandy English coins became less common even in those regions where they had previously been popular, that is north-west France. There seem to have been no imitation Short Cross sterlings struck in France. The authority of the Kings of France, vigorously exercised by Philippe-Auguste and his successors, insured that the coinage rights of French feudal magnates were restricted to the issues of deniers in as much as they were tolerated at all.

In Germany things were very different. The Emperor exercised only the most nominal control over the German lords spiritual and temporal who struck money. The arrival of English Short Cross coins in Germany, linked perhaps with diplomatic payments, was gradually followed by German imitations.

In the absence of die-studies the quantities of Short Cross imitations struck remain uncertain. However, it is clear that imitations account for only a very small proportion of the coins in Short Cross hoards found outside Germany. They rarely exceed 1%, and frequently do not even reach this figure, except for Scandinavian finds which do contain a slightly larger German element.[9] The hoards containing Short Cross in Germany tend to be predominantly German sterlings with a small English addition, e.g. Brummerlohe, Bünstorf, Friesoythe, and Hesseln. Hildesheim and Werl have a larger English element, commensurate perhaps with their later date. Some hoards, e.g. Coesfeld and Lechtingen have no English coins, but others, e.g. Detmold and Hillscheid are predominantly English. It would appear that c. 1230-40 Westphalian Short Cross types were plentiful but it is hard to believe that English Short Cross coins ever made up as much as 1% of the circulation in north-west Germany.[10] This impression is confirmed by the scarcity of references to sterling in Germany in the documentary sources of the first half of the century.

Trading and diplomatic links between England and Westphalia undoubtedly existed, yet at no time can these ties have been as strong as those which joined the Flemings and the English—a relationship which produced no imitations and no sterling hoards in the Short Cross period. Why then was the sterling type more readily adopted in Germany early in the century? The parity of sterling and the Köln pfennig is of paramount importance here. Struck at almost the same weight and fineness, sterling was able to circulate alongside the Köln issues. It should also be remembered that Westphalia was already familiar with a crowned facing bust and a cross and pellets reverse. The eleventh-century Dortmund deniers of Heinrich IV (1056-84) spring to mind. Ready access to the rich new supplies of silver from central Europe also fuelled two and four year cycles of <u>Renovatio monete</u> in Osnabruch and Münster;[12] There was thus a constant need for new varieties of types. The direct association of sterling imitation and English-based trade in the Short Cross period is not really helpful. Neither need the dropping of the imitation of the Short Cross type in Westphalia around 1240 be regarded as evidence of a change in the nature of the Anglo-German trade. The phenomenon of Westphalian sterlings needs to be explained with a view to the German domestic monetary situation as well.

Since the presence of sterlings in certain parts of France and Germany may be mainly attributed to special factors other than trade, the absence of sterlings in the Low Countries in the Short Cross period is less extraordinary. It should also be recalled that in the first part of the century most of the centres of wool and cloth trade were in France and subject to the monetary policies of the French crown which excluded sterling. Moreover it is possible that the sterling coinage was only gradually established as an important international trading currency. In the first half of the thirteenth century merchants trading between England and Flanders may have recoined their money as they crossed frontiers, or kept appropriate balances in each country. However in this connection it is worth recalling Dr. Metcalf's observations[13] that the Flemish mints situated in the south, e.g. Lille, were much busier than those further north, e.g. Bruges. If sterling was coming to the Low Countries it was not apparently recoined on entry near the coast in any significant quantity, though perhaps English coin did come to Flanders from the south, via the Champagne fairs.

A review of the circulation of Short Cross in Europe should not forget the Scottish evidence. Even in Scotland where English coin was always readily accepted, Long Cross was far more plentiful than Short Cross.[14] It seems that the use of English sterling in trade outside England, though growing throughout the century, only really took off in the Long Cross period. At any rate after about 1250, the international role of sterling did become established and the hoards demonstrate that Britain, Ireland and part of northern Europe made up a Sterling Area where English coin was offered and accepted readily from Slype to Caithness and from Co. Mayo to Hildesheim and Ribe.

The appearance of large numbers of Long Cross sterlings in the Low Countries is a very significant development. Although partly to be explained in terms of changing patterns of use and growing European familiarity with English coin, it looks as if the English may have been spending more abroad in the second half of the century. And yet there is no evidence of a decline in the foreign exchange value of sterling in the thirteenth century, such as occurred in the 1330s;[15] also the proliferation of Long Cross imitations suggests that demand for sterling in Europe continued to exceed supply. All this seems to indicate that England's trade balance remained in credit, despite the apparent increase in expenditure abroad.

Of course it was wool which made this possible. But there were other factors which contributed to the widespread acceptibility of sterling in Europe. The petit denier coinage of the Low Countries was remarkably local in circulation, no more than a small proportion of Flemish coins occurring in Brabant hoards, and vice-versa.[16] But in the second half of the century it was also becoming normal to use sterlings throughout the Low Countries. The advantages were numerous; sterlings were larger coins, and more convenient for use in commerce. Even with the introduction of St. Louis' gros tournois, the sterling still had a place in the denominational structure; gros, baudekin (2/3 gros), sterling (1/3 gros), denier tournois (1/12 gros). Sterlings were equally acceptable in Flanders, Hainaut or Brabant, unlike the local deniers. Naturally they were also acceptable in England. This was not merely a practical convenience; it enabled merchants to avoid what was in effect a toll or tax on international trade, which forced the recoinage of money at each frontier.

Given these advantages it is not surprising that imitation Long Cross sterlings soon came to be struck in the Low Countries. Students of the Brabantine series may be interested in the Hazelrig hoard from Scotland which contained a WALT sterling in a context otherwise no later than c. 1272.[17] The great majority of the Long Cross sterlings struck in the Low Countries were produced not in Flanders, heart of the wool-cloth trade with England, but in Brabant which at this date was, comparatively speaking, something of a backwater. No doubt the English embargo on wool sales to Flanders in the 1270s contributed to the growth of Brabant as a cloth maker and a sterling producer.[18] Flanders and Hainaut launched their own highly successful and much imitated baudekins in the 1270s.[19] Brabant less of a market leader in its own right, struck sterlings but with the heraldic obverse borrowed from its own denier coinage.[20] Though depending on the reputation of sterling to ensure a good reception for the new issues the Brabant sterling with its denier obverse obviously sought a place more in the Low Countries' monetary system than in England. In the Long Cross period in the Low Countries almost no really deceptive imitations were produced.[21]

France, because of the monetary policies of St. Louis would allow no sterling imitations to be struck on her territory (which included most of Flanders). And there is only one French Long Cross hoard.[22] Nevertheless the negative hoard evidence should be treated with some caution, as the documentary evidence suggests sterlings were indeed used there. Whether French legislation explicitly permitted or proscribed the use of sterling (and at different times in the second half of thecentury it did both), the implication is clearly that sterling was being used.[23]

In Germany the documents, the hoards, and the imitations all indicate that sterlings were used. Hävernick has shown that in the third quarter of the century sterling was most widely used in those regions bordering on the Low Countries. However, Berghaus has also shown that sterlings were more popular where strong German coinages were scarce. Interestingly the Short Cross tradition of imitation was dropped in Westphalia after about 1240, but continued into the Long Cross period, south of the river Lippe. It has to be remembered that when sterlings were struck in remote areas, their manufacture was an important business in itself. We are so used to looking at coins as evidence of trade that we forget their manufacture and marketing was a trade in itself.

Outright copies were made in Lippe[24] in Germany and in Cunre[25] in Holland, and a small hoard of Long Cross forgeries—all die-duplicates—was found at Lede[26] in Belgium. Forgeries seem to have been produced mostly in areas with little economic importance of their own. Such backwaters attracted silver only by offering accurate sterling copies at substantially less than sterling prices. And the quantities of Long Cross forgeries were now becoming significant. It has been estimated that some 5% of the English and Anglo-Irish portions of the Brussels hoard consisted of forgeries.[27] This figure is much higher than that for imitations in the Colchester 1969 hoard.[28] The explanation for the difference may be explained by the comparative proximity of the Brussels hoard to the source of the imitations. However, these imitations are good enough to fool modern numismatists, and could and probably did infiltrate the English circulation. Another possible explanation could be that since the bulk of the Colchester hoard was put together before c. 1256, these excellent imitations became more plentiful later in the Long Cross series in the 1260s.

These first-rate imitations deserve more attention. Apparently struck at a respectable weight and fineness, and having the same legends as genuine English coins, they are not, even today, always recognised for what they are. The modern numismatist needs to see several thousand genuine coins, preferably from a large hoard, before the anomalous issues become apparent. A similar series of imitations afflicted the Edwardian coinage but students of the Short Cross coinage have found that although imitations of this sort do exist, they are not as plentiful as 5% of the English circulation. The two hoards from Ribe in Denmark are interesting in this respect. Looking only at imitations with English-type legends, the 1911 hoard of about 1200 English Short Cross contained 10 imitations, but the smaller 1958 hoard, with 165 English Short Cross had 3 imitations. If a Danish hoard late in the Short Cross period had 2% of imitations then this may safely be regarded as a maximum for the Short Cross coinage.

This review of the evidence, country by country, in the Short Cross and Long Cross periods imposes a rather rigid framework on the evidence. For example the distinction between France and Flanders is not always helpful, and at times may be positively misleading. Moreover, a sharp distinction between Short and Long Cross periods maymake sense in English numismatics, but in Europe the two coinages overlapped. Not only do Short Cross coins occur in European hoards after 1247,[29] but also many of the trends which I have characterised as essentially Long Cross developments—for example the increased circulation of English money in Europe—will have been under way from the 1230s and 1240s. The acceptance of sterling in Europe was a gradual process—hastened in some areas by factors such as the absence of rigorous monetary controls or the convenience of the Köln pfennig—sterling parity, and delayed in other regions by the existence of thriving coinages on quite different standards, buttressed by the authority of powerful rulers or established trading centres. But given Britain's near monopoly position in the wool trade, and the intrinsic quality of the sterling, the international role of the currency was firmly established by the 1270s.[30]

This brings us towards the point when Edward I's recoinage, and his subsequent ban on the export of sterling[31] radically altered the ground rules of European trade. In 1280 there were thousands of pounds worth of English sterlings in Europe; most of it was concentrated in the Low Countries, but significant quantities were also to be found in France, Germany and Scandinavia. It has been calculated that at least £1,000,000 which had been minted as English Long Cross Sterling was not available to be recoined in England in the years after 1279.[32] Some of the missing coin will have been lost or hoarded or simply worn away, but the vast majority of these Long Cross sterlings will simply have been exported from England. As much as £100,000 worth may have been in Scotland;[33] some £900,000 must have travelled to mainland Europe, though much of it may have been recoined there, rather than kept as sterling. At this time, most of this English coin in Europe seems to be associated with English trade—something which was not necessarily true of sterlings abroad earlier in the century. Although some sterling will have been held in Europe as a convenient medium of international payment, much of it will have been in the hands of merchants who required it to purchase British exports. Indeed much of the readiness of other merchants to accept sterling will have depended on the regular demand for it caused by the need to pay for wool.

For European merchants holding sterling in 1279, the change of type was something of a blow. Suddenly their coin was no longer acceptable in England without the payment of dues associated with recoinage. Of course the sign of the Long Cross was still a guarantee of good weight and fine silver, and as such the Long Cross type continued to be used in Europe on shield-sterlings after 1279. Long Cross sterlings circulated in Europe side by side with the new Edwardian type.[34] But as far as use in England was concerned large quantities of Long Cross sterling kept in Europe were frozen. This may be the explanation of the differential sterling exchange rate—new sterlings at 4 Brabant deniers, old sterlings at 3.[35] This very large discount is far more than can be explained by the possible lighter weight of the older worn coins and must reflect greater demand for the new type acceptable in England. Merchants wishing to acquire new sterling to carry out their business in England were further hampered by the introduction of new measures which prohibited the export of sterling from England. That they did in fact continue to export sterling cannot be doubted. The French mint authorities believed that some £50,000 of sterling had entered France in the 1280s.[36] But the possibility of searches, fines and confiscations must have been a factor in the minds of European merchants, and must have contributed to their willingness to buy continental sterlings. The fact that in the early 1280s sterling was specifically exempted from a ban on foreign coin in France[37] can only have helped European manufacturers of continental sterlings.

Apart from preparing the ground for the influx of foreign sterling the recoinage and associated rules of foreign exchange may be presumed to have had some effect on prices. Certainly wool prices fell in the early 1280s;[38] foreign buyers will either have had less new sterling to hand, or will have had to meet mint charges to convert their old coin to new. Either way the wool growers may be expected to have felt the pinch. Deflation in the economy at large at this time cannot probably be dissociated from the freezing of substantial sterling assets in Europe. Those holding Long Cross in England had no choice but to recoin at English mints, but the change of type may well have prevented Long Cross coins in Europe from flowing in and out of England as required, and as they had probably been doing for some 30 years by 1280.

Thus the third quarter of the century emerges as an important, and all too brief phase of open monetary policy, when English sterling was freely offered and received all over Britain and the Low Countries, crossing frontiers without let or hindrance, and flowing wherever the currents of trade might take it. England may have been closer to European monetary union in 1270 than she is today! Such freedom from the restraints more usually associated with medieval monetary policy must have contributed to the prosperity of commerce, and only been possible at a time when silver seemed plentiful and trade was fairly balanced.

However, an alternative interpretation is possible. If the large quantities of Long Cross in Europe do indicate a serious deterioration in the English balance of trade, then the ban on the export of sterling may have been a deliberate attempt to check excessive English spending abroad. Once again contemporary parallels spring to mind. On balance, however, the evident popularity of the sterling in Europe throughout the second half of the thirteenth century would seem to preclude a negative balance of payments argument. Moreover it is improbable that the English government of 1280 had any idea of the state of the country's balance of payments.[39] The attempt to contain silver within national boundaries is probably better seen as a typical piece of late medieval bullionism.

Indeed the English recoinage of 1279 may itself have been prompted by the poor mint output of London and Canterbury in the 1270s, which in turn could well have been brought about by the success of the new French gros, the baudekins of Hainaut and Flanders, and the sterlings of Brabant. There may also have been fiscal motives for Edward's recoinage which was certainly very profitable. Thus it may be that the clipping and the unofficial debasement of currency—the official justification for this recoinage, should be seen more as an excuse rather than as a cause. At any rate, the bullionism of the 1280s, whatever its cause, in its turn brought imitations, currency smuggling, searches, debasement and forgery on a scale hitherto unknown, and from the 1280s till the end of the sterling period, monetary policy in England, France and the Low Countries was inextricably linked with military and political as well as fiscal and economic policy. To some extent then, England brought the problems of imitations on her own head.

Mint output in England in the 1290s was probably lower than at any other time in the thirteenth century. This can partly be explained by the disruption of trade caused by war, but even before war broke out, the level of mint output seemed settled at new low levels.[40] This is probably linked with the very significant output of continental sterlings from Low Countries mints.[41] Most unusually, some thirteenth century mint figures survive from Hainaut which show that in late 1297 and early 1298, 17,940 marcs of sterlings were struck at Mons and 38,000 marcs were struck at Valenciennes (8 deniers fine, 15s to the marc, = £41,955).[42]

The sterlings of Jean d'Avesnes have been arranged into four classes.[43] The hoard evidence makes it clear that classes 1, 2 and 3 were in circulation before 1297, while class 4 was not. It is apparent that the £42,000 of sterlings mentioned in the documentary evidence as being struck at Valenciennes from July 1297 and at Mons from August the same year were in fact class 4 coins. From this position it ought to be a simple step to calculate the class 4 issues as a proportion of Jean d'Avesnes, other issues, and thence to calculate his total sterling output. Unfortunately there is only one hoard which will permit such calculations. The English recoinage of 1300 attempted to remove crockards and pollards from the circulation so the proportions of these coins in post 1300 hoards are not reliable. The three large Scottish hoards dated c. 1300 and consisting almost entirely of crockards and pollards—Galston, Kirkudbright, and Cleuchead should provide ideal data, but sadly only Galston was recorded in sufficient detail to permit the calculations I have in mind.[44] Less than a quarter of Jean d'Avesnes coins in this hoard were class 4, but with no other hoards for comparison, this figure may not be representative of the circulation at large. But if class 4 in fact made up as much as one third of Jean d'Avesnes' sterling issue then his total sterling output will have been £125,865. If Jean d'Avesnes was responsible for one third of all the crockards and pollards made in the Low Countries, a proposition supported by the hoards, it would imply a total output of £377,595 of crockards and pollards struck in the Low Countries in the 1290s. This calculated guess, for it is no more than that, compares interestingly with the firm figure of £37,990 of sterlings minted at London and Canterbury between July 1290 and October 1298.

A method of estimating the number of crockards and pollards circulating in England is to look at the mint output figures for 1300 when these coins were forced to the mints and booked in the accounts as English silver. Since no one took English coin to the mints except when the types were changed, or the weight of the new issues gave bullion holders an incentive to remint old English coin, it is clear that the "English silver" passing through the mints must either be plate, or crockards and pollards. An idea of the amount of plate going to be coined can be gained from the quantities of "English silver" occurring in the mint accounts between recoinages; it is generally small.[45] Of the £136,341 which passed through the mints of London, Canterbury, Bristol, Chester, Exeter, Newcastle, York and Hull as English silver at this time, it is likely that, say £130,000 consisted of continental sterlings. However many crockards and pollards may have escaped recoinage (there are a few in almost every 1300-30 English hoard), others may have been re-exported to Scotland or Europe, or have arrived at the mints after Michaelmas 1300, or have been voluntarily recoined as foreign silver before 1300. It should also be remembered that because of the baseness or poor weight of some of the continental sterlings, one hundred of these coins when recoined would make fewer English pennies.[46]

Nevertheless, it may be that only half the crockards and pollards struck in the Low Countries were in circulation in England in 1300. Many continental sterlings were retained for use in the Low Countries. The hoards,[47] and the documentary evidence[48] which is scarce since many crockards and pollards were often simply called 'sterlings' and so are indistinguishable from English coin, make it clear that continental sterlings had an important though short-lived role in Europe.[49] Crockards and pollards, and illegally exported Edwardian types, together filled the role previously played by Long Cross alone—providing the liquidity without which the wool trade must have ground to a halt. Moreover, the very large number of continental coins which did circulate in England in the 1290s suggests that almost all the silver which might normally be expected to have come to the English mints was in fact coined on the continent for use in England.

The circulation of continental coinage in England was bound to cause difficulties, for the monetary systems of mainland Europe were much more complicated than the English. It is likely that in the 1290s the same coins circulated in different ways on different sides of the Channel. The Marchienne hoard gives an interesting picture of sterling circulation in the Low Countries in a very short period c. 1296-7, and provides an interesting contrast with the nearly contemporary Mellendean[50] hoard from the Scottish border. Whereas Mellendean has examples of the whole range of crockards and pollards struck before its date of deposit, Marchienne has almost none of the earlier issues of Gui de Dampierre or Jean d'Avesnes, though their 1296-7 issues are plentifully represented. Marchienne also contained examples of the contemporary continental copies of crockards and pollards.[51] These are important in the first place because it is interesting that mints of the Cunre type should choose to imitate crockards and pollards when they could produce accurate copies of English sterlings; this may be further evidence of the domestic role of crockards and pollards in the Low Countries; that they were a coinage common enough, and good enough to be worth imitating. But these copies also raise the topic of debasement, for they, and the later types of sterling present in Marchienne, were increasingly debased. Herein lies the explanation for the very tight chronological parcel deposited at Marchienne, and for the comparative scarcity of Low Countries finds of crockards and pollards which were in fact briefly plentiful there. Whereas in England sterlings were the invariable medium of exchange, of good weight and purity, the monetary patterns in the Low Countries were much more complicated. Sterlings were only one of many denominations from a wide range of competing mints of different nations. Moreover some sterlings were of better weight and/or fineness than others. Accordingly in Europe the life-span of crockards and pollards may have been shorter, as it more frequently became advantageous to re-coin existing coin.

Thus the circulating medium in the Low Countries in the 1290s seems to have been very large. Moreover the variety of issues and the rapidly changing terms on which bullion was bought by half a dozen competing mints all within 50 miles of one another presents a picture of bewildering complexity when compared with the inflexible stability of English mint policy. This stability explains why English mints were such easy prey for the mints of France and the Low Countries in the 1290s, but it also explains the renewed prosperity of the English mints in the early 1300s and the new wave of continental imitation which followed it.

With the French debasement of the mid 1290s, rapidly followed by debased sterling issues from Jean d'Avesnes and Gui de Dampierre,[52] similarly occasioned by the expenses of war-time finance, it was scarcely surprising that the English mints should be starved of silver. Bullion holders naturally sought the best price they could get, which inevitably was offered by the debasing mints. However, in due course debasement brought discredit to a coinage. Moreover, as continental mints decreed ever higher face values for a given quantity of silver, the European face value of good sterling also rose. In the short run mints and merchants, who cashed in before the true value of debased coin became widely known, could take substantial profits. Yet in the long run debasement spirals had a damaging effect on confidence and on trade. The bullion holder soon learned to turn again to those mints and coinages which were untainted by the stigma of excessive debasement,[53] while merchants and rentiers alike cried out for a return to strong money.

Thus, while accepting that a principal cause of the boom in the English mints c. 1302-10 was the revival of the wool trade,[54] the importance of a reaction against debasement should not be forgotten. This was perhaps one of the last occasions when a pronounced swing to strong money was possible; later in the fourteenth century the European shortage of silver made debasement, and/or weight reduction the norm, even in England. Yet Kutna Hora, the last great Bohemian find of the period, and wool together made possible a last prolific flowering of the English sterling (1302-10), and French mint officials complained that because of the high value put on sterling in terms of money of account in France, the English mints could offer a higher mint price for silver than the debasing European mints.[55] By an interesting inversion which would have intrigued Gresham, good money could drive out bad.

The revival of English sterling brought a renewed wave of continental imitations. As with the pre-1300 issues, the mints producing imitation sterlings show a pronounced correspondence with those imitating baudekins. The most prolific imitators of sterling in the 14th century seem to have been as follows: Robert de Bethune whose Flanders sterlings are all of good metal, Louis of Bavaria who struck sterling of good metal at Aachen,[56] Valeran de Ligny and Gaucher de Châtillon who struck large numbers of sterlings, probably on a declining standard, in the period before c. 1320. Together with imitation sterlings in the name of Edward of England some of which are attributable to Gaucher and others,[57] all these continental issues seem to have supplied about 5% of the English circulation in the first quarter of the fourteenth century, which suggests that very approximately about £50,000 of foreign sterling was circulating in England at this time.

Ferry of Lorraine and John the Blind may provide a link between the relatively pure silver issues made before c. 1320 and the much baser Lushbournes made in Luxemburg, Lorraine and Toul in the 1330s. John the Blind's base issues seem to have been especially plentiful but their reputation probably excluded them to some extent from English hoards and quantitative assessments are therefore difficult.

These base imitations may have contributed to the crisis of confidence which afflicted sterling in the 1330s.[58] However other factors were probably more important. The beginnings of a severe silver shortage all over Europe, together with the expense of war in Scotland early in the decade, and with France after 1337 placed considerable pressure on the English currency. In 1335 the government did in fact debase halfpennies and farthings (to 10 oz fine instead of 11 oz 2 dwt). This is an interesting early English example of an attempted domestic debasement intended to leave the international medium untainted. European confidence was shaken nonetheless. Moreover when the major European war did break out trade in general suffered, and even Florence and its international currency experienced a period of crisis.

In 1344 the inevitable reduction in the weight of the penny took place, though an attempt was made to safeguard international trade and to increase the domestic supply by the introduction of gold. After the Black Death, the international role of sterling was further reduced by the introduction of the groat (made possible by the further weight reduction of the penny and the increased per capita money supply). In the second half of the fourteenth century, the international role of sterling was more and more restricted to Scotland and Scandinavia.[59]

To sum up, the English sterling was made possible by silver that was brought to England by the wool trade. As a reliable silver coinage it was much imitated in Europe, but it was the ill-advised English attempt to restrict the international role of sterling in the 1280s which brought about the greatest wave of sterling imitation. When silver became scarce, and the wool trade died, the period of the English sterling and its imitations came to a close.

NOTES

1. For London and Canterbury mint output in the Short and Long Cross periods, see C. E. Blunt and J. D. Brand, 'Mint Output of Henry III' BNJ xxxix (1970), pp. 61-6. For the Edwardian coinage see C. G. Crump and C. Johnson 'Tables of bullion coined under Edward I, II and III, NC 1913, pp. 200-245.

2. L. A. Lawrence, 'The Short Cross Coinage 1180-1247' BNJ xi, (1915), pp. 59-100.

3. F. Dumas and J. D. Brand, 'The British Coins in the Gisors (1970) Hoard', BNJ xl 1971, p. 29, where a number of Short Cross hoards amenable to detailed classification are set out, clearly illustrating the large size of class V and VI. It should be remembered that wastage will have affected the earlier classes more than those issued nearer the time of concealment of the hoard. Moreover classes I-IV may have suffered particularly heavy wastage because of Richard's Crusade, and John's recoinage of light weight coins.

4. The currency of sterling in southern Europe is another question. See D. M. Metcalf, Coinage in the Balkans 820-1355, (Thessaloniki 1965) pp. 139, 142, 164, 183, 229, 230. See also the Naxos hoard.

5. W. Hävernick, Der Kölner Pfennig im 12 und 13 Jahrhundert (Beiheft 18, zur Vierteljahrschrift fur Sozial und Wirtschaftsgeschichte, Stuttgart 1930), p. 108.

6. The Netherlands, lying closer to sterling-producing Westphalia, must be a more likely user of Short Cross sterlings than the provinces nearer France. The Holland deniers, using sterling types on small denier-sized coins, would argue that this region at least was familiar with the Short Cross sterling. The chronology of these Holland issues is, however, by no means certain, and it is possible that Short Cross deniers may have continued to be struck in Holland until as late as about 1265. (I am most grateful to Prof. Dr. H. Enno van Gelder and Drs. A. T. Puister for their advice on this problem.) Thus I am uncertain how far the use of the short cross on a coinage of different weight standard may be taken as evidence of the circulation of the prototype.

7. J. Yvon, 'Esterlins à la Croix Courte dans les Trésors Francais de la Fin du XIIe et de la Première Moitié du XIIIe siècle.' BNJ xxxix, 1970, pp. 24-60.

8. P. Berghaus, 'Die Perioden des Sterlings in Westfalen, dem Rheinland und in dem Niederlanden'. HBnNI (1947-51), pp. 34-53.

9. See 'France' hoard NC 1897, pp. 235-44. Gisors, BNJ xl, 1971, pp. 22-43. Montpellier, Yvon op.cit., and also Brand and Duplessy BNJ xlvii, 1977, pp. 77-91. Colchester NC 1903, 111-176. Norrbys BNJ xxvii, 1954, pp. 359-61. Ribe I NC 1916, pp. 378-98. Ribe II NNA 1971, pp. 38-59.

10. For German hoards see W. Hävernick, op.cit., and P. Berghaus, op. cit. Also see P. Berghaus Westfälische Münzgeschichte des Mittelalters, (Landesmuseum für Kunst und Kulturgeschichte Münster 1974).

11. The documentary evidence is summarised by W. Hävernick, op.cit., p. 132.

12. H. Buchenau, on the Lechtingen hoard, Mitt. d. Bayer Num. Gesell., 42, 1924, p. 53.

13. See above, pp. 14-15.

14. N. J. Mayhew, 'Money in Scotland in the thirteenth century' in D. M. Metcalf (ed.) Coinage in Medieval Scotland (1100-1600), BAR 45, 1977, pp. 85-102.

15. E. Ames, 'The Sterling Crisis of 1337-1339', J. of Econ. Hist., xxv, (1965), pp. 496-522.

16. This point is illustrated by the hoards summarised by J. Ghyssens in Les Petits Deniers de Flandre des XIIe et XIIIe Siècles, Brussels, 1971.

17. D. M. Metcalf, 'An Annotated Bibliography of Scottish Coin Hoards, c. 1100-1600' in D. M. Metcalf (ed.) Coinage in Medieval Scotland (1100-1600), p. 26.

18. On the growing importance of Brabant see J. de Sturler, Les relations politiques et les échanges commerciaux entre le duché de Brabant et l'Angleterre au moyen âge, (Paris), 1936.

19. J. Duplessy, 'Chronologie et circulation des Baudekins à cheval', RBN 1971, pp. 169-234.

20. A. de Witte, Histoire monétaire des Comtes de Louvain, Ducs de Brabant et Marquis de Saint Empire Romain, I (Antwerp 1894), pls. viii, 213-229, and ix, 230-247 bis.

21. On Cunre, an exception, see below.

22. Pontchateau hoard, see Yvon, op.cit.

23. RN 1929, pp. 220-222, 226, 1930, pp. 85, 88, 110.

24. P. Weweler, 'Lippische Sterlinge' in Festschrift zur Feier des 25 jährigen Bestehens des Vereins der Munzforscher und Munzfreunde für Westfalen und Nachbargebiete, (Münster 1938), pp. 41-53.

25. J. Chautard, Imitations des monnaies au type esterlin frappées en Europe pendant le XIIIe et le XIVe siècle, Nancy 1871, pp. 316-22.

26. J. Baerten, CENB 3 (1966), pp. 70-2.

27. R. L. Davis in a paper read to the British Numismatic Society on 25 April

1978. On imitations of the Anglo-Irish type see Michael Dolley and W. A. Seaby 'The Anomalous Long-Cross Coins in the Anglo-Irish Portion of the Brussels Hoard' in R. A. G. Carson (ed.) Mints, Dies and Currency: Essays dedicated to the memory of Albert Baldwin 1971, pp. 291-318.

28. Information kindly supplied by Miss M. M. Archibald.

29. For example, the Hildesheim hoard HBN II, 35ff.

30. J. A. Van Houtte, Economic History of the Low Countries 800-1800 London, (1977) p. 50 argues that sterling came plentifully to Flanders until about 1250. Thereafter in the absence of a regular supply of English sterling, the Low Countries began to produce imitations. In my opinion this assessment is not supported by the finds.

31. M. Mate, 'Monetary Policies in England, 1272-1307' BNJ xli, 1972, p. 56.

32. M. M. Archibald, 'Wastage from Currency: Long Cross and the recoinage of 1279' in N. J. Mayhew (ed.) Edwardian Monetary Affairs (1279-1344) BAR 36, 1977, p. 184.

33. N. J. Mayhew, 'Money in Scotland in the thirteenth century' in D. M. Metcalf (ed.) Coinage in Medieval Scotland (1100-1600), p. 92.

34. E.g. the Diest hoard, summarised by J. Duplessy op.cit., pp. 225-7, and the Grand-Halleux hoard, RBN 1891 p. 240, also summarised in Duplessy.

35. A. de Witte, op.cit., pp. 68-9. See also P. Spufford and Wendy Wilkinson, Interim Listing of the Exchange Rates of Medieval Europe, Keele, 1977, p. 260 where old sterlings at Rome in 1285 were cited at 160 solidi to the pound, and new sterlings at 200 solidi.

36. R. and M. Dhenin, 'Le Tresor de Boulogne-sur-mer', Revue du Nord LV, 1973, p. 246, quoting RN, 1924, pp. 109-28.

37. RN 1930, p. 85.

38. T. H. Lloyd, The Movement of Wool Prices in Medieval England, (Economic History Review, Suppl. 6. Cambridge, 1973).

39. Much of the information required to assess the nation's balance of payments did in fact lie in government files, but it is unlikely that they used these accounts for anything more than a check on the honesty of their officials.

40. It should be noted that wool prices declined 1290-4, but there was no apparent fall in the volume of exports, see Lloyd op.cit.

41. Flanders and Namur, Hainaut, Brabant and Loos, and Cambrai, to mention only the larger coinages.

42. J. Ghyssens, 'La Monnaie de Hainaut sous Jean d'Avesnes d'apres le registre B.3268 des Archives départementales du Nord à Lille.' RBN 1973, pp. 90-1.

43. N. J. Mayhew, 'La Chronology des Esterlins de Jean d'Avesnes Comte de Hainaut (1280-1304)' RN 1975, pp. 172-181.

44. Galston hoard, NC 1923, pp. 260-74. Kirkcudbright, NC xiii, 1851, pp. 86-94. Clenchhead, PSAS xxxii, 1898, pp. 295-6.

45. The fact that when non-monetary silver was converted to monetary use it passed through the mint accounts is not generally recognised by the supporters of the 'accumulated silver stocks' theory.

46. C. Johnson, The De Moneta of Nicholas Oresme and English Mint Documents, (1956), p. xxxix, has calculated that crockards and pollards were on average 72.5% fine on the basis of figures in the Liber Quotidianus, but this may be unduly pessimistic.

47. Hoogstraeten, RBN 1866, pp. 434-6. Marchienne, RBN I, 1845, pp. 77-81. Geel, RBN 1949, pp. 128-156 and Pulderbosch-Zoersel, RBN 1910, pp. 405-10.

48. For a rare mention of esterlin à tiestelette (1295) see J. Ghyssens 'Essai de datation des Premiers Esterlins de Brabant' Annales du Congrès de Liège de la Fédération Archéologique et Historique de Belgique II (Liège 1971), pp. 567-72.

49. It is worth noting from the European hoards that whereas Long Cross shield-type sterling imitations circulate alongside the local deniers, crockards and pollards generally did not. Had the denier issues ceased by the 1290s or were the shield and the head-type sterlings assigned different roles in the monetary system?

50. Mellendean hoard, NC 1913, pp. 57-118.

51. For a fuller study of these coins, Chautard's 'Enigmatic' types, see N. J. Mayhew 'The sterlings of Gui de Dampierre, and related enigmatic issues.' NC 1978, pp. 116-125.

52. For a study of Gui de Dampierre's debasement see Mayhew, ibid.

53. This is not to deny the case for controlled responsible debasement in some circumstances.

54. T. H. Lloyd, 'Overseas Trade and the English Money Supply in the Fourteenth Century' in N. J. Mayhew (ed.) Edwardian Monetary Affairs (1279-1344), pp. 97-9.

55. See J. Duplessy, op.cit., pp. 216-7, Document no. VII, though the precise date of this document is uncertain.

56. There are some interesting problems dating the sterlings of Louis of Bavaria. N. Klüssendorf, Der Aachener Wechster-Process p. 71, note 36, cites documentary evidence of Aachen sterlings in 1319. However, the English hoard evidence and the use of the title Imperator suggest a date after 1328.

57. N. J. Mayhew, 'Gaucher de Châtillon and the imitation of sterlings in the name of Edward of England' RBN cxxi, 1975, pp. 109-116, and 'The Sterlings of Gui de Dampierre and related enigmatic issues' loc.cit.

58. E. Ames, *op.cit.*

59. See for example the two huge post 1350 hoards Kirial *NNA*, 1970, pp. 37-168 and Montrave, *PSAS* xvi, 1882, pp. 466-71. But see also Klüssendorf *op.cit.* for documentary evidence for the frequent use of sterling in Aachen in the middle of the fourteenth century.

DEVALUATION, COINAGE AND SEIGNORAGE UNDER LOUIS DE NEVERS AND LOUIS DE MALE, COUNTS OF FLANDERS, 1330-84[1]

F. and W. P. Blockmans

Thirty years ago, Professor Hans van Werveke calculated, in a now famous lecture to the Royal Historical Society of London, the volume and profit of the coinage under Count Louis de Male of Flanders, 1346-84. He claimed that this Prince drew approximately one fifth of his income from his seignorage and therefore proceeded repeatedly to devalue. He suggested also that the considerable devaluations initiated by the Count had an unforeseen but nevertheless favourable effect upon Flemish exports.[2]

A number of weaknesses in this argument can however be pointed out. Firstly, no account has been taken of the effect of devaluations in other countries; not only as far as the attraction of precious metals is concerned, but also as regards the competitive position of Flemish industry. In fact the latter suffered more harm from the exorbitant increases of wool-export duties.[3] It cannot be proved therefore that the profit-seeking of the Prince was the principal determining factor in this monetary policy. Furthermore, the proportion of profits obtained from the seignorage in relation to the total income of the Count, cannot be precisely assessed due to the absence of information on the latter subject. Finally, the correlations between mint output, intrinsic value and the seignorage receipts have never been statistically demonstrated. Nevertheless, the studies of Spufford and Munro have confirmed the importance of the procedures initiated by van Werveke.

It is for these reasons that I shall attempt in the following paper to elaborate upon the data collected by van Werveke, also taking into account the period of the preceding sixteen years. Apart from gaining additional information, this period (1330-46) offers a number of interesting aspects:

1. An acute crisis was developing internationally, within the political, commercial, military and monetary systems. These factors influenced the position of the currency in West European countries.

2. From 1338 onwards the Count was almost completely powerless in Flanders, the government being in the hands of a commercial elite with a popular base in the leading towns.[4] The question as to the extent to which a particular monetary policy actually originates from the personal aims of a Prince and his councillors is now open to investigation.

3. Exact information concerning the Count's income is available for the period of 1332 to 1336, thus enabling the proportion of the seignorage to be calculated.

Our data are based upon a number of accounts of the masters of the mint and three statements of the coinage by the wardens. These documents were partially published by Gaillard in 1857[5] and are the oldest known documents of this type in the Low Countries. Both van Werveke and Ghyssens[6] have made use of them, although only partially. It appears, however, to be necessary to return to the original documents, not only for these accounts,[7] but also for the instructions, commissions, contracts and ordinances which have been traced in the chancery records.[8] My information concerning the Count's income is also based upon two unpublished accounts[9] and one unpublished survey of the Count's finances drafted by the General Collector in 1332 and brought up to date until the year 1336.[10] Some new information is now available for the period before the oldest preserved accounts. It is quite certain that both the master for the silver and the warden were in office long before the beginning of their oldest preserved account (13 September, 1334) since on 2 April, 1334 they were allowed to continue in Ghent, on the right bank of the Scheldt, in the German Empire, the functions for which they had been appointed at Aalst.[11] The master of the mint for gold, Falco da Lampaggio from Pistoia is known to have been appointed on 28 June 1335, one year earlier than his oldest account. The contract had a duration of three years, and considering the fact that he stopped minting gold in June 1338, one may assume that there had been one year of gold minting for which we lack statistical evidence (June 1335-June 1336).[12] Further indications permit the assumption that the same man occupied the position of master for gold as early as 1331.[13]

The first stage of the monetary policy of Count Louis de Nevers, for which new evidence is at our disposal, dates back to 8 August, 1331. At that moment new instructions for the production of silver coins were issued,[14] providing for a severe reduction in fineness, of 12 grains. Simultaneously, the value of the gold coins was lowered although their intrinsic value remained unaltered. This points to a double premium given to silver, more than one might expect on the basis of the general silver scarcity alone.[15] The three largest towns, (Ghent, Bruges, and Ypres) soon became aware of the debasement, since they ordered in December 1331 "the assay of the new coins struck at Aalst" and invited a Ghent goldsmith to bring the results to the Count's general collector.[16] Other institutions similarly reacted with reservation. In February 1332 the Count affirmed the new valuation as follows:[17]

1 groat tournois	= 12 d. parisis
1 florin	= 12 groats tournois
1 royal	= 15 groats tournois

The town accounts of Ghent show an analogous shift in the rates exactly in the first half of August 1331, thus within a week after the proclamation of the new ordinance.[18] The florin was previously valued at 13 1/3 gr. tourn. and the royal at 17 gr. tourn., which meant a rise of 10 to 12%. The Count thus conformed with the rates prescribed in France after the revaluations of April 1330.[19] There is more to this however. Since rents and fines were normally expressed in money of account on a silver basis and were paid in gold, the Count's income must have been considerably augmented by the imposed increase in value of the new silver coins. This explains the prompt reactions from towns and clergy, for it is to be noted that the Count expressly mentioned the compulsory application of the new rates for all debts owed to him.

This operation, consisting in a strong enhancement of the value of silver both by altering the silver to gold ratio and by lowering the intrinsic value of silver coins, took place in a period of monetary stability in France and massive silver exports from England through an adverse balance of trade.[20] The devaluations cannot under these circumstances be considered as defensive, but must be regarded as purely voluntary. The two aspects of the measure of 8 August, 1331 must have been intended to raise the Count's income through higher seignorage profits and a premium on all debts to him.

This interpretation is supported by the extremely precarious state of the Count's finances in this period. In the survey of April 1332 drawn up by the three most prominent financial councillors, the ordinary income is computed at £10,418 parisis, and the extraordinary at £15,112 parisis, the latter being mostly derived from the repression of the revolt of 1323-8. During a period of three years, from September 1328 to September 1331, £300,000 had been collected in Flanders and completely spent. The total debts contracted by the Count amounted to more than £360,000. The authors of the report concluded with a warning: "Si est nostre conclusion que, se vous voulez mener teille vie et continuer, faites pourcachier par autres que par nous."[21] Effectively, the Count permitted his councillors to levy more taxes and charge more fines, thus raising his total yearly income from £10,418 before 1328 to £25,530 in 1332 and to £64,279 in 1335-6.[22] Even though the 1335-6 account was closed with a profit, the overall debts to the general collector remained as high as £8,792. The fines imposed on towns and individuals as part of the repression after the revolt of 1323-8 contributed the most in raising the Count's income, as is shown in the following table:

Division of the Count's income 7.9.1335-7.11.1336

domain	£ 8,022	10.6%
transport[23]	4,359	5.7
justice	8,550	11.25
new rents and fines on insurgents	26,786	35.25
aid	1,298	1.7
diverse	26,977	35.5
	£75,992	101.3%

In this context, the profit-seeking motive for the monetary measures of August 1331 is beyond doubt: every seignoral right was exploited to the maximum in order to raise the Count's income.

But the Count was not able to pursue his policy as he might have wished. Probably the assay by the three towns made the debasement obvious. On the 13 March, 1332, he had to send new instructions to his warden of the mint at Aalst. Realising that the reduction of the alloy had become common knowledge, the Count now ordered the striking of groats and half groats with 6 grains more silver than those struck since August 1331. The warden was also ordered to cut one groat and two halves more out of a marc of Troyes. The alloy of the black silver pennies had to be lowered by three grains.[24] The devaluation was thus limited and acknowledged but nevertheless continued. About the gold coinage, we know only that it went on simultaneously from the 8 August, 1331 onwards. In November 1334, however, its output seems to have ceased.

Louis de Nevers' endeavour failed so early because of its lack of refinement; changing too much at once. Nevertheless, it is highly probable that he took large profits from his debasements from 1331 to 1337, a period of good money in France and of almost no coinage in England. His action may have largely contributed to the difficulties of Paris and London in maintaining their standards. As is shown in tables 1, 2 and 3, the French debasement of January 1337 forced Louis de Nevers to a defensive devaluation of both his gold and silver coinage which can be proved to have been extremely profitable during some eight months until February, 1338. From then onwards the returns diminished and the quickening French debasements were no longer followed in Flanders for reasons which we shall explore further.

Let us now turn to the surviving accounts for the period 1334-46. Considering the fact that all of the documents mentioned above, combined, still show large gaps, the question arises as to the completeness of our data.

> The accounts for the gold currency cover a period of only 2 years (1336-8); we have already pointed out that gold was probably struck under the same conditions one year earlier. Another period of nearly four months is also documented in 1343;
>
> for the white silver 4 years and 2 months are covered, further a period of 6 months in the year 1343 and 11 months in 1346;
>
> for black silver the accounts cover a consecutive period of 3 years and 9 months (1334-8).

In a total period of well over twelve years, due to the fact that the data do not cover the whole period, the supposition of more missing accounts arises for the period after November 1338. This suspicion is supported by the text of the treaty of 3 December, 1339 between the Duke of Brabant and the Count of Flanders, which provided for the issuing of a joint currency, although we have no account from this period at our disposal.[25]

I shall venture to answer the question of the completeness of our data by discussing the period from November 1338 to December 1339. No accounts for this period have been preserved and there are no serious indications concerning actual coinage in Flanders. Moreover, such activity seems to me to be extremely unlikely considering that Count Louis de Nevers had lost almost all control over his county and that from 12 February until 5 October 1339 he had retreated to France leaving the real power in the hands of Jacob van Artevelde and his followers.[26] During the two months in which Louis de Nevers returned to Flanders he was forced to sanction the policies of his opponents, including the sealing of the previously mentioned treaty with Brabant. The Count fled to France one day later however, on 4 December, 1339 and was never to regain his power in Flanders. Under these circumstances (taking into consideration that one of the parties immediately withdrew), one can ask oneself what sort of execution the treaty must have received. This question becomes even more important because of the absence of any accounts concerning the joint Flemish-Brabantine coinage. There are however surviving coins of a common type issued under the name of both Princes, mentioning the mints of Ghent and Leuven.[27] Ghyssens suggests, on the basis of the light weight and numismatic characteristics, that the common currency could not have been brought into circulation earlier than February 1341.[28] In my opinion, the mention of the names of the Count and therefore also of his mint on the surviving coins does not necessarily indicate that Louis de Nevers actually played an active role. Coins were also minted in Ghent in his name in 1343 and 1346, but really under the authority of the revolutionary government of the three towns. Was this also the case in 1339 and/or 1341? It is a possibility, but then one must assume that the accounts of the coinage were lost by chance, while accounts for the years 1343 and 1346 were deposited in the count's archives. Some of these factors lead to the formulation of a new hypothesis, namely that the conventional groat was not coined in Flanders at all but only in Brabant, with of course a legal tender in Flanders and also in other principalities, such as Hainaut. The following facts support this possibility:

—A coin of the 'socius' type, which had been adopted in the Flemish-Brabant treaty, had been struck in Flanders since 1337.[29] Because of the massive production of this coin (table 2), it is possible that there was no direct need for new production.

—As a result of the retreat of the count, the revolutionary leaders were confronted unexpectedly with a legitimacy problem; should they use their own authority to mint coins? It seems unlikely that they would have decided to do so as early as December 1339. Generally speaking such a situation would lead to reservedness, hesitation and delay.

—The master of the mint, Falco da Lampaggio from Pistoia, who had worked until November 1338 for the Count of Flanders, went only a short while afterwards into the service of the Duke of Brabant, and thus embodied the unity of the coinage following the Flemish example. It is possibly for this reason that the Flemish put their confidence in the Brabantine coin. It must be noted however, that only a very small number of groats of the conventional type are preserved.

—The text on all the preserved coins shows the names of the mints of Ghent and Leuven, in this order. This undoubtedly points to their production in Brabant. Furthermore, whilst the formula 'MONETA FLAND' was current in Flanders, it remained the practice in the Duchy to mention the name of the mintingplace. A greater number of the latter remained in use, especially Antwerp, Brussels and Leuven, but also Maastricht and Halen. This detail equally indicates production in Brabant, albeit following the Flemish example. The mention of Ghent as one of the mints is part of the fiction already introduced by using the Count's name.

If it now appears plausible to suggest that no coins were minted in Flanders either during the year 1339, or after the treaty in December of the same year, then one can elaborate this argument to cover the end of the period under discussion, namely the year 1346. The Count had ceased to play a political role in the county. It was not until years later, in April 1343, that the revolutionary leaders began issuing money in his name, and then obviously only when they were forced into this position by the spectacular devaluations of the French currency (table 1).

Table 1. Debasement of silver coinage in England, France and Flanders 1330-46

	England	France		Flanders		
	t	t	f	t	f	Ag-Au ratio
1330	243d.	48	11d. 12g.	?	11d.	?
1331				57	10d. 12g.	?
1334				57½	10d. 6g.	12.6
1335	253d.					
Jan. 1337		96	10d. 16g.			
May 1337				60½	9d.	10.9
Oct. 1338		96	8d.			
Jan. 1340		105	7d.			
Apr. 1340		108	6d.			
Jan. 1341		84	6d.			
Febr. 1341		96	6d.			
June 1342		120	6d.			
Apr. 1343				66	8d.	12.1
Oct. 1343		60	12d.			
July 1344	266d.					
1345	268d.					
Jan. 1346	270d.			66	7d.16g.	11.3
Apr. 1346		180	3d. 18g.			

t = taille
f = fineness

Making allowance for gold coins struck in 1335, we can sum up our hypothesis as follows:

Coinage was not necessarily struck during the periods between 1334 to 1346 for which there are no surviving accounts. An explanation as to why there should have been no minting even appears to be possible. This would imply that the data shown in tables 2, 3 and 4 reflect the complete mintage in Flanders for a period of a good twelve years, with the exception of one year as far as gold is concerned. On the other hand, we can ascertain that coinage of white and black silver went on continuously from 1331 onwards under the conditions shown by the ordinances and appointments. For gold, an intermission may have occurred between 1332 and 1335.[30] On the basis of this it is possible to make a comparison with the data computed for the reign of Count Louis de Male (table 5). It appears thus, that the latter had much more gold and white silver minted, but four times less small change. This contrast probably also applies to the period 1331-34 for which only qualitative evidence is available.

Although the profit motive as an explanation for the monetary policy of Louis de Male has been seen to be insufficient, it should not on the other hand be neglected. A high income from minting made it possible to urge the master of the mint to strike small change on which no seignorage was taken.[31] We have already emphasised the fact that during the thirties Louis de Nevers found himself in great financial difficulties and that he used every means available to raise his income. It becomes difficult to ignore the element of profit-seeking when one takes into consideration how the Count, who was reproached by his financial counsellors for wastage, managed in 1337 to increase his seignorage on gold currency threefold and on silver currency sevenfold.

Especially for silver, the debasement of that year resulted in considerable seignorage receipts during some eight months, after which period the Count was forced to reduce his profit margin in order to continue to attract bullion. As far as the volume of the silver coinage is concerned, production was highest during the eight months following the debasement of 25 May, 1337 and thereafter steadily slowed down, as is shown in the following average production figures <u>per diem</u>:

16.9.34 - 26.4.37	86.6 pure marcs
25.5.37 - 15.2.38	127.6 pure marcs
19.2.38 - 10.6.38	65.2 pure marcs
24.6.38 - 7.11.38	49.3 pure marcs

The total profits from the seignorage during the most active period of Louis de Nevers' coinage represent, on the other hand, no more than a modest proportion of his income. During a good four years, 1334-8, the profits from the seignorage amounted to £18,192 parisis, out of which 90% was derived from the coinage of silver. This figure can be increased to £18,267 parisis if one adds an extrapolated figure for the seignorage on gold in 1335-6. On a yearly basis this amounted to roughly £4,407 parisis. These receipts can be compared with the Count's total yearly income in 1335-6 and with the general survey of 1332:

	total income	average seignorage receipts as %
1332	£25,530	17.26
1335-6	£64,279	6.86

Between these very divergent figures, the choice is difficult. Since the considerable increase in the count's total income after 1332 was less than proportionally produced by seignorage receipts, the ratio of nearly 17% for 1332 seems closer to normal than the later figure.

It is against this background that the minting profits of Louis de Male can be compared with those of his father (tables 5 to 8). From 1346 until 1354, his profits stayed at approximately the same level as those of his father during the period 1334 to 1338. From 1354 until 1362 however, he collected four times as much seignorage; from 1362 to 1366 three times as much, and from 1366 to 1374, twice as much.[32] Intentionally or unintentionally, but definitely not unnoticed, the coinage meant a substantial source of income and replaced the considerable fines which had been levied by his father.

The correlation coefficients between coin output and seignorage receipts (1334-84) are positive and significant:

gold	0.744
silver	0.651

The weaker correlation for silver than for gold can be explained by the fact that the intrinsic value of silver was much more often, and more drastically, altered (nearly 1:20 as against 3:4). On the other hand in the case of gold, the seignorage rate was changed with nearly all the mutations and sometimes in a dramatic way (nearly 1:22) as is shown in the following table.

(based upon the data in tables 2, 4, 6 and 7)	Gold	Silver
Total number of mutations under review	32	23
Alteration of intrinsic value alone	2	5
Alteration of seignorage rate alone	22	8
Alteration of both	7	10
Alterations of:		
fineness: number	9	12
extreme values	18-24	5¾d.-11d.
taille: number	4	5
extreme values[a]	(35¼)52-63 1/3 (66)	57½-72
seignorage rate: number	29	18
extreme values	6-130½	1-10

(a) In brackets: values of exceptionally introduced types of coins

It is equally obvious that for gold the reduction of the intrinsic value correlates strongly with an increase of the seignorage rate. On the contrary, for silver alterations of the intrinsic value in most cases do not correlate with an adaption of the rate of seignorage; when it occurs, the correlation is not always negative, as shown in the following table:

	Gold	Silver
Correlation of the alterations:		
I.V.—and S.R. +	5	5
I.V.—and S.R. -	-	2
no correlation	2	10

(I.V.: intrinsic value; S.R. : seignorage rate; -: decrease; +: increase.)

From this we may conclude that the manipulation of gold currency was mainly operated by changing the rate of seignorage while the intrinsic value was the main variable for silver. Nevertheless in both cases the seignorage receipts of the counts underwent a firm impulse from the volume of mint output.

The correlations between the rate of seignorage and mint output are demonstrated in the next table. The output has been analysed through both the *per diem* figures and the duration of each issue. It has to be noted that these lasted much longer for silver than for gold, and that the quantities of silver alloy minted were also considerably higher.

	Gold		Silver		
Issue lasting:	<3 months	>3 months	<5 months	6-16 months	≥20 months
S.R. 0					
+ and +	1	5	-	3	1
- and -	2	7	1	2	4
+ and -	4	2	1	2	-
- and +	4	2	1	5	-
Totals	11	16	3	12	5
		27			20

(S.R.: seignorage rate; 0: coinage output; +: increase and/or high level; -: decrease and/or low level.)

The full interpretation of these figures requires more data concerning the prices of bullion. Nevertheless, some patterns of decision-making can be discerned:

—the combination of high seignorage rates and high output evidently depends on favourable market circumstances; the effects work out in the medium term;

—lowering seignorage rates and equally lowering output can be profitable for the count; his moderate gain is a stimulus to attract bullion long-term;

—high seignorage rates and low output do not last long because of shortage of bullion;

—low seignorage rates can stimulate the output for a while, depending on market conditions.

A specifically succesful application of these mechanisms was the introduction of a new type of coin, usually of lower fineness and weight than a former one in which people had lost their confidence after a series of debasements. Such new issues scored sometimes feverishly high output figures thanks to the high price the mintmasters could offer for bullion at the expense of a further—still invisible—debasement. The mouton in 1356-57 and again in 1363, the heaume in 1368, the silver lion in 1365-67 and the groat in 1369-70 are examples of great long lasting issues, with exceptionally high *per diem* output and equally high seignorage profits.

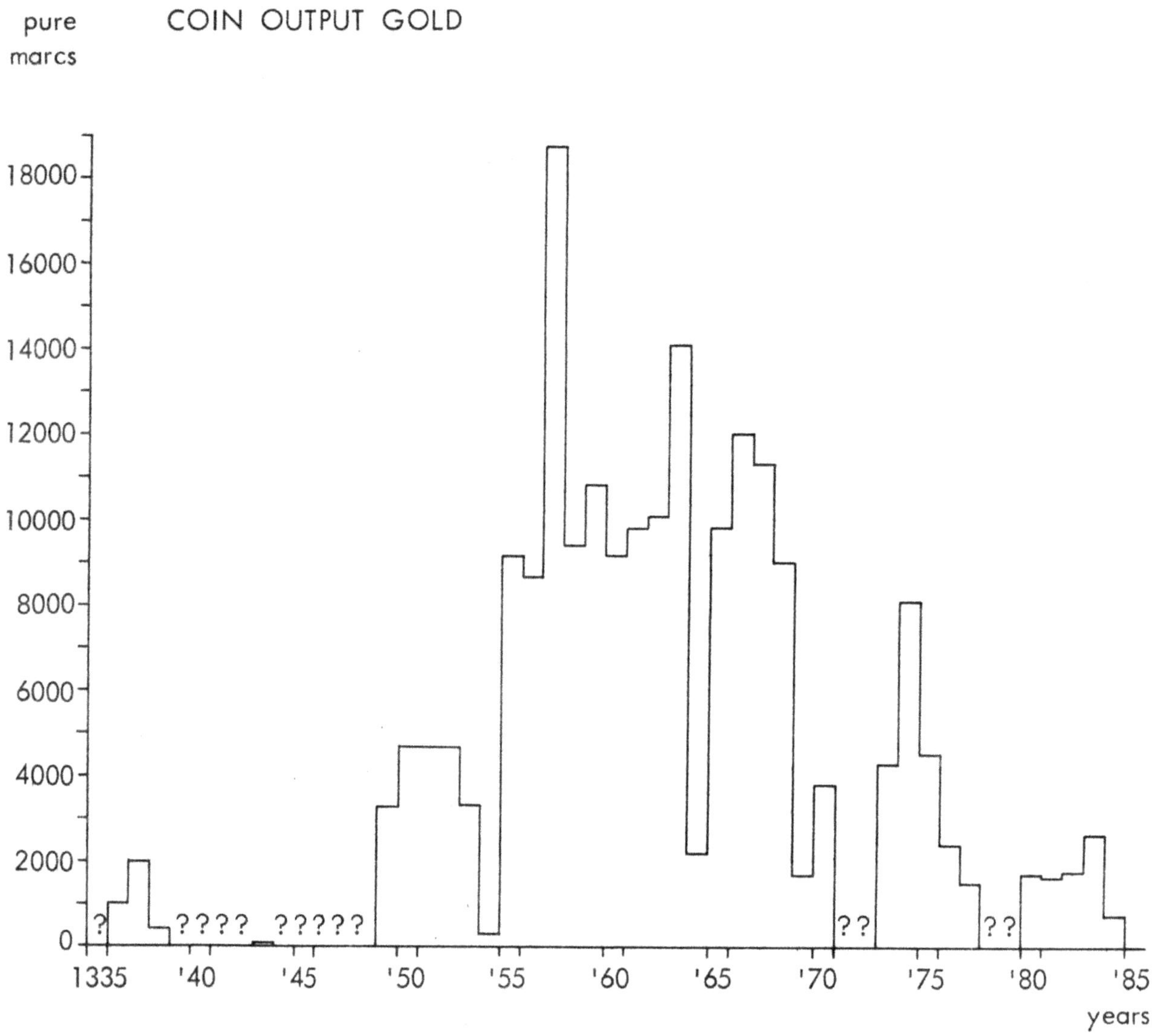
pure
marcs
COIN OUTPUT GOLD
18000
16000
14000
12000
10000
8000
6000
4000
2000
0
?
????
?????
??
??
1335
'40
'45
'50
'55
'60
'65
'70
'75
'80
'85
years

Graph 1.

Let us turn now to the global output figures (table 8 and graphs 1 and 2). The correlation coefficient of gold and silver coinage in marcs of pure metal is moderately positive: 0.555. The production of silver is relatively higher in the years 1335-38, 1345-53, 1365-70 and 1379-85, and consequently more regular than gold issues. Louis de Male obviously had a great deal of luck thanks to the international monetary crises that made possible huge profits on gold coinage from 1356 to 1361. After the restoration of the French coinage under Charles V, however, the extravagant Flemish output and seignorage receipts vanished.

To what extent can international monetary mechanisms serve as an explanation of the changing monetary policy during the period 1330 to 1346? The English Parliament had issued in 1335 a strict prohibition on the export of both bullion and coin. At the same time Edward III devalued his smaller silver coins.[33] Although this could have especially affected the Flemish trade, these regulations appeared to have been difficult to enforce. The English coinage, which had fallen into decline during the previous decades, nevertheless saw in 1336 a strong revival, which must to a certain extent have had disadvantageous effects on the supply of bullion in Flanders.[34] It was however only after the great devaluation in France in January 1337, the first in six years, that the Flemish currency was devalued. During this one year, the Count received on average 1d. par. per groat, half or quarter groat which was minted. Herein lay by far the greatest profit obtained from the whole coinage during the years 1334 to 1346.

The mechanism is thus complex: Louis de Nevers seems primarily to have been purely seeking his own profit. In 1337, external pressure and the export of bullion forced him to devalue his currency further, which for a few months appeared to be especially profitable. Afterwards however, he became in turn the victim of in particular, the French devaluations. The last phase of the operation appeared, as far as the gold was concerned, far less successful, possibly again due to the English bullionist policy.

Apart from the already familiar political motives, it now becomes possible in the light of this, to explain more fully the stagnation of wool exports during the period 1336 to 1337. With the arrival of Edward III in Brabant and later, in 1338, also in Flanders, the situation changes. As a means of payment for his political and military goals, he flooded the Bruges market with wool and made continuous appeals to financiers. He initiated thus a colossal flow of capital, concentrated upon Bruges as the most important money market in West Europe.[35] Money flowed therefore readily into Flanders making the minting of any of their own coins unnecessary for years. During the next stage we see the typical effects of war upon the coinage. Hoarding made gold coinage lifficult, whilst the need for small change increased. There was furthermore ι noticeable rise in the price of silver, especially during the years 1337 and 340 to 1341.[36]

The extent to which the monetary policy of the revolutionary government iffered from that of the Count remains as one of the final points to be discussed.

The production of white silver was entrusted in 1343 to Percheval du orche from Lucca, who, during the years 1334 to 1337, was also the Count's

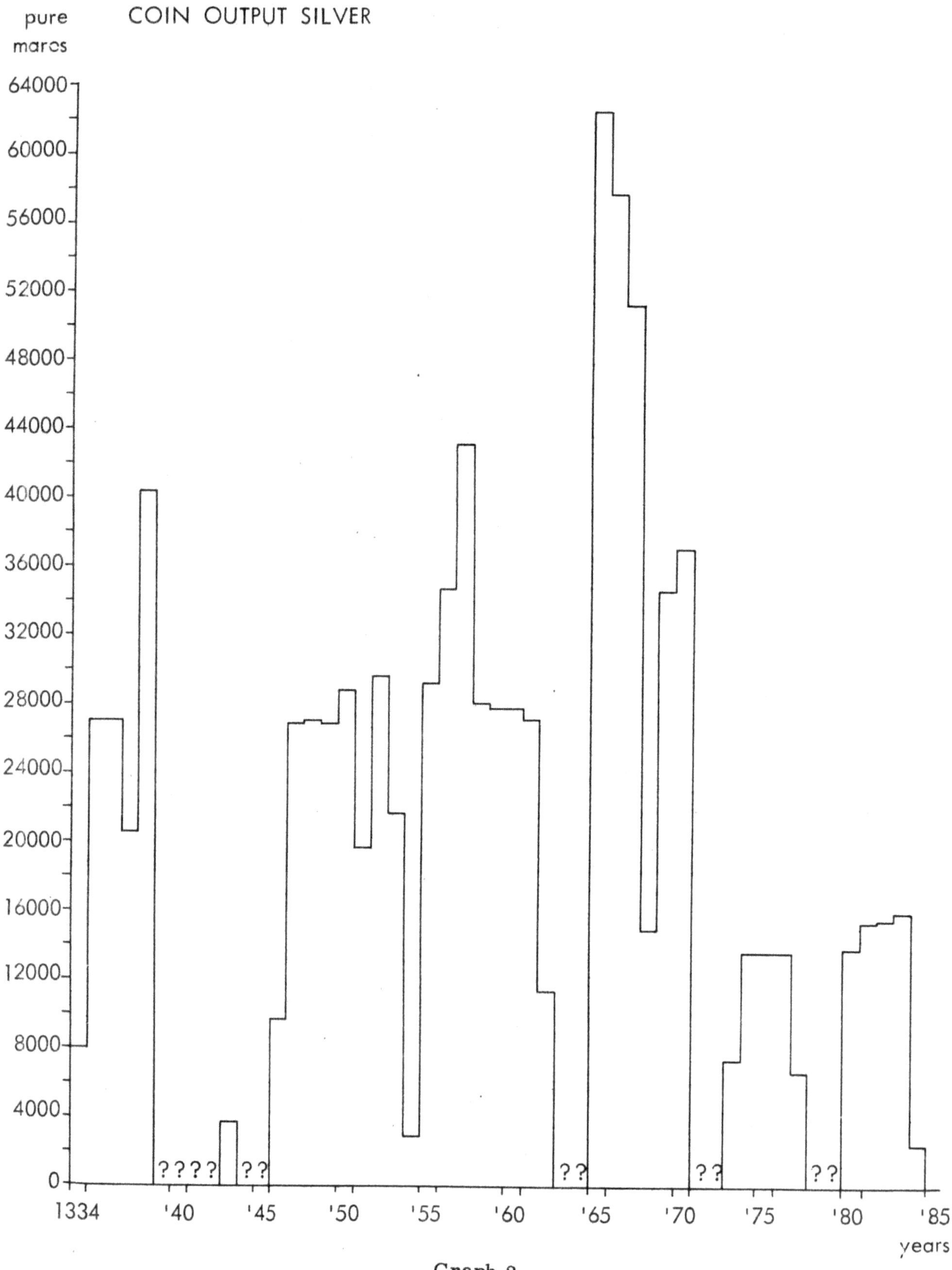
pure marcs
COIN OUTPUT SILVER
64000
60000
56000
52000
48000
44000
40000
36000
32000
28000
24000
20000
16000
12000
8000
4000
0
????
??
??
??
??
1334
'40
'45
'50
'55
'60
'65
'70
'75
'80
'85
years

Graph 2

master of the mint in Ghent. It is noteworthy that this man, during the period July 1344 to July 1346, fulfilled this same function for the King of England, after the latter had repudiated his debts to Florentine bankers.[37] In 1346 the three leading towns of Flanders called upon a member of Percheval's family to become master of the mint.

Characteristic of this coinage, which in the contemporary accounts is described as 'of the three towns', are the low seignorage rates, the reduced intrinsic value and the modest amounts minted. The attention of the public was drawn to the debasement by the inscription MONETA NOVA COMITIS etc.[38] It was obviously necessary to respond to the speedy collapse of the French silver currency, which in April 1343 had reached its lowest point. The considerable increase in English coin output from 1341 onwards, must also have contributed to the scarcity of silver in Flanders, since 94% of the bullion was of foreign origin.[39] It is remarkable, therefore, that the revaluation of the French currency during the years 1344 to '46 was not followed in Flanders.

In January 1346, a groat was issued containing still less silver than the previous one. Owing to a minimal seignorage, it was still possible to attain a reasonable output. One may here point to the three devaluations which the English silver currency underwent from July 1344 to January 1346, as a result of which the English production of silver coins attained, for a short duration, a higher level than had been attained for thirty years. In Brabant and Hainaut, debasements equally took place in 1345.[40] The Flemish coinage of 1346 can therefore not be regarded as purely profit-seeking vis-a-vis France; it was defensive against devaluations in England and in the beighbouring principalities. Finally, it is noteworthy that the towns did not strike small change, probably because they lacked the mint revenues to press the mintmasters on this point. this point.

Count Louis de Nevers tried to draw maximal profits from his coinage. At least during some months in 1337 and '38 he was certainly successful in this. He may also have drawn an extensive income from his debasements in 1331 and '32. In those years his seignorage receipt represented a considerable part of his total income. On the other hand, the monetary policy of the leading towns did not strive towards high seignorage receipts but appears to have been essentially determined by external circumstances. It did not manage, however, to provide the poor people with small change, in contrast to both Louis de Nevers and the Florentine revolutionary government.

As far as the reign of Louis de Male is concerned, our analysis equally aimed at a more precise insight in the motives and instruments of monetary policy. The suggestion of profit-seeking by the count and his advisers has now become a certainty. Of course, their decisions depended on the market situation, for which they could not be held solely responsible. But within that framework, they obviously took <u>all</u> the possibilities of profit which were presented to them.

The international effects of the monetary policy of the period were most likely increased by the sharp insight which existed among certain Italian specialists, who through their consecutive service to different masters were able to benefit on either a personal or family level by the profit-seeking of their masters.

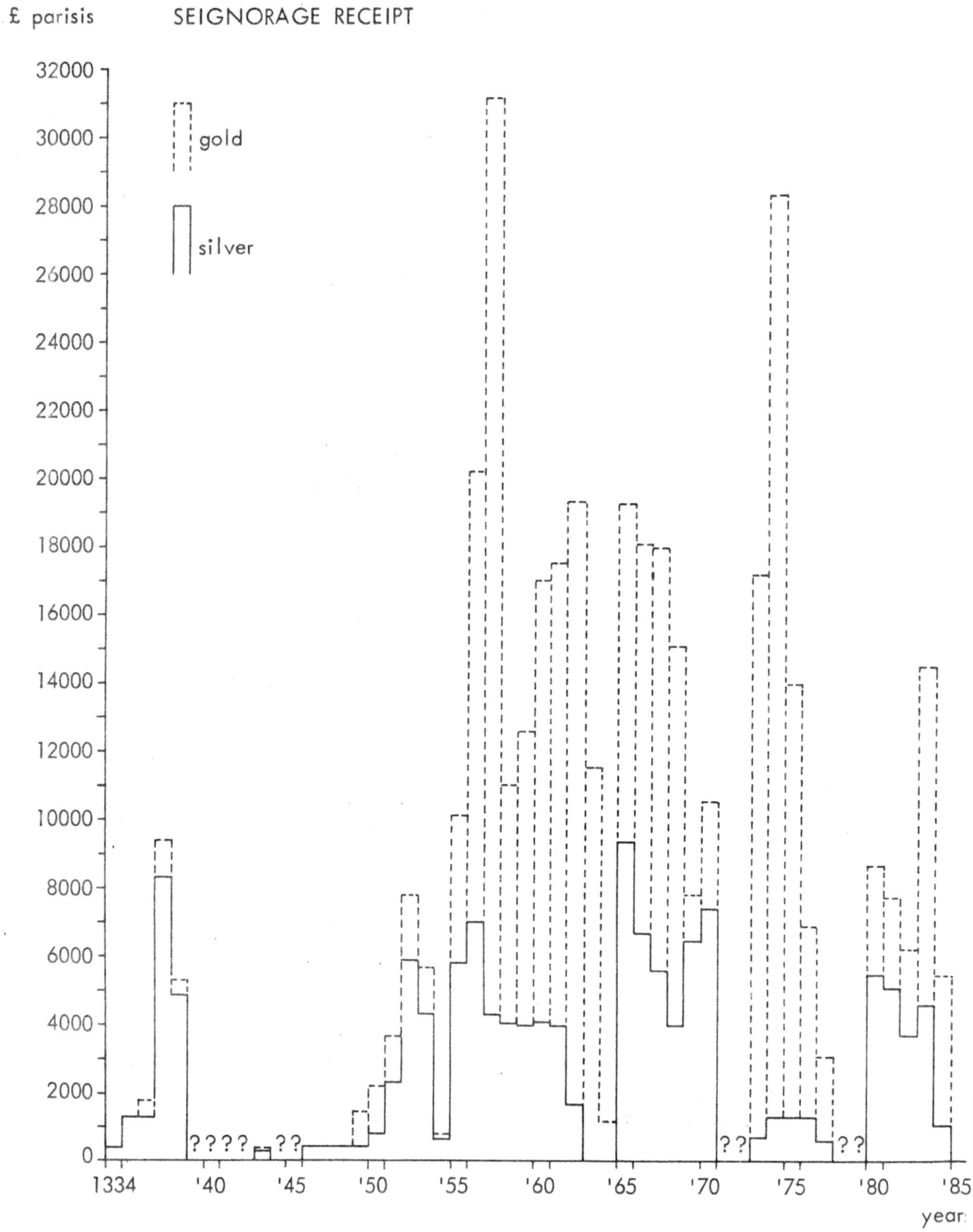
£ parisis
SEIGNORAGE RECEIPT
32000
30000
28000
26000
24000
22000
20000
18000
16000
14000
12000
10000
8000
6000
4000
2000
0
gold
silver
? ? ? ?
? ?
? ?
? ?
1334
'40
'45
'50
'55
'60
'65
'70
'75
'80
'85
year

Graph 3

Table 2. Coinage of white silver and seignorage in Flanders 1331-1346

Period	No. of days	fineness	pure marcs of Troyes	taille	rate of seignorage	seignorage receipt (in £ parisis)	no. of coins	per diem output (in marcs)
8.8.31-12.3.32	218	10d.12g.	?	57	1 gr.	?	?	?
13.3.32-?	?	10d.6g.	?	57½	1 gr.	?	?	? (a)
16.9.34-26.4.37	955	10d.6g.	70,829	57½	1 gr.	3,541 9/-	9,535,685	74 (b)
25.5.37-15.2.38	267	9d.	27,429	60½	7 gr.	9,600 3/-	} 2,801,564	103
19.2.38-10.6.38	113	9d.	7,301	60½	5 gr.	1,825 6/-		65
24.6.38-7.11.38	137	9d.	5,619	60½	5 gr.	1,404 17/-	453,296	41
	4 yrs. 53 d.		111,178			16,171 15/-	12,790,645	
16.4.43-17.10.43	185	8d.	3,768	66	2 gr.	376 16/-	373,032	20
20.1.46-20.11.46	305	7d.16g.	6,969	66	1 gr.	353 8/-	719,994	23

(a) in quarter and half groats; the taille is in all cases calculated in proportion to the groat

(b) in groats, half groats and quarter groats

Table 3. Gold coinage and seignorage in Flanders 1336-43

Period	no. of days	pure marcs of Troyes	taille	rate of seignorage	seignorage receipt (in £ parisis)	no. of coins	per diem output (in marcs)
28.6.35-?	± 1 yr.	(2,184) (a)	71 2/3	9 gr.	(984)	?	?
16.6.36-27.1.38	592	3,028	71 2/3	9 gr.	1362 2/-	217,000	5.115
28.6.37-9.1.38	197	170	53½	27 gr.	229 19/-	9,250	0.863
5.3.38-8.6.38	96	252	53½	18 gr.	220 16/9	13,500	2.625
	3 yrs.	3,450 (5,634)			1812 17/9	239,750	
16.4.43-9.8.43	116	27	53½	12 gr.	16 4/-		0.233

Table 4. Coinage of black silver in Flanders 1331-1338

Period	no. of days	fineness	marcs of alloy	taille	no. of coins
8.8.31-12.3.32	218	1d. 21g.	?	264	? (b)
13.3.32-?	?	1d. 18g.	?	264	?
16.9.34-26.4.37	2 yrs. 223 d.	1d. 18 g.	6,213	264	1,640,232
25.5.37-10.6.38	1 yr. 17 d.	1d. 18 g.	3,044	268¾	805,899
	3 yrs. 270 d.		9,257		2,446,131

(a) Extrapolation on the basis of the data for the following period.

(b) Value: 1d. parisis.

Table [illegible]. Average per annum of the coinage in Flanders

	1334-1346			1346-1384		
	weight total	weight average p.a.	number of coins p.a.	weight total	weight average p.a.	number of coins p.a.
gold	851 kg (1385.5 kg) (a)	70.917 kg (426.308 kg)	19,979 (119,875) (b)	48,867 kg	1,643 kg	413,391
white silver	29,869 kg	2,489 kg	1,156,972	195,994 kg	5,262 kg	c. 3,625,000
black silver	330.745 kg	27.562 kg (88.199 kg)	203,844 (652,302)	?	?	46,472

In brackets: (a) an extrapolation for 1335-36 is included.
(b) p.a. during period of effective coinage.

Table 6. Gold coinage and seignorage under Louis de Male, 1346-1384

This table is an extension and a revision of those published by van Werveke, "Currency manipulation," p. 120, and "De muntslag," p. 22 and p. 26. There are several reasons for the differences. The source material has been extended to the acts published by T. de Limburg-Stirum, Cartulaire de Louis de Male, 2 vols., Bruges, 1898-1901. Some supplementary data are drawn from accounts which had not been analysed thoroughly (20.12.1354-9.5.1355-24.11.1355, 22.11.-3.12.1356, 20.4-22.10.1359) or had been overlooked (7.8.1380-3.5.1382, see explicit statements in "De muntslag," p. 16 (sub nr. 51) and p. 19) (Lille, ADN, B 612/7751, 7796, 7834 and 20932; Brussels, ARA RR 2140).

On the other hand, our total figures are lower than van Werveke's because he seems to have accounted the marc of Troyes as 245 grams (see his equation in "De munstslag," p. 23 and also his De Gentsche stadsfinanciën in de Middel eeuwen, Brussels, 1934, p. 107 which leads to an overestimation of about 0.1%.

His results were more seriously affected by a number of miscalculations (see also the different figures in his two publications on the subject). It should be stressed, however, that we are very much indebted to the work done by our illustrious predecessor.

The dates in the first column concern the period of effective mintage unless this is lacking in the document. A letter "A" before the dates indicates the period of the account; a letter "A" or "M" behind the dates refers to the latter date, stating that it is the end of the account ("A"), or of the mintage period ("M").

Period	Coin	Currency (in groats)	Fineness (in carats)	Pure marcs of Troyes	Taille	Rate of seignorage (in groats/marc)	Seignorage receipt (in £ parisis)	No. of days	*per diem* output (in marcs of Troyes)
A 6.5.1349-1.1.52	écu	22	23 1/4	12,700 2 oz.	54	6	3,810 3/-	989	12.842
A 15.1.52-6.9.53	écu	23½	23 1/4	7,925 1 oz.(a)	54	9	3,204 4/8	599	13.231
A 20.12.54-24.11.55	écu	24	22 1/4	9,529 4½ oz.	54 1/3	12	5,717 14/6	340	28.028
20.2.56-13.8.56	écu	24	22 1/4	2,226 6 oz.	54 1/3	18	2,004 1/6	176	12.652
12.8.56-3.12.56	mouton	28	24	7,418 3½ oz.	52	28	10,378 19/6	114	65.074
10.12.56-11.2.57	mouton	28	24	3,096 4 oz.	52	46 2/3	7,225 3/-	63	49.151
11.2.57-4.3.57	mouton	28	24	1,442 2 oz.	52	42	3,028 18/-	22	65.557

(contd.)

Table 6 continued

Period	Coin	Currency (in groats)	Fineness (in carats)	Pure marcs of Troyes	Taille	Rate of seignorage (in groats/marc)	Seignorage receipt (in £ parisis)	No. of days	*per diem* output (in marcs of Troyes)
11.3.57-4.11.57	mouton	28	24	13,336 4 oz.	52	28	18,671 5/3	239	55.801
19.9.57-12.10.57	écu			594 5 oz.				24	24.776
11.11.57-24.8.58	mouton	28	24	7,269 1½ oz.	52	14	5,088 7/11	287	25.328
24.8.58-22.10.59	mouton	28	23½	11,200 ½ oz.	52½	14	8,836 5/3	425	26.353
22.10.59-1.2.60	mouton	28	23¼	2,900 2 oz.	52½	14	2,092 9/6	71	40.849
9.11.59-8.2.60	royal		24	272 5 oz.	66	1½ roy.	490 19/-	90	3.029
8.2.60-14.3.60	mouton	28	22¼	1,915 3 oz.	53	38	3,639 6/-	36	53.205
14.3.60-25.7.60	mouton	28	22¼	3,670 6 oz.	53	28	5,539 4/6	133	27.600
25.7.60-16.9.61	mouton	28	22¼	8,638 7 oz.	53	20	8,638 16/6	396	21.815
16.9.61-4.12.61	mouton		21½	557 6 oz.	53	36	1,003 19/-	80	6.972
16.9.61-13.9.62	franc	27	24	13,602 4½ oz.	63⅓	36	24,484 12/7	363	37.473
12.-27.9.62	franc	27	24	300	63⅓	40	360 -/-	16	18.750
A 15.10.62-22.12.62	franc	27	24	742 ½ oz.	63⅓	27	1,001 16/6	69	10.755
7.1.63-14.3.63	franc	27	24	442 1 oz.	63⅓	18	397 18/3	67	6.599
14.3.63-21.7.63	franc	27	24	1,665 6 oz.	63⅓	27	2,248 14/9	161	10.346
A 22.7.63-12.9.63	franc	27	24	4,982 ½ oz.	63⅓	18	4,483 7/-	53	94.001
12.9.63-23.10.63	mouton		19½	1,925 2 oz.	53½	35	3,369 2/-	42	45.839
23.10.63-11.11.63	mouton		19½	212 5 oz.	53½	63	818 6/-	20	10.631
11.11.63-29.1.64	mouton		19½	2,186 7 oz.	53½	28	361 13/-	80	27.325
29.1.64-4.3.64	mouton		19½	1,009 3 oz.	53½	14	706 11/-	36	28.038
4.3.64-11.5.64	franc	27	24	418 3 oz.	63⅓	18	376 13/-	69	6.063
A 10.2.65-17.12.67 M	lion	40	24	30,622 6 oz.	45¼	20	30,622 £10/-	1039	29.473

(contd.)

Table 6 continued

Period	Coin	Currency (in groats)	Fineness (in carats)	Pure marcs of Troyes	Taille	Rate of seignorage (in groats/marc)	Seignorage receipt (in £ parisis)	No. of days	*per diem* output (in marcs of Troyes)
A 10.2.65-28.6.65	½ lion		24	320 3½ oz.	90½	20	320 8/-	139	2.305
A 8.2.66-12.3.67	lion (b)		18	1,543 1½ oz.	45¼	8	616 5/6	398	3.878
19.12.67-18.6.68	heaume	54	24	9,673 7 oz.	35¼	60	11,885 4/7	182	53.153
19.12.67-21.1.68	1/3 heaume	18	24	47 4 oz.	(105¾)	60	85 10/-	34	1.397
22.9.69-5.8.70	Flanders		24	5,316 1½ oz.	58½	16	4,252 19/4	318	16.718
2.4.70-5.8.70	lion		24	210	45¼	22	230 18/6	126	1.666
A A 18.6.17.22.11.73	écu		24	55 4 oz.	54½	21½	59 14/-	159	21.583
				238 4 oz.		44	333 16/4		
				3,137 5 oz.		130½	12,942 13/-		
A 22.11.73-28.3.75 M	écu		24	10,541 2 oz.	54½	108½	36,153 17/-	472	22.333
29.3.75-26.6.76 A	écu		24	5,036 6 oz.	54½	80½	12,214 -/8	456	11.046
A 6.11.76-27.6.77	écu		24	2.027 4 oz.	54½	48½	3,294 14/-	234	8.665
A 30.1.80-7.8.80	écu		23½	421 7½oz.	54½	40	606 18/-	220	1.918
A 30.1.80-28.4.81 M	écu		23	1,832 4½ oz.	54½	102	3,361 14/6	453	4.045
28.4.81-18.8.83	écu		23	4,139 7 oz.	54½	82	5,819 15/-	844	4.905
7.9.83-29.2.84	écu		21½	2,309 3½ oz.	54½	180	12,471 11/-	176	13.122
Totals				199,657 marcs = 48,866.649 kg			263,249 13/7		

(a) Half and quarter écus included.

(b) "fais des moutons de Brabant"

Table 7. Silver coinage and seignorage under Louis de Male, 1346-1384

Period	Coin	Fineness	Pure marcs of Troyes	Taille	Rate of seignorage (in groats/marc)	Seignorage receipt (in £ parisis)	No. of days	Per diem output in marcs
24.11.1346-27.5.51	groat	6 d. 23½ g.	121,030 2 oz.	66	2	2,019 16/6	1646	74
7.8.50-27.7.51	1/3 groat	6 d. 12 g.	3,534 3 oz.	195	4	706 18/-	307	12
28.5.51-1.1.52	groat	6 d. 12 g.	16,818 6 oz.	66	2	1,681 17/6	218	77
28.5.51-1.1.52	1/3 groat	6 d. 12 g.	1,137 4 oz.	195	2	113 15/-	218	5
15.1.52-5.9.53	groat	6 d. 12 g.	50,461	66	4	10,092 6/6	598	84
7.9.53-24.10.54	groat	6 d. 8 g.	2,543 7 oz.	?	5	635 19/-	413	6
20.12.54-24.11.55	groat	6 d. 4 g.	30,297 2/3 oz.	69	4	6,059 10/-	339	89
20.2.56-3.12.56	groat	6 d. 4 g.	31,857 2½ oz.	69	4	6,331 10/-	285	112
10.12.56-4.11.57	groat	6 d. 4 g.	41.316 5 oz.	69	5	10,329 3/8	330	125
4.11.17-18.10.59	groat	6 d. 4 g.	54,834 ½ oz.	69	3	8,120 4/7	714	77
22.10.59-4.12.61	groat	6 d.	58,627	70	3	8,793 15/-	774	76
4.12.61-27.9.62	groat	6 d.	13,812 4 oz.	72	3	2,071 17/6	331	42
12.4.65-8.2.66	lion	8 d.	71,666 5 oz.	57	3	10,750	303	237
8.2.66-11.12.67	lion	8 d.	99,542	57	2	10,954 3/-	671	148
21.1.68-28.3.68	lion	7 d. 12 g.	5,125	57	8	2,050 -/-	67	76
28.3.68-18.6.68	lion	7 d. 12 g.	9,718 6 oz.	57	4	1,943 15/-	83	117
21.4.69-9.8.69	lion	7 d. 4 g.	8,719 3½ oz.	57	3	1,289 5/-	111	79
22.9.69-25.5.70	groat	6 d.	62,725	72 ?	4	12,545 -/-	246	255
18.6.73-27.6.77	lion	6 d. 12 g.	54,368 2½ oz.	57	2	5,437 -/-	1470	37
30.1.80-28.4.81	double groat	6 d.	18,495	58	8	7,420 -/-	454	41
28.4.81-3.5.82	double groat	6 d.	15,787 4 oz.	58	6	4,736 5/-	370	43
22.5.82-11.9.83	double groat	6 d.	21,775	58	4	4,355 -/-	477	46
12.9.83-29.2.84	double groat	5 d. 18 g.	6,588 4 oz.	58	10	3,294 5/-	171	39
Total			800,781½ marcs					
		=	195,993.67 kg					

Table 8. Coin output and seignorage receipt for gold and silver per year, 1334-1384

	Gold		Silver	
	coin output in pure marcs of Troyes	seignorage receipt in £ parisis	coin output in pure marcs of Troyes	seignorage receipt in £ parisis
1334			8,010	400
5	?	?	27,071	1,354
6	1023	460	27,145	1,357
7	2029	1070	20,520	8,376
8	398	283	40,349	4,894
-	-	-	-	-
43	27	16	3,768	377
-	-	-	-	-
46			9,763	434
7			26,838	448
8			26,912	449
9	3326	998	26,838	448
50	4687	1406	28,680	816
1	4687	1406	19,649	2,314
2	4631	1872	29,534	5,907
3	3294	1332	21,641	4,364
4	336	202	2,902	672
5	9193	5516	29,225	5,845
6	8677	14791	34,611	7,020
7	18729	27421	43,016	4,300
8	9403	6887	28,031	4,151
9	10828	8504	27,726	4,116
60	9173	12860	27,723	4,158
1	9869	13522	26,695	4,004
2	10148	17752	11,267	1,690
3	14114	11548	?	?
4	2219	1214	?	?
5	9869	9870	62,442	9,366
6	12026	11264	57,586	6,706
7	11300	11308	51,180	5,632
8	9012	11089	14,843	3,994
9	1688	1351	34,472	6,440
70	3838	3133	36,972	7,394
1	?	?	?	?
2	?	?	?	?
3	4325	16400	7,286	729
4	8152	27958	13,500	1350
5	4567	12578	13,500	1350

(contd.)

Table 8 (continued)

			Silver	
	coin output in pure marcs of Troyes	seignorage receipt in £ parisis	coin output in pure marcs of Troyes	seignorage receipt in £ parisis
1376	2451	5556	13,537	1354
7	1542	2506	6,546	655
8	?	?	?	?
9	?	?	?	?
80	1777	3093	13,689	5,491
1	1698	2593	15,346	5,090
2	1790	2517	15,428	3,747
3	2650	9806	15,872	4,613
4	787	4252	2,312	1,156

NOTES

1. The greater part of the documentation for this paper was assembled during the years 1960-2 by my father, the late Professor Frans Blockmans. My contribution has consisted mainly in writing the interpretation, taking into account recent views on this subject. I must add, that the opinions expressed here are in several respects adverse to those of my father, due to the criticism which has been formulated during the last decade against the purely voluntary approach to medieval devaluations. I am very much indebted to Dr. Maurice Vandermaesen who helped me substantially with the consultation of the chancery register for the period 1331 to 1332 (A.D.N., B 1595/2), which was unknown to previous students.

2. H. van Werveke, "Currency manipulation in the middle ages: the case of Louis de Male, Count of Flanders," in Transactions of the Royal Historical Society, 4th series, XXXI, 1949, 115-127, reprinted in his Miscellanea mediaevalia, Ghent, 1968, 255-267; De Muntslag in Vlaanderen onder Lodewijk van Male, "Mededelingen van de Koninklijke Vlaamse Academie voor Wetenschappen, Letteren en Schone Kunsten van België, Klasse der Letteren", XI, 5, Brussels, 1949, 27 p.

3. P. Spufford, Monetary problems and policies in the Burgundian Netherlands, 1433-1496. Leyden, 1970, 14-15; J. H. Munro, Wool, cloth and gold. The struggle for bullion in Anglo-Burgundian trade 1340-1478. Brussels-Toronto, 1973, 5-6, 39-41.

4. M. Vandermaesen, Lodewijk II van Nevers, in Nationaal Biografisch Woordenboek, 5, Brussels, 1972, 523-534.

5. V. Gaillard, Recherches sur les monnaies des comtes de Flandre depuis les temps les plus reculés jusqu'à l'avènement de la maison de Bourgogne. Ghent, 1857, Pièces justificatives XVII-XXIII, 31-63.

6. J. Ghyssens, "Le monnayage d'argent en Flandre, Hainaut et Brabant au début de la Guerre de Cent Ans," in *Revue belge de Numismatique*, CXX, 1974, 109-191.

7. Brussels, Algemeen Rijksarchief, Rekenkamer, Rolrekeningen (ARA, RR) 788-793; H. Nelis, *Chambres des Comptes de Flandre et de Brabant. Inventaire des Comptes en rouleaux*. Brussels, 1914, 54.

8. Lille, Archives départementales du Nord, série B, (ADN, B) 1595^2, 1565, 1566.

9. Brussels, ARA, RR 4 and 5; Nelis, *op.cit.*, 9.

10. Lille, ADN, B 1569; this important document has been discussed by P. Thomas, "Une source nouvelle pour l'histoire administrative de la Flandre. Le registre de Guillaume d'Auxonne, chancelier de Louis de Nevers, comte de Flandre," in *Revue du Nord*, X, 1924, 5-38.

11. Lille, ADN, B 1565, nr. 404, f° 63r°.

12. Lille, ADN, B 1565, nr. 456 f° 70 v°

13. A first indication is the duration of three years; furthermore, the total absence of formality or personal details in the contract of 28 June, 1335 concerning Falco da Lampaggio ("nostre amé F.L."), whereas seven months earlier the appointment of the master of the mint for silver was for a period of one year only, formulated more precisely: "nostre amé vallet Perchival du Porche de Lukez." Most important are the two fragments of the survey of the Count's finances in 1332 (see Note 10) where coins are described as "tiercelet de Faucon" and "Faucon for", (ADN, B 1569 f° 62). They probably point to the mintmaster's first name, the latter quotation suggesting a strong coin dating from either before the devaluation of August 1331, or after the revaluation of March 1332 (see p. 71). In any case, the florins had, since mid-August 1331, the same value of 12 groats tournois as in the contract of 28 June 1335. (J. Vuylsteke, *Gentsche stads- en baljuwsrekeningen 1280-1336*. II. Ghent, 1900, 746 l. 1-2 and 750, l. 39-40).

14. Lille, ADN, B 1592^2 f° 82v°-83r°: instructions to the master and the warden of the mint at Aalst and to the local bailiff to ensure the application of the new ordinance.

15. J. Day, in *Past and Present*, 1978.

16. Vuylsteke, *op.cit.*, II 805 l. 4-8 and 17-18.

17. On 11 February 1332, the Count informed the Abbot of Saint Nicholas at Tournai, at the request of the Dean of Saint Donatian at Bruges, about these exchange rates which were to be applied to all debts to the Count (ADN, B 1592^2 f° 117r°).

18. Vuylsteke, *op.cit.*, II 746, 750 and A. Van Werveke, *idem*, III *Register*, 1256-7, 1269.

19. E. Fournial, *Histoire monétaire de l'Occident médiéval*. Paris, 1970.

20. See table 1 and T. H. Lloyd, The English wool trade in the Middle Ages. Cambridge, 1977; also his "Overseas trade and the English money supply in the Fourteenth Century," in N. J. Mayhew (ed.), Edwardian monetary affairs (1279-1344), British Archaeological Reports, 36, Oxford, 1977, 104.

21. Lille, ADN, B 1569, f° 60r°-70v°; Thomas, op.cit., 12 and 27; F. Blockmans, "Le contrôle par le prince des comptes urbains en Flandre et en Brabant au Moyen âge," in Finances et Comptabilité urbaines du XIIIe au XVIe siècle. Pro Civitate. Brussels, 1964, 307-8, 315-319.

22. Brussels, ARA, RR 5; to achieve a yearly income, the sum of the account of 7.9.1335-7.11.1336 has been reduced to 12/14.

23. The 'transport' is a general tax of £8,000 parisis per year on the county of Flanders due to the Count on the occasion of the restitution to the King of France of the Castelries of Lille, Douai and Béthune in application of the treaties of Athis-sur-Orge (1305) and Pontoise (1312).

24. Lille, ADN, B 1595^{2} f° 84r°.

25. Placcaerten ende ordonnantien van de hertogen van Brabant, 1, Antwerp-Brussels, 1648, 546.

26. Vandermaesen, op.cit.

27. Description by Ghyssens, op.cit., 130-5.

28. Ibid., 123-4, 132.

29. Ibid., 186-7.

30. On 8 August, 1331 Jacques de Beernem was appointed as the warden of the mint at Aalst; his instructions then concerned both gold and white silver coins. The instructions addressed to him on the 13th of March, 1332, however, do not mention gold. His appointment as the warden of the mint in Ghent on 24 November, 1334 is for silver, black and white (ADN, B 1595^{2} f° 83r° and 84r°; 1565 nr. 475 f° 74v°).

31. Louis de Nevers urged the masters of the mint Jehan de Septare and Percheval du Porche on 8 August 1331 and 13 November 1334 in the same terms: 'Et est assavoir que de petites mailles noires dessus nommées li maistres dessus diz ne sera tenu de nous rendre nulle chose, mais il sera tenus de faire ent et ouvrer convenablement, tant qu'il devra souffire à nostre dit pays." Lille, ADN, B 1565 nr. 474 f° 74r° and 1595^{2} f° 82v°.

32. Van Werveke, De muntslag, 27.

33. Munro, op.cit., 23-4, 34.

34. J. Craig, The Mint. A history of the London mint from A.D. 287 to 1948. Cambridge, 1953, 61-4 and 410-1; Lloyd, "Overseas trade," 98.

5. E. B. Fryde, "Financial resources of Edward III in the Netherlands, 1337-40," in Revue belge de Philologie et d'Histoire, XLV, 1967, 1157-69.

36. Ghyssens, *op.cit.*, 136.

37. Craig, *op.cit.*, 65-7.

38. Ghyssens, *op.cit.*, 127 and 135.

39. Lloyd, "Overseas trade," 98.

40. Ghyssens, *op.cit.*, 167-71.

MONETARY CONTRACTION AND INDUSTRIAL CHANGE IN THE LATE-MEDIEVAL LOW COUNTRIES, 1335-1500

John H. Munro

I Monetary Contraction in Late-Medieval Europe and the Low Countries

Only a minority of economic historians would argue that late-medieval Europe experienced a severe monetary contraction, severe enough to have become at least a partial cause of that era's 'great depression'. The preponderant majority of those historians who support the thesis of a late-medieval depression or secular economic decline contend that its fundamental causes were 'real', not monetary: above all Malthusian crises and a sharp demographic decline; and/or severe economic dislocations from a succession of famines, plagues, other epidemics, and a widespread warfare that Europe had not experienced since late Carolingian times. When W. C. Robinson rashly argued, in 1959, that monetary forces were chiefly responsible for that depression, the acknowledged and most eloquent champion of the 'real' school, Prof. Michael Postan, responded with a devastating critique that silenced Robinson, evidently forever.[1] Since then those few historians who have dared espouse a 'monetarist' position in the depression debate have proceeded with greater caution than Robinson. Indeed the most notable of these historians, Prof. Harry Miskimin of Yale, has adroitly and imaginatively combined the chief 'real' and monetarist arguments by according primacy of importance to Postan's demographic theses and assigning monetary factors only a secondary role in deepening and prolonging the late-medieval depression.[2] Nicholas Mayhew of Oxford on the other hand has attacked Postan's key arguments much more directly in a seminal article of 1974 that convinced me at least to desert the Postan camp on monetary issues—ans so contradict my own earlier writings.[3] But Mayhew has wisely refrained from supporting all of Robinson's arguments on the direct role of monetary forces in causing the depression and has chiefly confined his arguments on monetary contraction to England.

The most recent contribution to the debate is John Day's "The Great Bullion Famine of the Fifteenth Century", Past and Present, no. 79 (May 1978), which provides the most elaborately documented and convincing evidence yet that most of late-medieval western Europe experienced such a monetary contraction.[4] Thus, while Miskimin and Mayhew utilized only English mint data, Day has presented graphs and other indices to demonstrate roughly similar trends in the coinage outputs of England, the Low Countries, France, Italy (Florence, Genoa), Spain, (Aragon, Navarre, Valencia) Sardinia and Lübeck. For other parts of Europe he has furnished considerable literary evidence of a 'bullion famine'. But in his view this famine became widespread and severe only from the 1390s, a much later date for the onset of contraction than that suggested by Miskimin, Mayhew, or by several earlier historians—principally Marc Bloch, Henri Laurent, and Albert Feavearyear.[5] Furthermore, since Day's primary objective was to document the existence of this bullion famine across Europe, severe limitations of space in an already condensed article of 52 pages prevented him from offering more than a brief explanation for the monetary contraction.

His principal explanation, though later combined with other arguments, is in fact the traditional one: a large deficit in Europe's balance of payments with the Islamic Near East. Although it is statistically impossible to provide a complete and accurate accounting of Europe's balance of payments in the late Middle Ages, Day's case is a thoroughly sound one, in my view, buttressed by considerable evidence. Furthermore it is fully supported by the prodigious, meticulously researched publications of that eminent Orientalist Eliyahu Ashtor. For the late fifteenth century, Ashtor estimates that western Europe imported an approximate annual average of 660,000 ducats worth of oriental spices and other merchandise from Syria and Egypt; and that to obtain these eastern goods merchants from Venice, Genoa, Marseilles, and Barcelona exported about 260,000 ducats worth of European manufactures and the remaining 400,000 ducats, in specie.[6] That specie drain to the Near East would have amounted to roughly 1,420 kg of gold or 16,500 kg of silver a year. As tables 3-5 and 8 indicate, only very rarely in the fifteenth century did the aggregate mint outputs of England and the Burgundian Low Countries combined match such a volume of precious metal exports.

Nevertheless, as the fundamental cause of late-medieval Europe's monetary contraction, a number of questions about this specie outflow remain to be answered. Why did Day's 'bullion famine' commence only in the late fourteenth century? Did western Europe begin to incur large trade deficits with the Near East only from that time, as Ashtor himself very cautiously suggests? Ashtor has certainly demonstrated that Venetian imports from Syria and Egypt grew by at least a third over the fifteenth century. Venetian specie exports may thus have mounted proportionately; but some of that Venetian commercial expansion, to account for over two thirds of Europe's trade with the Levant by 1500, was at the expense of Genoa, Marseilles, and Barcelona.[7] Did the Islamic Near East diminish in relative importance as a market for higher priced European manufactures in the course of the fifteenth century? Both Ashtor and Udovitch have demonstrated that Mamluk Egypt suffered depopulation, contraction, deflation, and severe depression in that era. Ashtor notes that the composition of Italian exports to the Levant changed in this era to become 'mainly olive oil, cheap and dried fruits, copper (for small coins), and cheap cloth'. Udovitch believes that the Levant itself suffered an overall balance of payments deficit as precious metals poured increasingly eastwards to buy spices and oriental luxury goods for both domestic consumption in the Near East and re-export to the West.[8] Had western Europe, on the other hand, previously been able to balance its deficits with the Near East by trade surpluses with Tunisia, the Maghreb, and Morocco, once a commercial source of considerable amounts of 'Sudanese' gold from the Niger?[9] Did those supposed surpluses diminish or disappear from the later fourteenth century? Furthermore did western Europe also develop balance of payments deficits with the Baltic regions and Russia - in purchasing grain, lumber, naval stores, and luxury furs especially, as Miskimin suggests?[10] Finally, did western Europe's balance of payments deficits become a serious problem, in absolute or relative terms, only in conjunction with other late-medieval economic difficulties?

The only historian who has offered a viable, all-encompassing explanation for the growth of a European balance of payments deficit and a consequent monetary contraction in the context of the late-medieval depression is Harry Miskimin. In full accordance with Postan, he first contends that demographic disruptions and sharp population declines produced a severe agrarian depression during the fourteenth century, altering the terms of trade in favour of the urban industrial sector, thus 'making it a magnet for the nation's bullion'. He also argued, without contradicting the Postan theses, that the depopulations 'led to an increase in per capita wealth' and permitted some survivors to become particularly wealthy from inherited cash balances. When so many reacted to the various plagues and other late-medieval catastrophes, and to their suddenly acquired wealth, in a spirit of hedonism by increasing their consumption of luxury goods, especially those imported from the Near East by the Italians, the inevitable result in Miskimin's view was a growing 'outflow of bullion that in turn generated the monetary shortage so much commented upon after the Black Death'. In basing his theory so directly upon English evidence he did indeed directly contradict Postan's strongly stated views that late-medieval England consistently enjoyed a favourable balance of trade and thus (presumably) a bullion influx.[11]

In a recent article, from the proceedings of the First Oxford Symposium, Mr. T. H. Lloyd has largely supported Postan's contentions about medieval England's favourable trade balances, at least for most of the fourteenth century.[12] Mr. Lloyd's article is a brilliant tour de force, and his contentions may well be correct; but I find some of his assumptions and especially the price multipliers rather too arbitary. From my own research in the enrolled and 'particular' customs accounts from Edward I to Henry VIII, I am not so confident that accurate trade balances can be computed for any period. In the first place, England's major exports (wool, cloth, tin) and a major import (wine) are recorded only by volume. How can the value of wool exports be accurately calculated when the best of some 30 varieties of wool cost over four times as much as the cheapest, and when prices fluctuated from year to year; or the value of cloth exports, of many varieties, when prices ranged from 10s - 15s a cloth to £3 or £4, excluding scarlets (from £8 - £12)? How can export and import values for other goods be distinguished when their values are globally combined in the 3d Petty Custom and the Poundage accounts? How useful indeed are these accounts when the Petty Custom of 1303 applied only to alien merchandise, when Poundage commenced only in 1347 and was consistently imposed only from the 1370s, when several goods and all merchandise of the Hansards, the largest group of foreign merchants, were usually exempted from Poundage?[13] Much less can we accurately compute the more important balance of <u>payments</u>, including remittances of papal taxes and other ecclesiastical dues - which Parliament so vigorously condemned in the late Middle Ages - military and diplomatic expenditures abroad, spending by travellers and pilgrims, and bullion movements instigated by various monetary and price stimuli? In any event, Lloyd admits that England's 'favourable' trade balances were probably diminishing from the 1360s or later. He thus implicitly offers us the possibility that England did suffer trade deficits in the fifteenth century, when the aggregate volume of wool and cloth exports, despite some upsurges in the 1420s and early 1440s, indisputably fell. They reached their nadir in the early 1460s, with a volume that was only 47 percent of that achieved in the 1390s.[14]

While Miskimin was also unable to provide statistical proof for his assertions on English balance of payments, he did support them by citing a considerable volume of bullionist and anti-luxury, anti-Italian legislation. Indeed his list can be amplified considerably by many more such statutes and ordinances to demonstrate that from at least the 1330s parliaments were frequently alarmed by the 'great dearth of money'. The period of most intense bullionism was from the 1360s, when parliament first banned the export of both precious metals in all forms without royal licences, to about the 1490s, as I have argued elsewhere.[15] As early as 1381, a parliamentary commission declared that a deficit in the balance of payments was directly responsible for the current dearth of coinage (along with foreign debasements).[16] Late-medieval parliaments and popular literature in general blamed most especially Italian merchants, bankers, and papal tax collectors for a constant and most deleterious outflow of precious metals. Clearly they did not share the 'real' school's ebullient optimism on matters monetary in late-medieval England.

To counteract these supposed specie outflows, parliaments resorted chiefly to two major remedies: a series of Employment Acts requiring aliens to export as much in value in goods as they imported or remitted abroad by bills of exchange; and several bullionist impositions on the wool trade, England's dominant export, which variously forced the wool Staplers to supply the mints with some of their receipts in bullion and to exact full payment in ready English money.[17] There is no evidence that these measures were at all successful in protecting and augmenting England's money supply. But they are significant in revealing late-medieval bullionist concerns - and also for the harm that they caused English trade, as will be noted in Part II.

Across the channel, the late-medieval Low Countries evidently also experienced chronic deficits in their balance of payments with Italy, according to Raymond de Roover, who utilized the more concrete evidence of Italian bills of exchange transactions. But he also discovered that Flanders usually enjoyed a surplus in its trade with Spain, permitting some merchants to settle their Italian debts with credits accumulated in Spain, via trilateral bills.[18] But it hardly seems possible that Spanish trade before the sixteenth century was as important as the Italian. Whether or not the Low Countries had an overall deficit or surplus in their balance of payments cannot, of course, be ascertained.

A continuous balance of payments deficit would not have produced monetary contraction had late-medieval Europe been able to replenish its precious metal stocks from within, by mining (and of course have them distributed through international trade). But the general consensus of historians is that European silver mining, having received no significant technological improvements since Roman times, experienced sharply diminishing returns in various parts of Europe from the late thirteenth and early fourteenth centuries. Many mines shut down entirely because of rising costs, virtual depletion, or flooding. To be sure, some new silver and especially gold mines were developed in fourteenth-century Bohemia, Hungary, Bosnia, and Serbia; but their combined additional outputs do not appear to have counteracted the prevailing trend elsewhere of falling metal outputs, according to Nef and others. Not until South German engineers devised two technological breakthroughs, mechanical drainage pumps to eliminate flooding and a lead-chemical process to separate the metals in argentiferous cupric ores, so plentiful in central Europe, did silver mining again enjoy a major boom, from the 1460s to the 1530s.[19]

The well documented slump in late-medieval mining was indeed the major argument for a monetary contraction put forward by the earlier generation of 'monetarists'. Not even the current proponents of the 'real' school will deny the extent of this slump. But they have rejected its significance on two seemingly unassailable grounds. Prof. Postan has contended, in the first place, that by the 1320s or so, after three centuries of rising mining production, 'the total stock of silver in Europe, in relation to the annual output, must have been truly enormous': 200-300 times the annual increments from mining. Secondly any mining output slump was more than counteracted by the devastating depopulations, of 30 to 40 percent or more, in fourteenth-century Europe.[20] 'Men were dying', comments David Herlihy, 'but coins were not', so that per capita coinage supplies should have risen.[21] Or, in terms of the aggregates of the Fisher Equation of Exchange, $M.V = P.T$, the volume of transactions would have declined much more than M, permitting a more than adequate money supply for a highly contracted economy - if one ignores possible balance of payments deficits, and Velocity changes.

But recently one's confidence in the theory of large accumulated metal stocks, those immortal moneys, has been undermined by a number or articles by C. C. Patterson, Marion Archibald, and Nicholas Mayhew, especially. For they have demonstrated that precious metal losses from wear and tear in circulation, unretrieved hoards, shipwrecks, and so forth must inevitably produce drastic reductions in a country's coinage supply unless that coinage was frequently and abundantly replenished by fresh mintings. Patterson believes that in medieval Europe the average annual rate of metal loss from coins was perhaps 1.0 percent; earlier Sir John Craig had estimated such weight losses at a more conservative 0.2 percent, though admitting that it could have reached 1.0 percent at times. Mayhew, adopting the more conservative estimate, argues that a decennial loss rate of 2.0 to 2.75 percent in early fourteenth-century England would have meant that 'seven tons of silver vanished into thin air through wear alone every decade'. He further points out that recoinages to restore the lost weight per coin meant further silver losses 'in the fire' from the minting process.[22] Coins do die.

Physical deterioration of the coinage by wear and tear, and especially by the common, nefarious practices of clipping and 'sweating', could further contract and damage the money supply by curtailing mint production and by encouraging the export of precious metals. Thus, so long as large numbers of underweight or fraudulent coins circulated at their decreed values, by tale, merchants would inevitably respond by discounting the entire coinage, good and bad alike. They would thus bid up the market price of bullion in money-of-account values, thereby eliminating the agio or premium that coins normally commanded over bullion, by virtue of their portability, convenience, and pre-established values. Such a premium was necessary to cover the costs of minting (brassage and seignorage); and without it, merchants would instead take their bullion to foreign mints offering more attractive prices. Or they would utilize good coin with plate and bullion in foreign trade, reserving the inferior coins for domestic trade. By such processes of Gresham's Law, the coinage standard and money supply would thus continue to diminish until the prince either imposed a total recoinage and renforcement on his subjects, at their expense, or took the easier road of debasing the coinage in weight and/or fineness to match the current inferior standard, and so restore the coinage premium. The latter method also had the advantage of attracting foreign bullion, if the prince offered more coins, a better price for the metal concerned, than competing mints.[23] Consequently many late-medieval countries periodically alleviated a scarcity of coinage through debasements - even though many were actually undertaken for fiscal motives (seignorage profits) rather than monetary ones. But these debasements in turn would worsen the monetary plight of their neighbours, provoking them in turn to engage in *guerres monétaires*. Indeed western Europe, after having enjoyed monetary stàbility for almost all the thirteenth century, was then plagued by over two centuries of such *guerres monétaries*, first provoked by Philip the Fair's debasements of 1295-1306.[24] Furthermore very severe debasements and the rampant inflations they generated sometimes ended up exacerbating Europe's monetary stringency. By undermining faith in the coinage, they provoked 'flights from money', increased hoarding, and disrupted trade. Contrary to some opinions, medieval merchants consistently demanded sound money. Certainly in late-medieval France and the Low Countries debasements so enraged nobles and merchants alike that the prince was often forced to restore a 'strong coinage', which necessarily contracted the money supply, with often brutal deflationary consequences, as in Flanders in the 1390s and 1430s.

Another damaging way by which mint manipulations affected the money supply was in 'favouring' one metal over the other at the mint by debasing it more heavily, or by raising its official money-of-account price, and thus by increasing its mint ratio. An influx of the one metal attracted by debasement could be mirrored by an outflow of the other 'disfavoured' metal, in a variant of Gresham's Law. Thus Prof. Andrew Watson has contended that late-medieval Europe suffered large outflows of silver to the Islamic Near East by adopting strongly pro-gold mint ratios, while Muslim mints were favouring silver (except in fact from *c.* 1400 to 1410, when their gold prices rose strongly).[25] The theory that mint-ratio alternations could instigate large-scale international bullion movements has been disputed by many eminent historians, Harry Miskimin and Ashtor in particular.[26] Certainly the critics are correct in contending that there were many barriers inhibiting arbitrage trades in precious metals: the refusal of mints to exchange metals in bullion form, and the bullion of one metal for coin of the other, often; the costs of brassage and seignorage in minting; money-changers' fees, and transportation costs; and the prospects of bullion seizures at the frontiers or of receiving fraudulent coin when making exchanges. The operative mint ratio was not one of the official values (coinage 'traites') but of the ratio of the bullion price of one metal to the coined value of the other. To account for all these costs, the differences between such ratios at two or more mints had to be large to promote bullion flows.

Nevertheless even small differences in mint ratios could affect the international distribution of precious metals by encouraging merchants to have their metals minted in those countries offering the highest exchange values for gold and silver respectively in terms of other commodities. Thus merchants were able to realize some arbitrage profits through normal foreign trade in goods, buying some for silver in one country, say, and selling them for gold in another. The available evidence does not indicate that the very imperfect market economies of medieval Europe were able to establish equilibrium prices for both metals and goods soon enough to eliminate such arbitrage profits.[27]

To support the contention that these mint-ratio alterations did influence the direction of international bullion movements, a simple statistical test may be employed: Chi-Square contingency tables. The one presented here in table 9 express the quinquennial average values of coinage outputs in each metal, in England and the Low Countries, in constant pounds sterling (1411-63 values) over the 80 year period 1420-99. Over this entire period, gold accounted for 66.1 percent of the total value of English mint output and 44.1 percent of the Burgundian output (compared to 82.9 and 70.8 percent respectively in the previous eighty years, 1340-1420). According to the relative mint ratios shown in tables 6-7, gold was more highly valued by the English mints until June 1425, then by the Burgundian mints until March 1465, and then finally once more by the English mints. Table 6 also indicates that during the decade 1485-95 Maximilian's mints again attempted to assert the stronger claim to gold. But monetary affairs in the Low Countries were then greatly disturbed by the chaotic civil wars of 1483-5 and 1488-92, which included mint competition from the rebel Flemish towns. The accounts of the Dordrecht and Mechelen mints show that Maximilian's pro-gold policy, with some drastic increases in that metal's price, was only momentarily if impressively successful in 1488-90.[28] Much of that high output may of course largely represent domestic remintings; and that could be true of most periods of extensive debasements. If we are to assume that such debasements and mint-ratio alterations had no significant effect on the relative flow of the two metals to the two countries' mints, that other factors, such as the structure of foreign trade, quite independently determined what proportions of mint outputs would be in each metal, we should expect that the ratios of the values of the gold and silver coinages in each or most of the quinquenniums, in both countries, should very roughly correspond to these long term (80 year) ratios. To test this null-hypothesis of independence, we use a contingency table with expected and actual mint output values for each quinquennium. If the computed $\chi^2 = \sum \frac{(f_o - f_e)^2}{f_e}$ is small, as tested by Chi-Square significance tables, then we must accept the null hypothesis of independence (from mint-ratio alterations). The chi-square statistics computed here for both the English and Burgundian mint-tables are so very high, far beyond the range of the significance tables, that we have no hesitation in rejecting this null hypothesis.[29] Finally, and more importantly, table 9 shows that for almost all of the quinquenniums, except for that of the previously mentioned civil war era, each country minted more of the 'favoured' metal than the amount expected by the contingency test, and in rough accordance with the relative mint ratios. Note in particular, for its importance in the analysis of Part II, how the preponderance in gold minting shifted from England to the Low Countries after 1425, and then back to England after 1465.

As Watson has pointed out, most northern European countries pursued pro-gold policies during the later Middle-Ages, though offering much higher gold prices in the middle decades of the fourteenth century than thereafter. England was perhaps the most consistent and resolute in 'favouring' gold, from the first successful striking of that coinage in January 1344 until the early sixteenth century.[30] Since gold was obviously acquired at the expense of silver, and since silver was the basis for most countries' domestic commerce, wages and salaries, and money-of-account systems, northern Europe's pro-gold monetary policies may have become, to some extent, agents of monetary contraction and deflation, except when and where counteracted by silver debasements. Attributing such deflation to pro-gold policies in both England and the Low Countries seems to be particularly pertinent for the middle third of the fifteenth century, from 1435 to 1465, as will be discussed in Part II. Yet it would be unfair to place the entire blame upon the English and Burgundian governments; for in this period, as table 7 shows, the free market prices for gold at Antwerp were generally rising, indicating that merchants and other princes were often outbidding them for gold.

Why merchants or princes should have placed such high values on gold has yet to be fully explained. Gold provided, to be sure, a far more suitable medium for long-distance trade than silver. It had a far higher purchasing power per ounce than silver, and a far greater international acceptance, since it was much less subject to debasement, if only because international merchants were much more likely to test high-value coins than retail merchants in domestic trade were to examine petty silver coins. Despite these unquestionable advantages, it is difficult to contend that international trade greatly expanded in the late middle ages in general, or even came to command a greater share of monetary exchanges, to justify these strong pro-gold policies. In any event international merchants found even more effective methods of transacting their trade, in bills of exchange and letters obligatory, except when they suffered trade deficits. If international trade did not necessarily demand more gold, then warfare, diplomacy, and other state and ecclesiastical expenditures obviously did, and at a rising rate in the later Middle Ages. When such state expenditures were international, gold again was the preferred medium. Finally, because gold did serve as the predominant international medium, and because it had long symbolized imperial grandeur, gold offered better proof of sovereignty and power than did the frequently debased silver coinages.[31] The chief motives behind northern Europe's pro-gold policies were probably more political than purely economic; the economic consequences were probably more harmful than beneficial.

The remaining possible causes of monetary contraction in late-medieval Europe are all closely related and may be more succinctly summarized: a reduction in the coinage velocity, increased hoarding, and a greater use of gold and silver as industrial materials for luxury display. None of these purported causes can, to be sure, be statistically verified. J. D. A. Thompson and others have maintained that proportionately more coin hoards can be dated to various periods in the late Middle Ages than to the adjacent eras, though others have commented upon the absence of coin hoards during the most severe fifteenth-century 'bullion famine' of c. 1440-65.[32] Coinage velocity changes are the most difficult of all to document. Yet it seems almost certain that many forces combined to depress coinage velocity at certain periods:

the sharp fall in the number of spenders with depopulations; the disruptions and contractions of trade, international and regional, by famines, plagues, warfare, rebellions, piracy, and brigandage, with the collapse of effective order in many parts of Europe; and then the retreat of parts of depressed agrarian Europe from a monetized market economy. Finally, various government reactions to monetary scarcity and fiscal stringency in the form of bullionist legislation, especially the almost universally imposed bans on precious-metal exports, undoubtedly had some effect in curbing the international flow of specie. At the same time, such bullionist measures also encouraged the use of the aforementioned bills of exchange and letters obligatory to obviate the transport of specie; while also restricting metal flows, they may have augmented coinage velocity, as several historians argued, by economizing on the use of specie within countries. But surely any widespread use of these bills was restricted to a very few international trading centres dominated by Italians. It remains to be proved that credit, whose use still remained a direct function of the specie supply, expanded sufficiently to counteract the evident contraction in late-medieval European coinages.[33]

A special and severe case of reduced coinage velocity was hoarding, which was a perfectly natural and obvious reaction to the many severe crises, dislocations, and general insecurity that frequently afflicted late-medieval Europe. Hoarding was also a rational response to falling prices and depressed market conditions in general. Such views on coinage velocity and hoarding do not, however, appeal to those who espouse the thesis that an increased consumption of eastern (and Russian) luxury goods, producing balance of payments deficits, was the chief cause of monetary scarcity. Yet the two theses are not contradictory and mutually exclusive. Some segments of society - aristocrats, the rich or well-to-do burghers - may have engaged in this 'conspicuous consumption', while others, the peasantry especially, responded to crises by hoarding; and an era marked by hedonistic spending sprees, in particular the very inflationary post-Plague era of the 1350s and 1360s, may have been followed by an era of dolorous parsimony and hoarding by the majority, as suggested by the subsequent deflations from the 1370s to the early fifteenth century.[34] Furthermore, the increased use of gold and silver in resplendent luxury display, a phenomenon attested to by most art historians, is hardly inconsistent with the Miskimin thesis.[35] That is certainly a rational and aesthetic form of hoarding. At the same time, however, we must also admit the likelihood - as Postan rightly enjoins us to do - that periodically war-time taxation, government borrowings, and even those late-medieval cyclical movements that temporarily restored some prosperity, would have stimulated some dishoardings.[36]

One problem concerning coinage velocity remains: to what extent was any decline in coinage velocity in late-medieval Europe merely a passive response to economic contraction in general, to declining economic tempi; and to what extent was monetary scarcity a contributory cause of depression or 'secular decline'? That question is obviously impossible to answer with any certainty. But if hoarding is a rational response to falling prices, extensive hoarding would certainly have accelerated that deflation, which in turn would have squeezed profit margins, curtailed investments, and bred a pessimistic business psychology. Indeed any form of monetary contraction could have induced deflation with such consequences. In more concrete terms, deflation would have increased the burden of debts, the costs of both previously borrowed capital (in repayments) and then future borrowings (in rising interest rates). Deflation also evidently increased the relative costs of skilled labour in those guild protected industries in which wages fell less than wholesale prices. Indeed historically wages generally move much less than the changes in price levels. These factors together in late-medieval Europe would have further encouraged a retreat from the money economy and have exacerbated, if not caused, the periodic cyclical depressions of that era. Thus we can only agree with Marc Bloch that monetary phenomena must be considered 'as a seismograph that not only registers earth tremors, but sometimes brings them about'.[37]

My task in this monetarist debate for the Third Oxford Symposium on Coinage and Monetary History is much less ambitious than John Day's or Harry Miskimin's. It is merely to demonstrate further evidence of monetary contraction in the late-medieval Low Countries in Part I and in Part II the industrial changes that various but related monetary forces might have induced and encouraged. My own statistical calculations for both the Low Countries and England have led me to choose an earlier date than Day's (but later than Mayhew's) for the commencement of a general and persistent, long-term decline in mint outputs: the 1370s.[38] In my view that decline reached its nadir in the 1460s (coinciding thus with the nadir in English wool and cloth exports); but not until the early sixteenth century did both countries fully recover the coinage volumes of the thirteenth and earlier fourteenth centuries. Since I fully agree with Prof. Postan and many others that the European economic contraction commenced long before the 1370s, I must therefore disagree with Robinson in assigning any primary role to monetary forces in directly precipitating that secular economic decline. Statistical justification for my conclusions about long-term monetary trends and monetary contraction can be found first in table 10, which should then be supplemented by the quinquennial average coinage outputs in Tables 2-6, 8-9. Although my mint data are necessarily confined to England and the Low Countries, my statistics do cover a longer period of time (England, from 1235; Flanders, from 1335) than Day's, and are more complete for both countries, especially in the fourteenth century.[39] Like Day, I have given gold and silver mintings in kilograms of pure metal. To present aggregate coinage outputs in units reflecting the weight of metals struck and not just in money-of-account values, which are distorted by periodic debasements and <u>renforcements</u>, especially in the Low Countries, and to provide a comparable measurement for both countries, I have used a constant pounds sterling: this time English gold and silver values for 1351-1411, the longest period of monetary stability of the entire period analyzed, and one dividing it in two. Then long term averages, up to 100 years, were computed. If we look first at the English data, and choose any combination of periods offered in the table, we can discern a very clear and consistent pattern of minting decline from the thirteenth to the end of the fifteenth centuries, with a much greater decline indicated in the fifteenth than in the fourteenth century. The most severe decline, especially for silver, occurred in the 100 years 1370-1469. Total coinage output in constant pounds sterling averaged only 59.1 percent of that of the previous 100 years, 1270-1369, and only 45.3 of the 1335-69 average; and even when measured in current pounds sterling (not given in the table), the average coinage output of 1370-1469 was only 76.8 percent of the preceding 100 years' mean.[40] If the greater part of the population decline had occurred by the 1370s - and admittedly some historians now dispute that - it would seem difficult to argue that per capita coinage supplies in debased currency were maintained, let alone increased, over the late Middle Ages.[41] The statistics for the Low Countries, despite the much different, debasement-ridden monetary history of that region, demonstrate an even starker coinage decline, especially when one notes that up to the 1420s only Flemish mint outputs are given, while thereafter virtually all of the Burgundian Low Countries' mint outputs are included. Thus the mean of the total coinage struck in 1370-1469 was only 38.8 percent of the 1335-1369 mean; and the mean of 1400-1499, the lowest of the four periods given in the table, was only 32.9 percent of the 1335-1369 mean. If one were to contend that the earlier period is too heavily biased by the debasements of Louis de Mâle, it is instructive to compare their power to draw metals into the Flemish mints with the debasements of Philip the Good, Charles the Rash, and Maximilian in the fifteenth century:[42]

Prince	Decade of Debasement	Mean Annual Value of Mint Output in constant £ sterling	Percentage of Value of 1355-64 Mint Output in constant £ sterling
Louis de Mâle	1355-64	143,545.4	100.0
Philip the Good	1425-34	82,738.3	57.6
Charles the Rash	1470-79	45,036.4	31.4
Maximilian	1480-89	33,120.2	23.1

Those who would deny any connection between mint outputs and the money supply would have to explain why so much less metal was evidently passing through the Burgundian mints in the fifteenth century than in the Flemish mints <u>alone</u> in the fourteenth. Finally, the accompanying graphs present both the volumes and values of Burgundian mint outputs in the fifteenth century and their long-term trends (1420-1499), using 'least-squares' regression lines. All four trend lines are downward sloping: kilograms of gold and silver, current pounds groot values, and values in constant pounds sterling. The rates of decline would appear to be greater than that of the Low Countries' population, as projected by historical demographers.[43]

Nevertheless it would admittedly be quite dangerous in principle to use mint outputs as anything more than very general indicators. They should not be taken as statistical proxies of the money supply. In the first place, one must clearly distinguish between mint outputs resulting from trade and balance of payments surpluses or the level of economic activity on the one hand, and those from debasements and recoinages on the other. A <u>renforcement</u>-coinage, for example, might result in very large coinage outputs yet actually contract the money supply by reminting many inferior coins into fewer good ones. A debasement would of course expand the money supply, but not necessarily proportionately, for several reasons: (1) by reminting some part or most of the current circulation into a greater number of coins (2) by attracting foreign bullion to the mints, in offering better prices for

Graph I: Burgundian Low Countries: Gold and Silver Mint Outputs in Kilograms of Pure Metal in Quinquennial Averages. 1420-4 to 1495-99

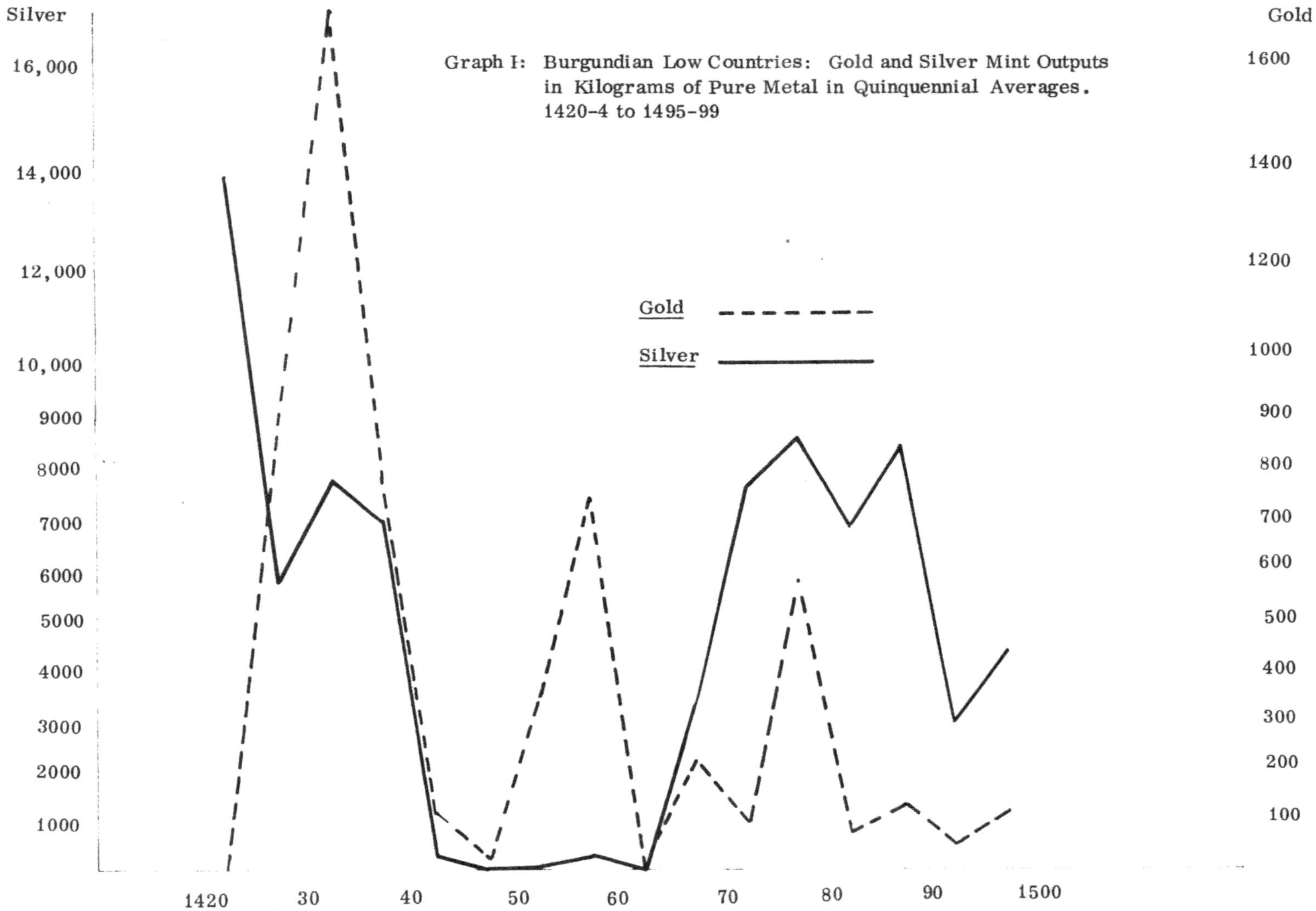

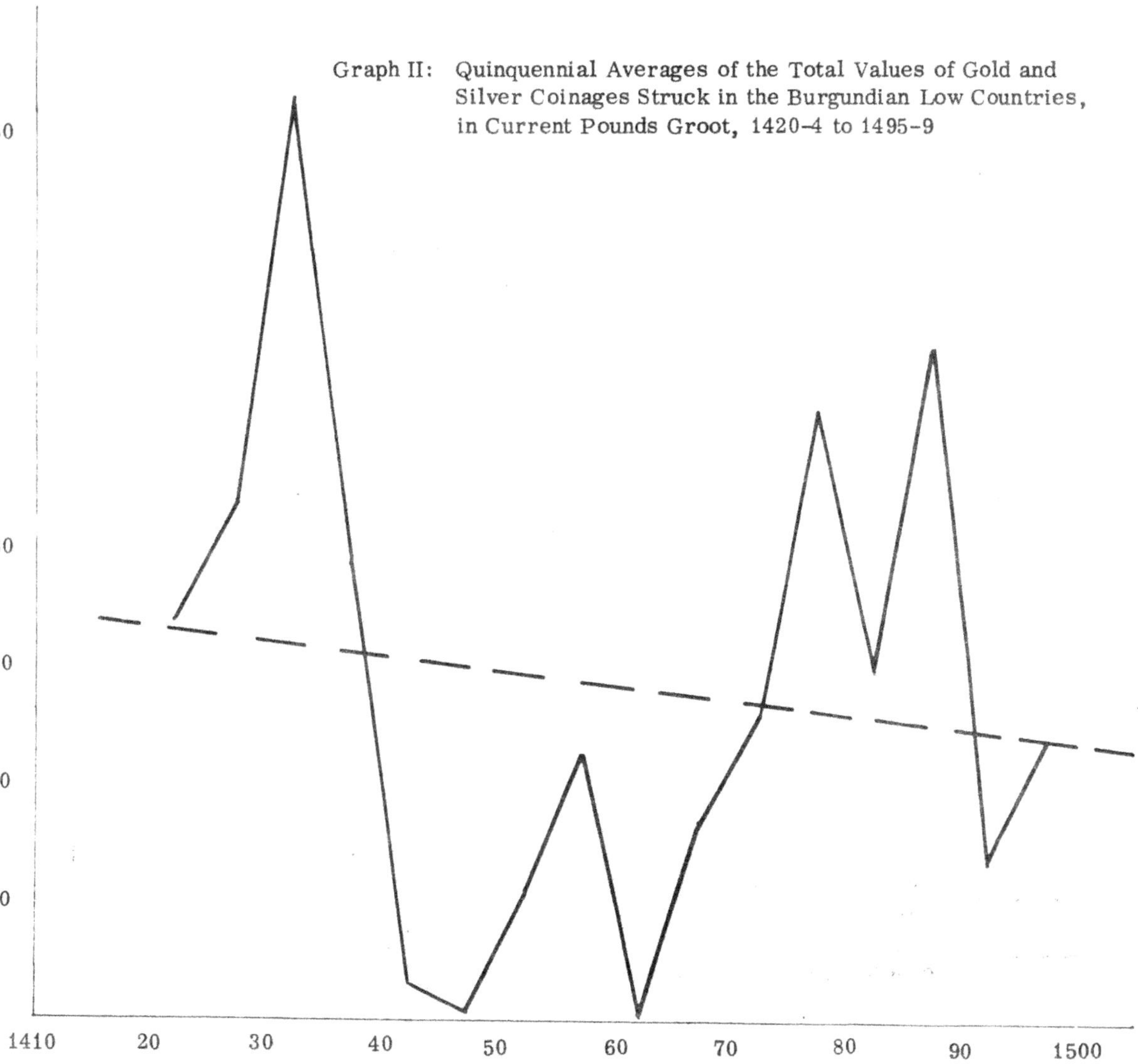
Graph II: Quinquennial Averages of the Total Values of Gold and Silver Coinages Struck in the Burgundian Low Countries, in Current Pounds Groot, 1420-4 to 1495-9
150
80
60
40
20
1410
20
30
40
50
60
70
80
90
1500

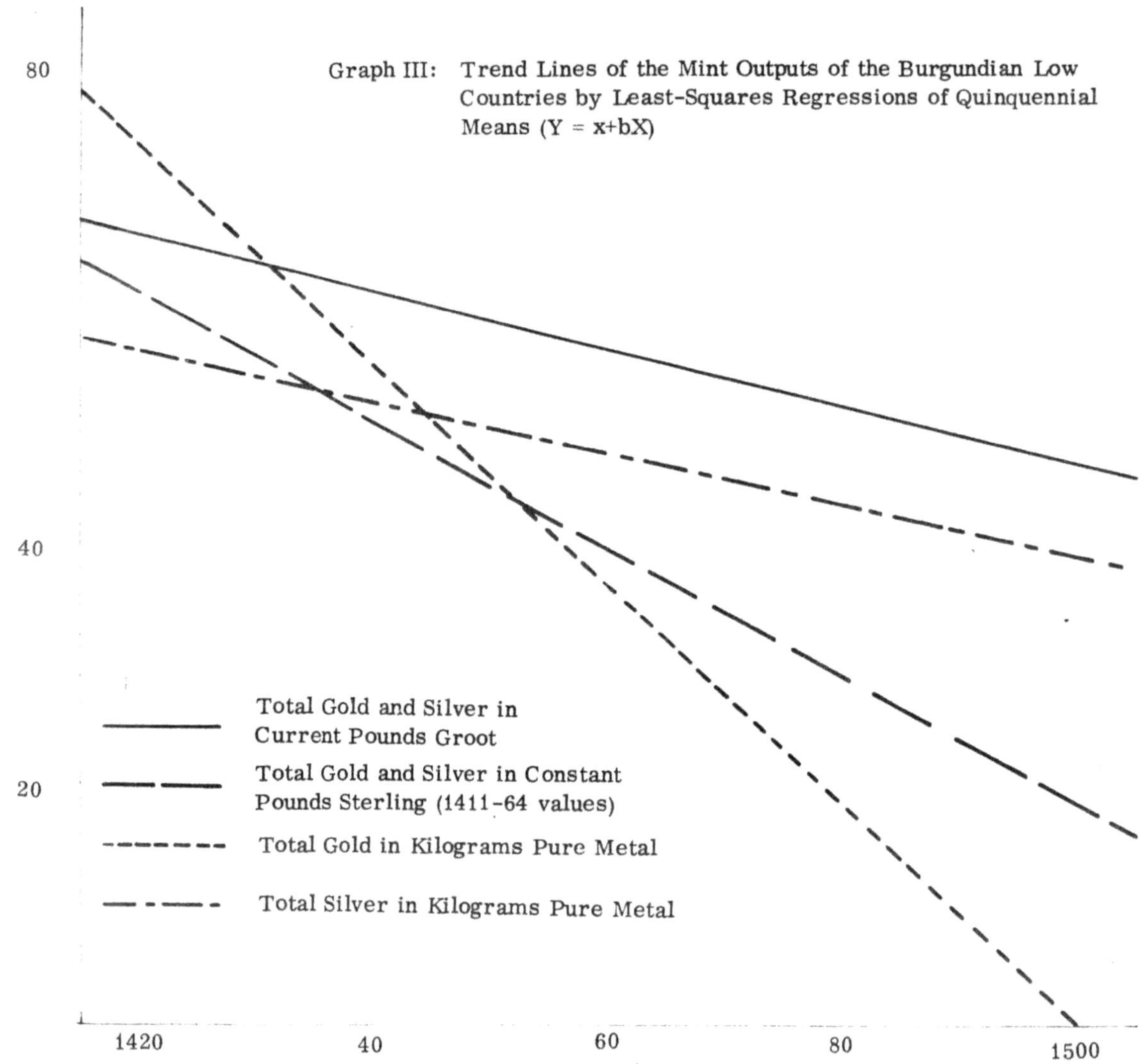
80
40
20
Graph III: Trend Lines of the Mint Outputs of the Burgundian Low Countries by Least-Squares Regressions of Quinquennial Means (Y = x+bX)
Total Gold and Silver in Current Pounds Groot
Total Gold and Silver in Constant Pounds Sterling (1411-64 values)
Total Gold in Kilograms Pure Metal
Total Silver in Kilograms Pure Metal
1420
40
60
80
1500

the metal than competitors, (3) by similarly encouraging domestic dishoardings, (4) by promoting a favourable trade balance, from the resulting fall in the exchange rate, which would cheapen exports and raise the cost of imports. But that monetary expansion might well be short-lived. Many of the newly debased coins might be sent abroad, especially if they were counterfeits of good foreign coins, to places where ignorance of the debasement would facilitate their acceptance.[44] Furthermore, as noted in analyzing mint-ratios, a debasement of one metal would likely cause some outflow of the other metal. On the other hand, a country's money supply might be temporarily expanded by an inundation of debased foreign coins and counterfeits whose circulation and inflationary effects would eliminate the premium on the domestic coinage, and soon force a closure of the mints. Such a closure would not in itself reflect a monetary contraction; but any long-term failure to restore minting, to replenish the coinage, would undoubtedly produce such a contraction, so powerful were the forces of wastage (Patterson-Mayhew Law) and of Gresham's Law, already discussed.

Finally, we should not expect to find that any changes in the money supply would produce proportionate changes in the price levels - and, contrary to frequently expressed opinion, not a uniform change in prices.[45] For relative price changes and changes in the price level depend upon a combination of factors: (1) changes in coinage velocity, (2) change in supply of credit, (3) changes in the volume of transactions, (4) the income elasticities of demand for various commodities on the part of those whose money incomes rose or fell from changes in the money supply, (5) elasticities of supply of the various commodities so demanded, (6) price elasticities of demand and supply of various commodities with any subsequent economic changes induced by the foregoing. Indeed we can never hope to disentangle the real and monetary forces at work in price-level changes, whether the changes are inflationary or deflationary, with constant changes in relative prices.

For all these reasons alone, therefore, it would seem quite pointless to seek any correlation between mint outputs and prices. Yet surprisingly such mathematical correlations, with good to excellent levels of statistical significance, can be found in the fifteenth-century Burgundian Low Countries. For intensive examination I have chosen the period 1420-99, when the Burgundian mint accounts are reasonably complete, and when a good price series is available in the Van der Wee price index, modelled directly on the famous Phelps Brown and Hopkins index for southern England.[46] I have thus correlated the current value of the aggregate mint outputs in current Flemish pounds groot (X) with the Van der Wee price index (Y), lagged by one year to allow changes in the money supply to take effect. As table 17 shows, the correlation is the weakest for the entire period, 1420-99, yet is still statistically significant at a respectable 3 percent level. That the correlations are stronger for all the post-1435 periods is not surprising, because the Van der Wee index is based entirely upon Brabantine prices; and not until the monetary reform of 1434-35 was the Brabantine monetary system effectively integrated with that of Flanders and the other Burgundian Low Countries. For the period 1420-34, Van der Wee's prices were converted into Flemish groots at exchange rates that may have been, moreover, artificial.[47] The strongest correlation appears to have been that for the period 1435-63, one of monetary stability, with only one significant debasement, of gold in 1454. The r^2 or coefficient of determination of 0.323 means that virtually a third of the variation in prices can be explained by the variations in mint outputs; and the significance level, or probability of errors, is less than 1 percent. But even the period 1435-99, marked by 23 debasements and two _renforcements_, provides very respectable correlations with an even lower significance level, of 0.22 percent. Finally, table 18 shows very high correlations of the Van der Wee price index (in five-year averages) with the official values of silver and gold, significant at the 0.06 and 0.001 levels respectively, indicating that price levels were very responsive to debasements and renforcements. We are thus entitled to use such monetary and price data with some reasonable confidence as analytical tools to aid in interpreting the Low Countries' economic history in the fifteenth century.

II Industrial Change in the Late-Medieval Low Countries: Textiles

In view of the analysis in Part I, how did monetary changes and monetary policies influence the course of change in one of the Low Countries' principal industrial sectors, and the most famous one, textiles? The general outlines of the transformations that occurred over the fourteenth and fifteenth centuries have become a commonplace of European economic history: the decline and fall of the traditional urban luxury draperies, based on English wools, which had once dominated European and Mediterranean markets; and their ultimate replacement by the so-called _nouvelles draperies_ and _draperies légères_, both largely rural in origin, producing medium quality woollens and cheap, coarse worsted or serge-type fabrics respectively.

The Flemish luxury draperies in particular suffered a series of disasters in the course of the fourteenth century: invasions, rebellions, and civil wars in Flanders from 1297 intermittently to 1320; and then in 1323-28, 1338-49, 1359-61, 1367, 1370, 1377; and worst of all 1379-85.[48] At the same time, the industry suffered losses of markets in France, Italy , and England; disruptions, then contractions of other established markets by plagues, warfare, and periodic depressions; mutually destructive disputes with the German Hanseatic League, which had become the Flemish industry's chief customer. Perhaps the most serious blow of all came from England: first, from the 1330s a tremendous increase in export taxes on wools, averaging 40 percent of the wholesale price; and, as a partial consequence, the growth of English competition in the cloth trade. The greatest advantage of the English clothiers was not the much vaunted fulling mill or a rural industrial location but a sharp differential in export duties. For their cloths bore only a minimal 2 percent duty, while their wools were purchased domestically tax free. Counting not only export taxes but shipping and freight charges, and the prices charged by the quasi-monopolistic Calais Staple Company, the Flemish found that those same fine English wools cost them more than twice as much. This English wool, it must be stressed, was the prime determinant of luxury quality in these textiles, along with dyestuffs; and, apart from 'grain' in scarlet dyeing, this wool was the single most costly input for the Low Countries' draperies, accounting for 65-75 percent of the wholesale price before finishing.[49] Thus even those other rivals of the Flemish luxury draperies, periodically taking advantage of the latter's disruptions, finally also succumbed to the English competition; for they too had made themselves too dependent of fine English wools. Yet it would be dangerous to exaggerate the role of English cloth competition: because then one has the difficulty of explaining why this competition took more than a century to ruin its rivals, from the mid-fourteenth to the late-fifteenth century.

It would also be quite unwise to pretend that monetary forces were the crucial factor in the downfall of the Low Countries' luxury draperies. Undoubtedly various 'real' factors, including indeed the consequences of demographic decline, were more important. Yet monetary forces and policies did have some role to play in these commercial-industrial transformations that is worthy of investigation. If we may commence with Flanders in the 1330s, their initial role seems to have been beneficial, according to Prof. Hans Van Werveke.[50] He argued that the Flemish cloth industry received a considerable export stimulus from the several silver coinage debasements of Counts Louis de Nevers (1322-46) and Louis de Mâle (1346-84), even though most were undertaken for purely fiscal motives. The major debasements, ten of them, occurred between May 1337 and December 1363, reducing the silver content of the double groot by 56.8 percent (3.484 g to 1.504 g). In April 1365 the coinage was strengthened in fineness (6 to 8 deniers argent-le-roy); and between then and 1384, the coinage was debased five more times and twice strengthened, with an overall reduction in fineness (most of the weights are unknown) of 25 percent.[51] In general, the consequent fall in exchange rates should have temporarily stimulated cloth exports. In particular, Van Werveke argued, the Flemish drapers gained by paying their artisans in silver coin of rapidly diminishing value, while selling their cloths for stable foreign gold. But since English wool commanded such a very large proportion of production costs, and since both wool and dyestuff costs were rising with devaluation, one wonders what cushion the drapers gained from debasements, and to what extent they could afford to sell for less in terms of gold, at least once previous inventories had been exhausted. Furthermore, a chronic struggle over wages between the weaver-drapers and the fullers' guild seems to have been a major factor in several of the very destructive Flemish urban rebellions of this era.[52] Nevertheless considerable support for Van Werveke's contentions can be found in tables 1 and 2, which present quinquennial averages of the various Ypres cloth seals (which must not be aggregated to avoid double or triple counting),[53] sales of the Ghent drapery tax farms, English wool and cloth exports, and the mint outputs of England and Flanders. They certainly indicate a considerable recovery and boom for at least the Ypres cloth industry, and also generally buoyant English wool exports, from the 1350s to the 1370s; the Ghent cloth industry shows no real signs of decline before the late 1360s. Overall this was the very era of intensive debasement that produced exceptionally large mint outputs in Flanders. But for Europe as a whole, this was also a very inflationary era in general, and evidently one of general commercial boom that might be attributed inter alia to the aforementioned 'inheritance effects' and post-Plague spending sprees, and perhaps to the 'multiplier' effects of military financing.[54]

From the later 1370s a very sharp deflation besets England, then Spain and Italy, spreading to other parts of Europe over the next decades and on into the fifteenth century.[55] For England itself deflation and low stagnant prices generally prevailed (except in the 1430s, 1480s) until the early sixteenth century. In Flanders, as tables 1 and 2 suggest, a very sharp fall in Flemish mint outputs in the 1370s was followed by an evidently serious decline in Ypres' cloth production. The decline of the Ghent drapery, as indicated by the tax farms, began earlier, in the mid 1360s, and was much more precipitous, as tax farms sales fell 76 percent by the mid 1380s.[56] Similarly, but less drastically, English wool exports fell 37 percent from the late 1360s to the mid 1380s, and then another 6 percent by 1400. All of these falling indices correlate with other evidence, monetary and real, for a severe cyclical depression in northern Europe during the last three decades of the fourteenth century.[57]

Unfortunately the Ghent and Ypres statistics both terminate in 1384, towards the end of the so-called second Artevelde rebellion, led by Ghent. That six-year civil war, which came to involve English and French military forces as well, was the most disastrous by far to afflict fourteenth-century Flanders; and undoubtedly it must bear considerable responsibility for the sharp fall in production indices after 1379.[58] The aftermath of the civil war further worsened the plight of the Flemish cloth industry: a harsh peace imposed in December 1385, provoking continued unrest, the refusal of many foreign merchants to return to the staple port of Bruges until the 1390s, and a complete Hanseatic embargo of Flanders, over reparations claims arising from the war, from 1388 to 1392. That embargo was especially harmful in permitting the English and Dutch cloth trades to make decisive breakthroughs into Hanse markets in northern Germany, the Baltic, and eastern Europe.[59]

A final if not terminally crippling blow came from Duke Philip the Bold's monetary policy. After four debasements in <u>guerre monêtaires</u> with France, Brabant, and other neighbours, Duke Philip reformed the coinages in 1389-90, brutally strengthening silver by 31.8 percent and gold even more, by 41.7 percent (thus altering the mint ratio in favour of silver.)[60] Whatever the preceding pattern of prices, Flanders then joined England and others in a sharp deflation and falling mint outputs that lasted until the next round of debasements in 1416-18 and the 1420s especially.[61] For the Flemish cloth industry, the consequences of Duke Philip's 1390 monetary reform were directly opposite to those of debasement. Thus exchange rates rose, sharply raising cloth export prices; or alternatively, those drapers pricing their cloths in gold <u>nobles</u> would have suffered severe losses by the ducal fiat reducing the noble from 8s 6d groot to 6s 0d groot. Furthermore, since most drapers were debtors, requiring extensive credit to finance their operations, they were also burdened in having to repay debts - and indeed also in having to pay wages - in the new strong silver groots, occasioning bitter outcries from the Flemish burghers in the 1390s. Attempts to force down wages certainly provoked serious riots in Flanders; and wages generally did not fall in proportion to the <u>renforcement</u> and general fall in prices.[62] In the meantime, despite a general economic contraction, the English cloth trade was clearly benefiting from the Flemish problems: as table 1 shows, its exports had climbed more than three-fold from the 1370s to the late 1390s.

All this might well suggest that the Flemish cloth industry was on the verge of extinction by the end of the fourteenth century, as some historians, injudiciously extrapolating from the Ypres statistics, have asserted. But the German historian Hektor Ammann has painted a rather different picture, based upon voluminous research in sources emanating from the Baltic, Germany, central and eastern Europe, and covering what had become the major market for the Low Countries' draperies. For this whole area in general, he rather surprisingly maintained that the Flemish draperies, having fallen behind the Brabantine industries during the fourteenth century, had recovered to reclaim first place during the early fifteenth century; the older, traditional draperies, moreover, were still more prominent than the smaller nouvelles draperies. After the now second-ranking Brabantine draperies, led by Mechelen, Brussels, Vilvoorde, and Lier, came the Dutch draperies, headed by Leiden. The English, therefore, ranked an astonishingly poor fourth.[63] Table 12 does not contradict Ammann's contentions for the first three decades of the fifteenth century. Thus the number of drapers' stalls rented at the Ypres cloth halls shows a large increase in the second decade; and although the number did fall again in the 1420s, the 1425-29 average was still 90 percent of the mean prior to that upsurge. The value of the annual tax farm-sales for the Ypres drapery shows an even gentler decline, of only 6.5 percent from 1410 to 1429, while the values of the tax-farm sales of the Ghent and Mechelen draperies (admittedly much smaller than in the early fourteenth century) show increases of 77 percent and 28 percent respectively over these first 30 years of the fifteenth century. Only the Leuven drapery's tax farm, for the smallest and weakest of the old urban industries, does not conform to these trends; and even there the decline does not (again) become significantly worse until the 1420s.[64]

The English customs accounts for these three decades, on the other hand, do provide further support for the Flemish evidence. Thus English wool exports to Calais, now accounting for most of the wool shipments, not only cease declining, but even enjoy a moderate rise of 6 percent, while English cloth exports on the other hand suffer a sharp set-back during the early fifteenth century, declining a third from 1395-99 to 1410-14. This temporary reversal in fortunes again suggests that English cloth competition was not the inexorable executioneer of the Low Countries' draperies. But that reversal was only temporary. English cloth exports began to recover after 1415, after the English victories in France; and by the late 1420s they managed to surpass their peak of the 1390s, though just barely. Perhaps a higher proportion of English cloth exports was now directed to the Low Countries, the expanding Brabantine Fairs of Antwerp and Bergen-op-Zoom especially. That influx greatly alarmed the drapery towns of Brabant and Holland, particularly because these Fairs gave the English cloth trade direct access to the important South German and central European markets. The Dutch and Brabantine towns thus clamoured for and won the same protection long enjoyed by the Flemish draperies: bans on the imports of all English woollens, imposed in July-August 1428, but subsequently allowed to lapse.[65]

Despite the fears of these draperies, all the evidence suggests that this decade of the 1420s was one of relative prosperity for the Low Countries; and evidence elsewhere suggests a general cyclical upswing, deviating from the secular trend of economic decline.[66] Significantly as tables 8 and 3-5 show, the mints in both England and the Low Countries were once more enjoying very large coinage outputs. Certainly they were not as large as those of the mid-fourteenth century; but, as Day has also shown for other parts of Europe, they were sufficient to relieve the bullion famine at least temporarily.[67] Both countries evidently benefited economically from the Treaty of Troyes alliance (1420) and the victories in France. But the large English mint outputs of the early 1420s also reflect the general recoinage of 1421-22 and the reopening of the Calais mint in July 1422. In the Burgundian Low Countries, the even larger mint outputs of the later 1420s were to a considerable extent the product of drastic debasements begun in 1425 - partly for fiscal reasons, partly as defensive reactions against foreign debasements. Thus Duke Philip the Good, armed with new mints at Namur and Dordrecht, had debased silver 16.1 percent and gold 29.6 percent, vastly more, by 1429.[68]

As tables 3-5 and 8-9 show, English mint outputs, gold especially, fell even faster than the rise in Burgundian mint outputs during the later 1420s - and into the early 1430s. The crown and Parliament once more became gravely concerned about bullion scarcities at this very crucial stage of the French wars, the time of Joan of Arc. But debasement was a recourse that Parliament had long opposed strenuously.[69] Instead, crown and Parliament retaliated against the Low Countries in September 1429 by resurrecting bullionist impositions on the vital wool trade known as the Calais Staple Bullion laws. They were the most severe ever enacted. In sum, they required the Staplers (1) to increase wool prices, reputedly by a third, (2) to sell wool only for good English coin or bullion, permitting no sales credit, and (3) to deliver a third of the price in bullion to the Calais mint. To enforce these measures and to reward a small clique of Staplers supporting this bullionist policy, the crown also had Parliament enact the so-called Partition Law requiring the Staplers to partition or divide up sales receipts not in accordance with their individual sales but rather with the amount of wool stocks by county that each merchant had brought to the Staple. Even if all sales were for cash, those smaller merchants would have had to wait, perhaps for years, to get their final penny. Consequently this partition system forced out of business the small dealers with minimal working capitals who had depended upon rapid turnovers to buy new stocks. According to Dutch charges, a group of 20 to 30 Staplers gained full control and imposed a rigid monopoly on wool sales.[70]

For the luxury draperies of the Low Countries, enjoying a brief Indian Summer of prosperity, the Calais Ordinances were a cruel blow. The sharp increase in wool prices was destructive enough, especiallysince their English drapery rivals were then enjoying falling wool prices at home, as table 12 indicates. But undoubtedly more crucial were the onerous bullion demands and the ban on credit at the Staple. Credit had been traditionally granted for two thirds of the wool price, in two bills or letters obligatory redeemable in six months and a year, in any good currency, at the fairs of the Low Countries. When the Staplers, and also the Merchants Adventurers in the cloth trades, collected their bills at these fairs, they did not usually bring back the proceeds in specie; instead they lent the funds to London Mercers at the fairs by buying from them bills of exchange payable in sterling at London. The Mercers then used the borrowed funds, in Flemish currency, to import goods from the Low Countries into England, using their sales proceeds to redeem their bills. Similarly the Staplers bought wools from the English growers by paying one third down in cash - sometimes raised by the sale of bills - and by supplying letters obligatory for the remainder. Since this credit system obviously curbed the influx of precious metals, one need not wonder why bullionist-minded English parliaments were so hostile to credit.[71] But without credit the wool and cloth trades, indeed late-medieval commerce and industry in the advanced regions could not have functioned as they did.

Had the Flemish and Brabantine drapers of the 1430s been the same rich, powerful merchants who had dominated the thirteenth-century industry and towns, men with large capitals, they might have been able to meet the Staple's bullionist demands without facing ruin. But not the small and capital-poor weaver-drapers of the fifteenth century, who then served as the industrial entrepreneurs. Merchant-dominated Leiden, with an active, aggressive cloth trade, and the growing Dutch fleets at their disposal, was perhaps the exception; and this drapery fared the best in the post 1430 era.[72] Elsewhere the small weaver-drapers were already heavily dependent upon merchants for credit, chiefly Hansards and Italians, but some domestic ones as well. In any case, to have borrowed even further so much more English coin and bullion - especially in the era of monetary constriction that followed - would certainly have meant punitive interest and exchange charges (in buying English coin and in selling other coin as bullion) on top of prohibitive wool prices extorted by the crown-backed monopoly at Calais.

Duke Philip the Good's subsequent monetary policy only served to exacerbate the plight of his draperies. To be sure, he did continue his debasements from 1429 to 1433; and perhaps these devaluations did assist cloth exports and eased the initial burden of the Calais laws for his drapery subjects (though also raising their wool and dyestuff costs). But then from October 1433 to mid-1434 he unified the several coinages of the Burgundian Low Countries; and in relation to his last Namur debasement of May 1433 he strengthened gold by 38.5 percent and silver by 29.6 percent, thus effectively raising cloth export prices by the former or latter, depending on what pricing system was used. Although silver was strengthened by a lesser degree, the monetary policy still remained pro-gold in relation to the pre-1425 ratios and the current English ones.[73]

Another significant aspect of the 1433 monetary reform was an ordinance severely curbing the activities of deposit bankers, who had been suspected of transmitting coin and bullion to foreign mints. According to de Roover and Van der Wee, a series of such ordinances subsequently extinguished deposit banking in the Burgundian Low Countries. In any event, this brutal <u>renforcement</u> of 1433-34 would have caused them serious damage by severely contracting the money supply, as analyzed in Part I, in turn reducing the bankers' cash reserves and credit resources.[74]

In this monetary reform, Duke Philip had promised not to alter the coinages for twenty years; and in substance he maintained this austere monetary policy for even longer, until May 1466. Indeed his government made it even more pro-gold by raising gold prices in March 1443, and then by debasing gold another 5.3 percent in January 1454.[75] The only concession he permitted silver was a minor debasement of <u>mites</u>, the small 'black' coinage, in October 1456.[76] That singular concession was clearly in response to a severe monetary scarcity afflicting the general populace. Indeed as tables 3-5 show, once the recoinages of the mid-1430s had been completed, mint outputs fell very sharply in the 1440s; and while debasement produced respectable gold outputs in the mid-1450s, silver outputs continued to slump, ceasing entirely in 1458. Finally, after receiving only a trickle of gold, the Burgundian mints closed in 1462, reopening only with the 1466 debasement.[77] This monetary stringency was hardly unique to the Low Countries. As tables 8-9 show, English mint outputs also plunged drastically in the later 1430s and 1440s. In the 1445 parliament a petitioner complained that the 'defaute' of silver was causing the realm 'grete hurt'. The crown then had the Tower Mint strike half-pence and farthings 10 percent lighter;[78] but to little avail. English minting reached its dismal nadir in 1448, and remained generally very low until Edward IV's debasements of August 1464 - March 1465.[79] Peter Spufford, furthermore, has shown that the Rhenish electoral mints were all closed for lack of bullion from 1443 to 1455 and 1461 to 1463.[81] Most recently John Day, citing a vast amount of evidence, has argued that western Europe as a whole suffered its most severe and widespread bullion famine of the Middle Ages during these very years, 'circa 1440-60'.[80] Finally a clear relationship between mint outputs and price levels in this same period can be seen in table 11: for both England and the Burgundian Low Countries, the sharp slump in minting was followed by significant deflation. And as noted in Part I, tables 17 and 18 present mathematical correlations between Burgundian coinage outputs and the Van der Wee price index, all of them statistically very significant.

What, therefore, were the industrial consequences of the Calais bullion laws, Philip the Good's monetary policies, the 'bullion famine', and the consequent deflation? Since Michael Postan, Eileen Power, Rose-Marie Thielemans, myself, and most recently Terence Lloyd have all discussed the history of the Calais ordinances, and since Lloyd especially confirms my view of their economic importance, only the barest outline of subsequent developments need to given here.[82] Not until June 1434, after completing his monetary reform, did Duke Philip finally retaliate, by banning all English cloth imports into the Low Countries. The Anglo-Burgundian alliance soon collapsed; and after Philip had made his peace with France, England attacked the Burgundian Low Countries. The ensuing war of 1436-39 virtually halted the wool trade and did considerable damage to the Low Countries' draperies. Throughout all this conflict the Calais Ordinances remained in force, even after the 1439 peace. Finally combined domestic English and Burgundian opposition, with stringently enforced bans on bullion exports, forced the crown to renounce the Calais Ordinances in 1442. But within three years or so the English had surreptitiously restored some part or form of these ordinances, provoking yet another Burgundian ban on English cloth in 1447-52. Finally, twelve years later, in 1459, an Anglo-Burgundian agreement was reached requiring the Burgundians to exclude all non-Staple wools in return for complete abrogation of the hated Calais laws. But just four years later, in 1463, the new Yorkist monarchy of Edward IV, facing both fiscal and monetary stringency, enacted a modified version of the Calais laws, provoking the third Burgundian ban on English cloth in 1464. Not until 1473, after Philip's son Charles helped restore Edward IV to his throne, creating a debt to repay, did Parliament formally revoke and forever abolish the Calais ordinances, and explicitly permit the use of credit at the Staple.[83] From subsequent, often vociferous complaints about high wool prices at the Staple, however, one suspects that the monopolistic organization may have been largely left intact.[84]

By the time that the Calais Ordinances were finally repealed, the damage done to most of the Flemish and Brabantine draperies de luxe was clearly irreparable. In the long interim many more of their markets had been lost forever to the English cloth trade, and many drapers and artisans had been permanently forced out of the industry by high costs. Undoubtedly a report of the Hanseatic kontor at Bruges had greatly exaggerated in contending, so early as 1433, that because of 'the terribly severe' Calais Ordinances, 'and the costliness of wool, more than half of the drapery industry [in Flanders] has perished.'[85]

Yet in view of the statistics presented in tables 12 and 14-16, that Hanse report provides a very prescient description of the industry's plight over the next forty years. Thus by the mid-1470s, the number of drapery stalls rented at the Ypres cloth halls had fallen to just 16 percent of the number occupied on the eve of the Calais laws. The mean value of the various drapery tax-farm sales for Ypres, Ghent, Mechelen, and Leuven, which can be taken only as general indicators, similarly show sharp declines after 1430, especially from the 1440s, though varying in degree, and though partly attributable to depopulations as well.[86] Even more eloquent evidence of decline, and a much more precise measure, can be found in the steep plunge of the English wool trade to Calais after 1430, by almost one half; and exports for the rest of the century averaged just 55 percent of the pre-1430 volumes. Certainly the very high cost of English wools is clearly evident in the sharply rising prices of Flemish luxury woollens after 1430—despite the subsequent general deflation—as indicated by tables 14 and 15. These two tables are equally instructive in demonstrating that certain cloths made from non-English wools at Leuven, Neuve-Eglise, and some other nouvelles draperies by no means experienced the same rise in prices; indeed their prices barely rose at all, and then fell with the general deflation.

The next table, table 16, by comparing English and Flemish cloth prices very approximately in equivalent pounds sterling, certainly indicates a very large and growing gap between these price series, giving the English an insuperable advantage. Only in the last quarter of the fifteenth century, when the final victory of the English cloth trade had been fully assured, did English cloth prices rise significantly. Even then these prices averaged only about a third of the Flemish prices, which only the very rich could afford. Yet the English cloth trade's road to victory was far from being straight and smooth after 1430, as table 12 indicates. Though cloth exports continued to expand rapidly, they reached their peak in the early 1440s, having doubled their volume in just thirty years; they then quickly lost almost all these gains, as cloth exports fell 46 percent by the early 1460s. These twenty years were of course the very era of medieval Europe's worst bullion famine, the era of deflation, and according to several historians, of severe depression.[87] The English cloth trade also suffered from the Lancastrian government's political adventures and military defeats, which cut English merchants off from cloth markets in Gascony, Scandinavia, and the Baltic.[88] The Flemish draperies were of course much too weak both to weather the storms of this depression and take advantage of the English setbacks. Even worse, the Flemish and Brabantine draperies also suffered severely from a dispute with the Hanseatic League. In trying to extort new privileges from Flanders and Brabant, the

Hanse imposed a seven-year embargo against them, from 1451-57. Instead, it was the Dutch cloth trade, conducted by aggressive, enterprising merchants and expanding fleets, which took decisive advantage of the English and Flemish-Brabantine difficulties to invade the Baltic, North German, and Polish-Russian markets.[89]

As table 12 indicates, from the 1460s, an era of general if gentle economic recovery, the English cloth trade resumed its expansion, while most of the Flemish and Brabantine urban draperies continued to decline. Again monetary policy may have intervened to accelerate these changes. In August 1464 Edward IV debased the silver sterling coinage by 20 percent and the gold coinage, by March 1465, even more, by 25 percent.[90] The sudden upsurge in English cloth exports suggests that they had received a strong tonic from these devaluations. When Duke Philip the Good followed suit in May 1466, he debased silver by only 12.7 percent, far too little to match England's new export advantage. But because he debased gold by even less, 3.3 percent, his coinage alterations in conjunction with England's had the effect of altering the mint ratios to favour silver strongly once more (as before 1425).[91] That decisive change occurred at the same time that radically new mining technologies, discussed in Part I, had succeeded in producing a major silver-copper mining boom in South Germany and Central Europe. The Burgundian mints, aided by several more debasements, now attracted not only considerable quantities of silver, as tables 3-5 show, but also, as Van der Wee has noted, South German merchants to Antwerp, where they eagerly sought out English cloth as their return cargo.[92] At the same time, English cloth merchants, having been excluded from Gascony, Hanseatic territories, and always Flanders, just as eagerly flocked to Antwerp as their chief remaining gateway to the continent. Significantly London, accounting for the bulk of England's trade with Antwerp, increased its share of total cloth exports from 40 percent in the 1450s to 70 percent in the 1480s and 1490s.[93] This South German trade in English cloths from Antwerp was especially disastrous for most of the Brabantine draperies, which had strongly depended upon the Rhenish, South German, and central European markets. Equally injurious for all the Low Countries' draperies was the development of dyeing and shearing industries in Antwerp and certain Dutch towns to finish English cloths, thereby robbing the Low Countries' draperies of their last remaining advantage: those crucial finishing techniques for which they had long been world famous. The rest of the story can be seen in table 12: especially the 2.5 fold growth of English cloth exports from the early 1460s to the early 1500s. Even in the 1480s, English cloth imports into the Brabant Fairs and Holland were considered veritably an immense flood - _inundacioni maris immensi_.[94]

The other major industrial transformations that were accelerated - not caused - by the combination of monetary and economic factors just discussed were the expansions of the so-called _nouvelles draperies_ and the _draperies légères_ or _sayetteries_. These two textile industries must not be confused as is so often done in the historical literature. The latter were either worsteds or mixed stuffs with a worsted warp (long-staple) and a woollen weft (short-staple); and were generally very light, coarsely textured, only partially fulled, unsheared, and were reasonably cheap. They were in fact the progenitors of Elizabethan England's 'New Draperies', though never using English wools but coarser wools of the Low Countries, France, and Germany.[95]

The Flemish *nouvelles draperies* on the other hand were totally unrelated. Like the traditional luxury draperies, they belonged fully to the woollen branch of the industry, using fine, short-stapled greased wools for both warp and weft. They were in fact medium-priced counterfeits of the true luxury woollens, produced by drapers who deliberately economized on the several stages of production: especially weaving, fulling, tentering and teaseling, shearing and dyeing. They certainly also economized on wool, the most costly input of all, by using smaller warp-counts, fewer wefts, and cheaper grades of English wool.[96] English wools were far from being homogenous; and the most expensive sold at Calais in the fifteenth century, from Herefordshire and Shropshire, cost over four times as much as the 'Middle wools' from Rutland and Holland, Lincs.[97] Some of the *nouvelles draperies* also used Scottish wools, once priced not too far below the English, or even some domestic wools for their lesser grade cloths. But, in my view, the various adverse conditions of the late-medieval economy hindered the sale of cheap textiles beyond the local market and thus favoured luxury production for export: more highly skewed income distributions; contracted and scattered markets; very high costs of transportation and marketing, especially with the various disruptions of established trade routes; high labour costs; and possibly high costs of working capital, with monetary contraction. Certainly with lower volumes of sales and higher unit costs of production and marketing, luxury production was economically much more viable than the very cheap-line textiles.[98] Thus if the *nouvelles draperies* were to compete effectively with other luxury woollens in international markets, their choice of wool was really very circumscribed. The counterfeiter of coins, after all, does require some gold or silver. Some *nouvelles draperies*, the more prestigious ones, adopted the same regulations as the true luxury draperies in strictly forbidding the use of any but fine English wools: in particular, Wervik, Kortrijk, Diksmuide, and Langhemarck, at least until two of them were forced to change in the course of the fifteenth century.[99]

Certainly the Low Countries' draperies never considered substituting Spanish wools for English wools when the latter became so heavily burdened with export duties from the 1330s. Spanish *merino* wools, to be sure, came to be regarded as the world's finest in early modern times. But the Flemish and Artesian drapery regulations of the thirteenth and fourteenth centuries contemptuously classed Spanish wools of the day with the very worst - *waterwulle*, *vlocken*, and other *faulx lanages*; as such, their use in any of the regular commercial draperies, even the cheap ones, was strictly forbidden.[100] These were not merino wools. According to the most recent scholarship, merino sheep, originating with the Banū Marīn or Merinid tribes of North Africa, conquerors of the Almohad empire, were not introduced into Spain until after 1340, when the last Merinid invasion was repulsed at the Battle of River Salado.[101] Undoubtedly some considerable time was required to develop the finer breeds of merinos, larger flocks, and the proper routes of the various *transhumantes* across Spain; for terrain, climate, and grazing conditions were equally important in producing the finest short-stapled fleeces. Not until the late sixteenth or seventeenth centuries do merino wools surpass the best Herefordshire and Shropshire wools in fineness.[102] But by the 1380s Spanish merino wools were considered good enough to be used in the Italian cloth industries of Verona and Prato, though ranking a poor fourth in value.[103]

In the Low Countries their use cannot be documented for so early a date. Undoubtedly centuries of contempt for Spanish wools greatly hindered acceptance of the new merino wools; and over such a long distance, information would have been much less trustworthy. But evidently some Flemish draperies were resorting to merino wools by 1420; for in that year a petitioner in Parliament complained that Spanish and Scottish wools were now being sold in Flanders in violation of a supposed agreement to exclude non-English wools so long as English cloth remained banned from Flanders.[104] The first extant regulation concerning Spanish wools was issued in September 1428 by the little rural _nouvelle draperie_ of Estaires on the Lys, which permitted their use in second grade cloths, but still required the best cloths to be made exclusively from the finer English wools.[105] The next month the Flemish and Castilians signed the first of their trade treaties to contain specific and prominent mention of Spanish wools.[106]

In my own view the necessary catalyst of change to overcome the residual prejudices against Spanish wools and to accelerate their adoption by at least the _nouvelles draperies_ was the sharp rise in English wool costs, resulting from the imposition of the Calais bullion laws in 1430, and then from Philip's subsequent policies and the Anglo-Burgundian war. Thus in March 1436, during that war, the Sovereign Bailiff of Flanders declared that:[107]

> English wool has become so costly that merchants cannot profit by it... And my lord [Duke Philip] has found that the wools of Spain and Scotland are beginning to be adopted in conformance with English wools, and these said wools are now being used to almost the same extent as the English wools used to be.

Then during the Anglo-Dutch peace negotiations of 1438, the Dutch ambassadors maintained that as a direct result of the Calais Ordinances English wools sales had fallen by one half while Spain and Scotland were selling three times as much wool in their towns as before.[108] Finally, during the 1467 trade negotiations with England, the Burgundian ambassadors warned that unless the Calais laws were revoked their draperies could no longer sustain the wool costs: they would either collapse or have to obtain their wools from entirely different sources.[109]

The true luxury draperies nevertheless still refused to consider the latter option, for fear that use of non-English wools would ruin their reputation and so cripple their remaining sales in aristrocratic markets. But since the _nouvelles draperies_ were in essence counterfeiting luxury cloths already, and since they had long been cutting corners, the substitution of Spanish for English wools was a much less painful sacrifice for them, especially if the alternative was extinction. Most of them, moreover, were still too young to have the rigid guild structures and complex production codes that so inhibited technological change in the old established urban draperies, codes that were designed to guarantee true luxury quality. Neither Neuve-Eglise nor Armentières, the most famous of the _nouvelles draperies_, who both came to use Spanish wools to great advantage, had such institutional barriers before the sixteenth century.[110] The following _nouvelles draperies_ have also been documented as adopting Spanish wools in the course of the fifteenth century: Poperinge, Aalst, Dendermonde, Oudenaarde, Menen, Geraardsbergen,

Comines, Wervik, Kortrijk, Warneton, Bailleul, Ninove, Tourcoing, Nieppe, Meteren, Eecke, Godeswaersvelde, Flêtre, Eeklo, Dranoûter, Kemmel, Wulvergem, and the nieuwe drapperie of the 1440s at Brussels and Leuven in Brabant.[111] Some nouvelles draperies evidently never did take up Spanish wools: Diksmuide and Langhemarck in particular.[112] Their output declined drastically over the fifteenth century, as did production at the prominent nouvelle draperie of Wervik, which took up Spanish wools too little and too late. In 1458, a group of Wervik drapers petitioned the duke for a repeal of their drapery ordinance requiring them 'to swear a holy oath yearly upon the cross to use none but English wools'. In 1463, after a lengthy investigation, ducal officials reported that the extremely high cost of English wools now justified the use of Spanish and Scottish wools. But Duke Philp would agree to authorize the use of such wools for only petits draps made by those drapers agreeing to have no contact with English wools.[113] Apparently about this time Kortrijk also made a very belated and incomplete switch to Spanish wools.[114]

As tables 12, 14, and 15 suggest, those nouvelles draperies that had adopted Spanish or other medium quality non-English wools much earlier and more willingly were able to maintain much lower prices and fared substantially better than the luxury draperies over the fifteenth century. Particularly striking are the completely opposite trends of the tax farm sales for the luxury draperies on the one hand and for the various non-woollen textile industries on the other, as shown in tables 12 and 13. For the latter, the high cost of English wools would hardly seem to be a relevant consideration. Yet one may argue that the Calais ordinances and associated economic factors did assist both the nouvelles draperies and the non-woollen textiles, the sayetteries and other draperies légères in particular, by encouraging a transfer of capital, labour, and entrepreneurship from the old draperies to these newer, more aggressive and flexible industries.

Of all these fifteenth-century economic transformations, the one requiring the least comment is the decline of the English wool trade. Yet it must not be thought that the English wool trade disappeared, nor even that the expansion of the nouvelles draperies and draperies légères meant a proportional fall in English wool exports. For, in the first place, many of the nouvelles draperies found that the optimum 'trade-off' between quality and price for the luxury market was achieved by mixing Spanish and English wools. The mid-fifteenth century author of the Libel of Englishe Polycye, despite his nationalist bias, was not entirely off the mark in maintaining that Spanish wool 'is of lytelle valeue, trust unto me, wyth Englysshe wolle but if it menged [mixed] be.'[115] Even in the sixteenth century, when the qualities of Spanish merino wools had undoubtedly improved, the leading nouvelle draperie, the famous Armentières, required that its draps oultrefins be made of two parts Spanish and one part English wool, of the best quality (Cotswolds, Berkshires, Lindseys).[116] In the second place, some remnants of the old luxury draperies did survive into the sixteenth century, principally at Mechelen, Ghent, and Brussels, and above all at Leyden (whose history is a case apart).[117] There were and always will be the very rich and the very powerful who will demand nothing but the best at whatever cost. Undoubtedly these sixteenth-century draperies still produced the best cloths, steadfastly maintaining those high standards of excellence that had earned them so much glory and so many customers in the past. But in the future, if the glory remained, most of the customers did not. The future had been claimed first by the English draperies and *nouvelles draperies* in the Low Countries; and then subsequently by the *draperies légères*, *sayetteries*, and then finally by the associated New Draperies of Elizabethan and Stuart England. These latter draperies produced for much broader, virtually mass markets in the sixteenth and early seventeenth centuries, whose expansionary economic movements, and indeed inflation, constituted a decisive reversal of all those forces of contraction that afflicted late-medieval Europe.

Clearly the structural changes in the economies of England and the Low Countries, and especially changes in the structure and orientation of European markets provided the fundamental causes of these industrial transformations. In particular the rebirth of the *sayetteries*, once so prominent in twelfth and thirteenth-century Flanders, certainly depended upon a massive increase in demand from the middle classes and a renewed access to the Mediterranean markets.[118] How dramatic these fifteenth-century industrial transformations were can be seen in the final graph IV, which provides production indices of the Ypres luxury drapery and the Hondschoote *sayetterie*. Note that the long-term trend lines, linear regression lines, intersect in the 1440s. Those regression lines provide further indication of the role played by the Anglo-Burgundian monetary conflicts. For before the imposition of the Calais bullion laws in the 1430s, the Ypres production indices were *above* the trend line, while the Hondschoote indices were *below* the trend line; and conversely from the 1430s, the Ypres indices fell below the trend line, while the Hondschoote indices rise above the trend, except during the civil war years of the late fifteenth century, when even extensive coinage debasements could not encourage exports enough to counteract the disruptive consequences of the Flemish rebellion for Hondschoote's *sayetterie* trade.

IV: Quinquennial Averages and Trend Lines of the Number of Drapers' Stalls Rented at Ypres and Value of Tax Farms for the Hondschoote Sayetterie 1400-04 to 1505-09

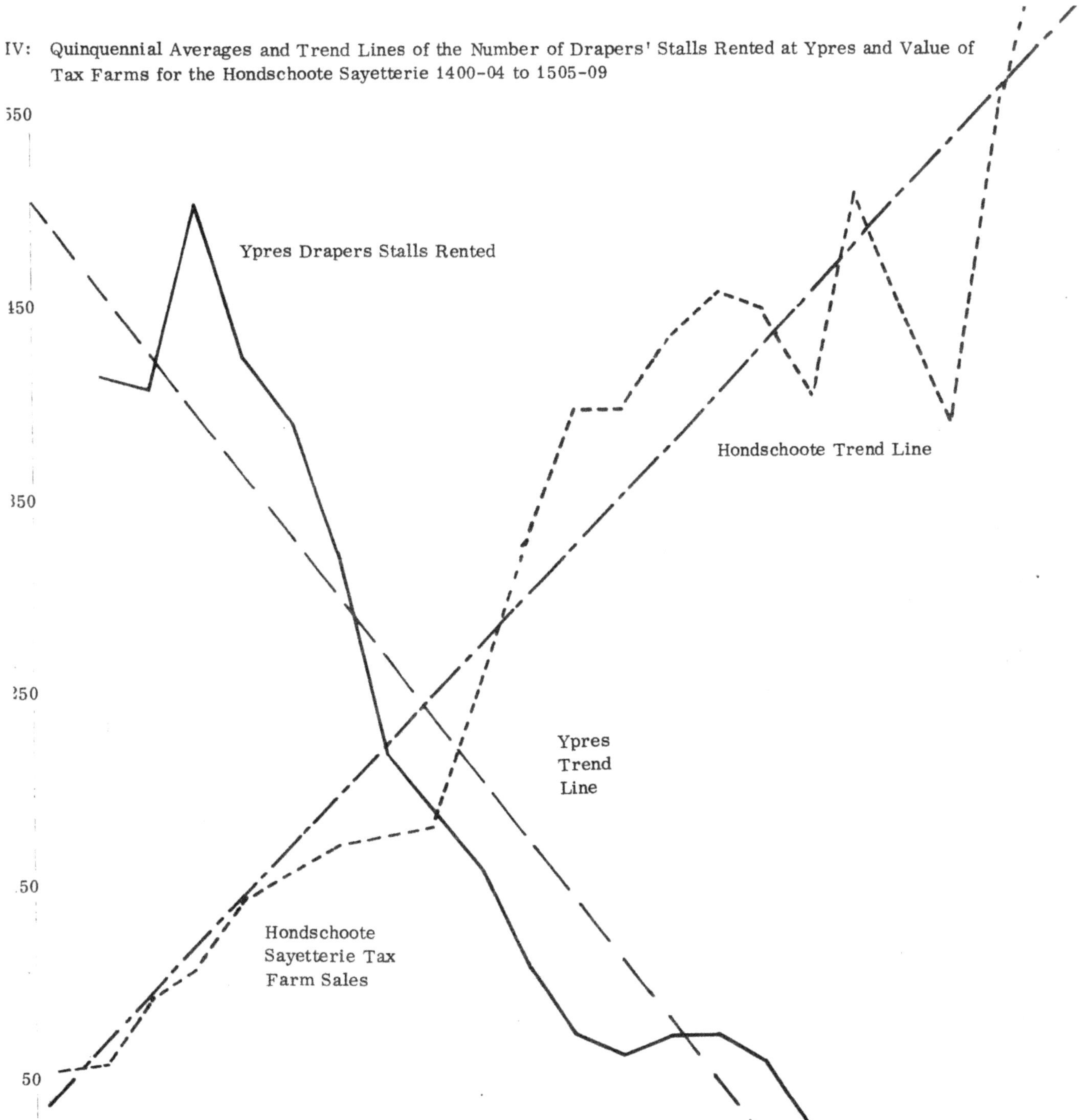

NOTES

PART I

1. W. C. Robinson, 'Money, Population, and Economic Change in Late-Medieval Europe', Economic History Review, 2nd ser. XII(1959), 63-76, followed by Michael M. Postan, 'Note', 77-82. See also M. M. Postan, 'Some Economic Evidence of Declining Population in the Later Middle Ages', Ec.H.R. 2nd ser. II (1950), 221-46, reprinted in his Essays on Medieval Agriculture and General Problems of the Medieval Economy (Cambridge, 1973), pp. 186-213; Postan, 'Rapport', IXe congrès international des sciences historiques (2 vols. Paris, 1950), I, 225-41, revised and republished as 'The Economic Foundations of Medieval Society', in Essays, pp. 3-27; Postan, 'Medieval Agrarian Society in its Prime: England', Cambridge Economic History of Europe, I (2nd ed. 1966), 560-70; Postan, 'The Trade of Medieval Europe: the North', Camb. Ec. Hist. II (1952), 191-256; Postan, The Medieval Economy and Society: An Economic History of Britain, 1100-1500 (London, 1972), pp. 27-40, 224-46; Robert Lopez, 'The Trade of Medieval Europe: the South', Camb. Ec. Hist. II, 338-54. The latest, most impressive and compelling restatements of the 'real' school's theses are John Hatcher, Plague, Population, and the English Economy, 1348-1530 (London, 1977) and Postan and Hatcher, 'Population and Class Relations in Feudal Society', Past and Present, no. 78 (Feb. 1978), 24-37.

2. Harry A. Miskimin, 'Monetary Movements and Market Structures: Forces for Contraction in Fourteenth- and Fifteenth-Century England', Journal of Economic History, XXIV (1964), 470-90; Miskimin, The Economy of Early Renaissance Europe, 1300-1460 (Englewood Cliffs, N.J. 1969; reissued Cambridge, 1975), especially pp. 25-72, 132-57; R. S. Lopez, H. A. Miskimin, and A. L. Udovitch, 'England to Egypt, 1350-1500: Long-term Trends and Long-distance Trade', Studies in the Economic History of the Middle East, ed. M. A. Cook (London, 1970), pp. 93-106. Cf. also R. S. Lopez and H. A. Miskimin, 'The Economic Depression of the Renaissance', Economic History Review, 2nd ser. XIV (1962), 408-26; Carlo Cipolla, R. S. Lopez, and H. A. Miskimin, 'Economic Depression of the Renaissance? Rejoinder and Reply', Ibid. 2nd ser. XVI (1964), 519-29.

3. Nicholas Mayhew, 'Numismatic Evidence and Falling Prices in the Fourteenth Century', Economic History Review, 2nd ser. XXVII (1974), 1-15. See also his 'The Monetary Background to the Yorkist Recoinage of 1464-1471', British Numismatic Journal, XLIV (1974), 62-73. For my earlier, anti-monetarist views, see John H. Munro, Wool, Cloth, and Gold: The Struggle for Bullion in Anglo-Burgundian Trade, 1340-1478 (Brussels and Toronto, 1973), pp. 11-18.

4. This issue of Past and Present reached me two days before I flew to England to deliver this paper. Our conclusions, though similar, were reached independently; and my basic ideas on monetary contraction were presented last year (30 Aug. 1977) to the Conference on Pre-Modern Monetary History, 1200-1750, at the University of Wisconsin, in my paper entitled 'Mint Outputs, Monetary Change, and Economic Contraction in Late-Medieval England and the Low Countries.' See also John Day, 'The Decline of a Money Economy: Sardinia in the Late Middle Ages', Studi in memoria di Federigo Melis, III (1978), 155-76.

5. Cf. Marc Bloch, 'Le problème de l'or au moyen âge', Annales d'histoire économique et sociale, V (1933), 1-34, reprinted as 'The Problem of Gold in the Middle Ages', Land and Work in Mediaeval Europe: Selected Papers by Marc Bloch, trans. J. E. Anderson (London, 1967), pp. 186-229; Bloch, Esquisse d'une histoire monétaire de l'Europe (Paris, 1954) pp. 35-77 [written before 1940]; Henri Laurent, 'Crise monétaire et difficultés économiques en Flandre aux XIVe et XVe siècles', Annales d'histoire économique et sociale, V (1933), 156-61; Albert Feavearyear, The Pound Sterling: A History of English Money, 2nd ed. rev. E. V. Morgan (Oxford, 1963), pp. 10-15. Cf. also W. A. Shaw, The History of Currency, 1252-1894 (London, 1896), pp. 1-60; A. Girard, 'Un phenomène économique: la guerre monétaire, XIVe-XVe siècles', Annales: E.S.C., II (1940); F. Graus, 'La crise monétaire du XIVe siècle', Revue belge de philologie et d'histoire, XXIX (1951), 445-54; Johan Schreiner, 'Wages and Prices in the Later Middle Ages', Scandinavian Economic History Review, II (1954), 61-73; R. Cazelles, 'Quelques réflexions à propos des mutations de la monnaie royale française (1295-1360)', Le moyen âge, LXXII (1966), 83-105, 251-78; E. Fournial, Histoire monétaire de l'occident médiévale (Paris, 1970).

6. Subsequently, however, Day does suggest that the balance of payments deficit became a serious problem for Western Europe only when declines in European mining and West African gold supplies reduced the available metal stocks. 'The Great Bullion Famine of the Fifteenth Century', Past and Present, no. 79 (1978), 3-12, 35-40, Cf. Eliyahu Ashtor, 'Observations on Venetian Trade in the Levant in the XIVth Century', Journal of European Economic History, V (1976), 533-86; Ashtor, Les metaux précieux et la balance des payements du Proche-Orient à la basse époque (Paris, 1971), pp. 65-96; Ashtor, 'The Venetian Supremacy in Levantine Trade: Monopoly or Pre-Colonialism?', Journal of European Economic History, III (1974), 5-53; Ashtor, 'The Volume of Levantine Trade in the Later Middle Ages (1370-1498)', Ibid. IV (1975), 573-612; Ashtor, A Social and Economic History of the Near East in the Middle Ages (London, 1976), pp. 319-31. The Venetian ducat = 3.56 g.

7. Ashtor, 'Venetian Supremacy', pp. 5-17, 23-40, 46-53; Ashtor, 'Volume of Levantine Trade', pp. 605-12, esp. p. 609 n. 94.

8. Abraham Udovitch (with R. S. Lopez and H. A. Miskimin), 'England to Egypt, 1350-1500: Long-term Trends and Long-distance Trade', Studies in the Economic History of the Middle East (1970), pp. 115-28; Ashtor,

'Venetian Trade' (1976), pp. 574-86 (quotation on p. 586); Ashtor, Economic History, pp. 280-331. In Les metaux précieux (1971), pp. 13, 41-53, 97-110, Ashtor had attributed the increasingly severe monetary scarcity of fifteenth-century Egypt to Mamluk military expenditures abroad and especially to hoarding, not to the balance of trade, which he believed remained favourable overall for the Levant (p. 96). But subsequently, in 'Volume of Levantine Trade' (1975), he seems to be agreeing with Udovitch in stating that 'one cannot believe that the balance of trade for the Levant itself was favourable' (p. 612). See also the other sources cited in n. 6 above.

9. Cf. Robert Lopez, 'Back to Gold, 1252', Economic History Review, 2nd ser. IX (1956), 232-40; Bloch, 'Problem of Gold' (n. 5 above), pp. 212-18; Ashtor, Les metaux précieux, pp. 15-29, 97-108; V. Magalhaes-Godhino, L'économie de l'empire portugais aux XVe et XVIe siècles (Paris, 1969); Marian Malowist, 'Quelques observations sur le commerce de l'or dans le Soudan occidentale au moyen âge', Annales: E.S.C., XXV (1970), 1630-36; E. W. Bovill, The Golden Trade of the Moors, 2nd ed. (London, 1968), pp. 13-44, 79-131; Pierre Vilar, A History of Gold and Money, 1450-1920 (London, 1976), pp. 30-61; Day, 'Bullion Famine', pp. 36-40, providing evidence of serious disruptions and diminutions of African gold flows to Europe from the later fourteenth century.

10. H. A. Miskimin, 'Long-term Trends' (n. 2 above), pp. 102-04; Miskimin, Economy (n. 2 above), pp. 138-42. In support of this view, see Artur Attman, The Russian and Polish Markets in International Trade, 1500-1650 (Göteborg, 1973), pp. 103-93, esp. pp. 103-18 on the influx of precious metals into Russia from the 11th century.

11. Cf. the publications of Miskimin, Postan, and Hatcher cited in notes 1-2 above.

12. Terence H. Lloyd, 'Overseas Trade and the English Money Supply in the Fourteenth Century', Edwardian Monetary Affairs (1279-1344), ed. Nicholas Mayhew (BAR 36, Oxford, 1977), pp. 96-124.

13. Public Record Office, Lord Treasurer's Remembrancer Exchequer, E.356/1-27, E.372 (various); King's Remembrancer Exchequer, Accounts Various, E. 122 series. Cf. also N. S. B. Gras, The Early English Customs System (Cambridge, Mass. 1918), pp. 59-139; H. L. Gray, 'Tables of Enrolled Customs and Subsidy Accounts, 1399 to 1482', in Studies in English Trade in the Fifteenth Century, ed. Eileen Power and Michael Postan (London, 1933), pp. 321-30; E. M. Carus-Wilson and Olive Coleman, England's Export Trade, 1275-1547 (Oxford, 1963), pp. 1-33, 194-207.

14. Lloyd, 'Overseas Trade',pp. 121-22. Cf. also G. A. Holmes, 'Florentine Merchants in England, 1346-1436', Economic History Review, 2nd ser. XIII (1960), 193-208; E. B. Fryde, 'Anglo-Italian Commerce in the Fifteenth Century', Revue belge de philologie et d'histoire, L (1972), 345-55. See also my tables 1 and 12 below.

15. 38 Ed. III stat. 1 c. 2 in Statutes of the Realm, I, 383. Cf. John Munro,

'Bullionism and the Bill of Exchange in England, 1272-1663: A Study in Monetary Management and Popular Prejudice', in The Dawn of Modern Banking, ed. Fredi Chiappelli (New Haven and London, 1978), pp. 169-243.

16. Rotuli Parliamentorum, III, 126-27: nos. 1-2. Cf. Feavearyear, Pound Sterling (n. 5 above), pp. 33-36; Jacob Viner, Studies in the Theory of International Trade (London, 1955), pp. 6-15; Munro, 'Bullionism', pp. 169-90 for its significance.

17. Cf. Munro, 'Bullionism', pp. 169-243; Munro, Wool, Cloth, and Gold (n. 3 above), chap. 1, 2, 4; Eileen Power, 'The Wool Trade in the Fifteenth Century', Studies in English Trade (n. 13 above), pp. 79-90.

18. Raymond de Roover, 'La balance commerciale entre les Pays-Bas et l'Italie au XVe siècle', Revue belge de philologie et d'histoire, XXXVII (1959), 374-86; de Roover, L'evolution de la lettre de change, XIVe-XVIIIe siècles (Paris, 1953), pp. 64-5; de Roover, The Bruges Money Market Around 1400 (Brussels, 1968).

19. John U. Nef, 'Silver Production in Central Europe, 1450-1618', Journal of Political Economy, XLIX (1941), 575-91; Nef, 'Mining and Metallurgy in Medieval Civilisation', Cambridge Economic History, II, 456-73; Graus, 'Crise monétaire' (n. 5 above), pp. 450-52; D. Kovacevic, 'Les mines d'or et d'argent en Serbie et en Bosnie médiévales', Annales: E.S.C., XV (1960), 248-58; Postan, 'The North', C.E.H., II, 211-12; Miskimin, Economy (n. 2 above), pp. 112-15; Day, 'Bullion Famine' (n. 6 above), pp. 35-36, arguing that the new mines may have compansated for the decline of the old up to about the 1360s.

20. Postan, 'The North', pp. 211-12 and his other publications cited in n. 1 above, esp. 'Note', pp. 77-82; Hatcher, Plague, pp. 52-54.

21. David Herlihy, Medieval and Renaissance Pistoia: The Social History of an Italian Town, 1200-1430 (New Haven and London, 1967), p. 125. For the immediate post-Plague era, the comment is perfectly valid.

22. C. C. Patterson, 'Silver Stocks and Losses in Ancient and Medieval Times', Economic History Review, 2nd ser. XXV (1972), 205-35; Marion Archibald, 'Wastage from Currency: Long-Cross and the Recoinage of 1279', Edwardian Monetary Affairs (n. 12 above), pp. 167-86; John Craig, The Mint: A History of the London Mint from A.D. 278 to 1948 (Cambridge, 1953), pp. xvi, 60; Mayhew, 'Numismatic Evidence' (n. 3 above), pp. 1-15.

23. Cf. Feavearyear, Pound Sterling, (n. 5 above), pp. 10-15; Munro, Wool, Cloth, and Gold (n. 3 above), pp. 25-30; John Munro, 'An Aspect of Medieval Public Finance: The Profits of Counterfeiting in the Fifteenth-Century Low Countries', Revue belge de numismatique, CXVIII (1972), 127-48. For an analysis of such discounting and consequent price increases, see Mavis Mate, 'Monetary Problems in England, 1272-1307', British Numismatic Journal, XLI (1972), 37-45.

24. Cf. A. Blanchet and A. Dieudonné, Manuel de numismatique francaise, II (Paris, 1916), chaps. 3-7; A. Grunzweig, 'Les incidences interna-

tionales des mutations monétaires de Philippe le Bel', Le moyen âge, LIX (1953), 117-72; Cazelles, 'Mutations de la monnaie' (n. 5 above), pp. 83-105.

25. Andrew Watson, 'Back to Gold—and Silver', Economic History Review, 2nd ser. XX (1967), 1-34, and esp. p. 18.

26. Harry A. Miskimin, Money, Prices, and Foreign Exchange in Fourteenth-Century France (New Haven, 1963), pp. 117-19; Ashtor, Les metaux précieux, pp. 31-36 (but a qualified agreement with Watson on p. 51); Ashtor, 'Recent Research on Levantine Trade', Journal of European Economic History, II (1973), 193. Cf. also Day, 'Bullion Famine', p. 6.

27. Cf. Munro, Wool, Cloth, and Gold (n. 3 above), chap. 2; graphs I-VI.

28. Cf. tables 3-9 below; Peter Spufford, Monetary Problems and Policies in the Burgundian Netherlands, 1433-1496 (Leiden, 1970), appendix III, pp. 183-85. Between July 1487 and January 1490, Maximilian raised the value of the gold marc (244.753 g.) from £26.400 groot to £50.087 gr., almost doubling it. Algemeen Rijksarchief, Rekenkamer, no. 17,882: no. 4; 18,242: no. 3.

29. At the 1% level of significance, χ^2 with 14 degrees of freedom $[(n_r-1)(n_c-1)]$ has a critical value of 29.14. Another, derived measure is the Contingency Coefficient,

$$C = \sqrt{\frac{\chi^2}{\chi^2 + N}},$$

in which 0 = perfect agreement. Values of C are given in table 9 below. Cf. Roderick Floud, An Introduction to Quantitative Methods for Historians (London, 1973), pp. 128-34, 138-9.

30. Watson, 'Back to Gold', (n. 25 above), pp. 21-31; Craig, Mint (n. 22 above), pp. 36, 59-75.

31. Cf. Bloch, 'Problem of Gold' (n. 5 above); Munro, Wool, Cloth, and Gold, pp. 43-64; Munro, 'Bullionism' (n. 15 above), pp. 169-243.

32. J. D. A. Thompson, Inventory of British Coin Hoards, 600-1500 A.D. (Oxford, 1956), p. xxvi and passim; Jean Lafaurie, Les monnaies des rois de France: Hughes Capet à Louis XII (Paris, 1951); Day, 'Bullion Famine' (n. 6 above), pp. 44-5; Spufford, Monetary Problems (n. 28 above), pp. 55-73.

33. Most historians agree that medieval forms of credit, in the absence of true negotiability and discounting, expanded V rather than M; but credit instruments were certainly in more widespread use than is commonly thought. Cf. Michael Postan, 'Credit in Medieval Trade' and 'Private Financial Instruments' in his Medieval Trade and Finance (Cambridge, 1973), pp. 1-64; de Roover, Lettre de change (n. 18 above) and his Money, Banking and Credit in Mediaeval Bruges (Cambridge, Mass., 1948); de Roover, 'New Interpretations of the History of Banking', Journal of World History, II (1954), 38-76.

34. Cf. E. H. Phelps Brown and Sheila Hopkins, 'Seven Centuries of the Prices of Consumables, Compared with Builders' Wage Rates', Essays in Economic History, ed. E. M. Carus-Wilson, II (London, 1962), 183, 194; Herlihy, Pistoia (n. 21 above), pp. 55-120, 122-30; Miskimin, Money (n. 26 above), pp. 53-71; E. J. Hamilton, Money, Prices, and Wages in Valencia, Aragon, and Navarre, 1351-1500 (Cambridge, Mass., 1936), graphs on pp. 53, 55, 57, 60, 102, 104, 106, 160, 163, 191; see also pp. 189-269; Leopold Génicot, 'Crisis: From Middle Ages to Modern Times', Cambridge Economic History, I (2nd ed. 1966), 677-94.

35. Cf. Miskimin, Economy (n. 2 above), pp. 134-43; Johan Huizinga, The Waning of the Middle Ages (London, 1926), esp. pp. 140-52; Philip Ziegler, The Black Death (London, 1969), pp. 240-88; R. S. Lopez, 'Hard Times and Investment in Culture', The Renaissance: A Symposium (New York, 1953), pp. 19-32.

36. Postan, 'Note' (n. 1 above), p. 78.

37. Bloch, 'Problem of Gold' (n. 5 above), p. 186.

38. Nicholas Mayhew has provided a very persuasive case for the contention that the 1320s mark the real beginning of the late-medieval monetary contraction, in 'Numismatic Evidence' (n. 3 above), pp. 1-15. His arguments have been supported by Michael Prestwich, 'Currency and the Economy of Early Fourteenth Century England', Edwardian Monetary Affairs (n. 12 above), pp. 45-58; and there can be no doubt that the era 1320-1345 was for England one of severe monetary scarcity. But, like that of the 1290s, this one may also be attributed to the effects of foreign debasement and counterfeiting and the crown's military and diplomatic expenditures abroad. In any event, the immense mint outputs that ensued in the 1350s and 1360s in England, the Low Countries, and France make it difficult to argue that the preceding era marked the onset of a long-term, European wide bullion famine—unless one were to argue that the vast mintings of the mid-century were a unique, unrepeatable phenomenon resulting from the 'inheritance effect' of the Plague and dishoardings necessitated by the Hundred Years' War. See table 1 below and Miskimin, Money (n. 26 above), pp. 87-88, 90, 93-4, 100-15, 143-44, 159; Cazelles, 'Mutations' (n. 5 above), pp. 88-94, 256-62; Edward Ames, 'The Sterling Crisis of 1337-1339', Journal of Economic History, XXV (1956), 496-522.

39. Day did not incorporate the Calais mint accounts of 1387-1403, recently published by Lloyd, the other provincial English mints, and the extra mint accounts of Louis de Mâle (Flanders) published by Van Werveke. See the sources to tables 2-9 below; and n. 51.

40. Mean of 1270-1369 = £47,661.88 (current); mean of 1370-1469 = £36,617.3 (current). From 1344 to March 1465 the English silver coinage was debased by 40.8 percent and the gold by 41.8 per cent. See Munro, 'Bullionism' (n. 15 above), table II.

41. For a contrary view, see Hatcher, Plague (n. 1 above), pp. 31-63.

42. See tables 2-9 and notes 50-51 below.

43. Cf. Hans Van Werveke, De Zwarte Dood in de zuidelijke Nederlanden, 1349-1351 (Brussels, 1950); Herman Van der Wee, The Growth of the Antwerp Market and the European Economy, Fourteenth to Sixteenth Centuries (3 vols. The Hague, 1963), I, appendix 49, 545-48; II, 7-9, 31-7, 61-7; Joseph Cuvelier, Les dénombrements de foyers en Brabant, XIVe-XVIe siècles (Brussels, 1912); Maurice Arnould, Les dénombrements de foyers dans le comté de Hainaut, XIVe-XVIe siècles (1956).

44. See Munro, 'Profits of Counterfeiting' (n. 23 above) and Pierre Cockshaw, 'De quelques imitations de monnaies au XVe siècle', Revue belge de numismatique, CXVIII (1972), 149-63; Bloch, Esquisse (n. 5 above), pp. 40-70.

45. So prevalent is this view that to combat it seems almost futile. But see Anna Jacobson Schwartz's review of F. C. Spooner, The International Economy and Monetary Movements in France, 1493-1725 (1972) in Journal of European Economic History, III (1974), 253: 'He subscribes to a familiar fallacy, namely, that a monetary explanation of inflation to be valid requires that all prices move in unison.'

46. Herman Van der Wee, 'Prijzen en lonen als ontwikkelingsvariabelen: Een vergelijkend onderzoek tussen Engeland en de zuidelijke Nederlanden, 1400-1700', Hulde aan Charles Verlinden (1976), pp. 413-47, forthcoming in an English translation in Acta Historiae Neerlandica; Phelps Brown and Hopkins, 'Seven Centuries' (n. 34 above).

47. I have used the exchange rates in Van der Wee, Antwerp Market, I, table XIII, 124-5. Exchange rates do not necessarily reflect domestic price ratios between countries.

PART II

48. See in particular David M. Nicholas, Town and Countryside: Social, Economic, and Political Tensions in Fourteenth-Century Flanders (Bruges, 1971); Henri Pirenne, Histoire de Belgique (eds. 1-5, 1902-32; new ed. in 4 vols. Brussels, 1956), I, 225-56, 287-94, 297-326, 339-40, 352-62; Hans Van Werveke, Gand: Esquisse d'histoire sociale (Brussels, 1946), pp. 29-69; Van Werveke, Jacques Van Artevelde (Brussels, 1943), pp. 23-119.

49. See John Munro, 'Industrial Protectionism in Medieval Flanders: Urban or National?', The Medieval City, ed. H. A. Miskimin, D. Herlihy, and A. L. Udovitch (New Haven and London, 1977), pp. 230-55 and tables 13.1-5, pp. 254-68; Munro, 'Wool-Price Schedules and the Qualities of English Wools in the Later Middle Ages, ca. 1270-1499', Textile History, IX (1978), and Munro, 'The Medieval Scarlet and the Economics of Sartorial Splendour', Cloth and Clothing in Medieval Europe: Essays in Memory of E. M. Carus-Wilson, ed. K. Ponting and N. Harte (London, 1979); and Edward Miller, 'The Fortunes of the Early English Textile Industry in the Thirteenth Century', Econ. Hist. Rev. 2nd ser. XVIII (1965), 64-82.

50. Hans Van Werveke, 'De economische en sociale gevolgen van de munt-

politiek der graven van Vlaanderen (1337-1433)', Annales de la Société d'Emulation de Bruges, LXXIV (1931), 1-15 and his 'Currency Manipulation in the Middle Ages: The Case of Louis de Male, Count of Flanders', Transactions of the Royal Historical Society, 4th ser. XXXI (1949), 115-27; both reprinted in his Miscellanea Mediaevalia (Ghent, 1968), pp. 243-67.

51. Hans Van Werveke, De muntslag in Vlaanderen onder Lodewijk van Måle (Brussels, 1949); Victor Gaillard, ed. Recherches sur les monnaies des comtes de Flandre, II (Ghent, 1856).

52. Cf. the sources cited in notes 48 and 50 above, especially those by Van Werveke; and also H. S. Lucas, The Low Countries in the Hundred Years' War, 1326-1347 (Ann Arbor, 1929), pp. 438-56, 480-93, 516-22.

53. Cf. Hans Van Werveke, De omvang van de Ieperse lakenproductie in de veertiende eeuw (Brussels, 1947); Raymond Van Uytven, 'Technique, productivité, et production au moyen âge: le cas de la draperie urbaine aux Pays Bas', Produttivita e tecnologie nei secoli XII-XVII (Terza Settimana di Studio 'Francesco Datini', Prato, April 1971), forthcoming. He estimates that Ypres' maximum cloth production was no more than 40,000 woollens per annum.

54. See the sources cited above in notes 2, 34-35.

55. See the sources cited in notes 34 and 46 above, and Tables 2-5, 7-8 below.

56. In March 1367, Louis de Måle granted the request of the Ghent weavers to restrict entry into their guild to local citizens, after the weavers had complained about the current industrial crisis, stating 'dat der neringhe van haren ambochte zere vercranet ende verarecht es'. Georges Espinas and Henri Pirenne, eds. Receuil de documents relatifs à l'histoire de l'industrie drapière en Flandre, 1re partie (4 vols. Brussels, 1906-20), II, 516-17, no. 477.

57. Cf. E. M. Carus-Wilson, 'Trends in the Export of English Woollens in the Fourteenth Century', Economic History Review, 2nd ser. III (1950), reprinted in her Medieval Merchant Venturers (London, 1954), pp. 252-61; G. A. Holmes, The Estates of the Higher Nobility in Fourteenth-Century England (Cambridge, 1957), pp. 115-20; Van der Wee, Antwerp Market (n. 43 above), II, 7-18, 28-30, 289-95, 309-14; and the sources cited in n. 34 above on deflation, and n. 58 below.

58. Cf. Nicholas, Town and Countryside (n. 48 above), pp. 203-21, 331-51; Richard Vaughan, Philip the Bold: The Formation of the Burgundian State (London, 1962), pp. 19-50, 168-73, 180-2; Fritz Quicke, Les Pays Bas à la veille de la période bourguignonne, 1356-1384 (Brussels, 1947), pp. 297-355.

59. Vaughan, Philip the Bold, pp. 168-82; Van der Wee, Antwerp Market (n. 43 above), II, 14-18; Munro, 'Industrial Protectionism' (n. 49 above), pp. 235-39. For an 'upzette van den wevers' in 1387, exodus of foreign merchants, and Hanseatic reparations claims, see Louis Gilliodts-Van Severeren, ed. Inventaire des chartes et documents de la ville de Bruges

(6 vols. Bruges, 1871-76), III, 233, no. 738 (1387); 224-35, no. 734 (1392); Gilliodts-Van Severen, ed. Cartulaire de l'ancienne estaple de Bruges (6 vols. Bruges, 1904-08), I, 324, 329, 335, 342-4, 359-61, 365, 367-68.

60. Hans Van Werveke, 'De Vlaamse munthervorming van 1389-90', in his Miscellanea Mediaevalia (Ghent, 1968), pp. 268-80; Pierre Cockshaw, 'A propos de la circulation monêtaire entre la Flandre et le Brabant de 1384 à 1390', Contributions à l'histoire économique et sociale (Université Libre de Bruxelles), VI (1970-71), 107-41; Van der Wee, Antwerp Market, II, 14-15; Munro, Wool, Cloth, and Gold, pp. 43-55, 198.

61. Nicholas, Town and Countryside (n. 48 above), pp. 338-39; Van der Wee, Antwerp Market, II, 14-18, 28-41. Cf. the price-tables and graphs in ibid. I and III respectively; and Charles Verlinden et al., eds. Dokumenten voor de geschiedenis van prijzen en lonen in Vlaanderen en Braband, XVe-XVIIIe eeuw (2 vols. Bruges, 1959-65); and the sources cited in notes 34 and 46 above.

62. Van Werveke, 'Muntpolitiek' (n. 50 above), pp. 246-54 (esp. graph on p. 248); Van Werveke, 'Munthervorming' (n. 60 above), pp. 274-75; Van der Wee, Antwerp Market, II, 141-18, 29-30; de Roover, Money, Banking, and Credit (n. 33 above), pp. 227-29; Gilliodts-Van Severen, Archives de Bruges (n. 59 above), III, 134-5, no. 706; 140-2 (Jan. 1390).

63. Hektor Ammann, 'Deutschland und die Tuchindustrie Nordwesteuropas im Mittelalter', Hansisches Geschichtsblätter, LXXII (1954), 1-61.

64. On the Leuven and other Brabantine draperies, see Raymond Van Uytven, Stadsfinanciën en stadsekonomie te Leuven van de XIIde tot het einde der XVIde eeuw (Brussels, 1961), pp. 337-91, 471-639; Van Uytven, 'De omvang van de Mechelse lakenproductie vanaf de XIVd tot de XVIde eeuw', Noordgouw: cultureel tijdschrift van de provincie Antwerpen, V (1965), 1-22; Van Uytven, 'La draperie brabançonne et malinoise du XIIe au XVIIe siècle: grandeur éphemère et décadence', Produzione, commercio, et consumo dei panni di lana (Seconda Settimana di Studio 'Francesco Datini' at Prato, April 1970, Florence, 1976), pp. 85-97; Robert-Henri Bautier, 'La place de la draperie brabançonne et plus particulièrement bruxelloise dans l'industrie textile du moyen âge', Annales de la société royale d'archéologie de Bruxelles, LI (1966), 31-63.

65. Munro, Wool, Cloth, and Gold, pp. 6-9, 69-70; Munro, 'Industrial Protectionism' (n. 49 above), pp. 229-48.

66. Van der Wee, Antwerp Market (n. 43 above), II, 31-59, 314-17; Munro, Wool, Cloth, and Gold, pp. 73-75; and sources cited in n. 34 above.

67. Day, 'Bullion Famine' (n. 6 above), pp. 32-35, 40-44.

68. Munro, Wool, Cloth and Gold, pp. 65-92, 198-211.

69. Ibid., pp. 34-45; Munro, 'Bullionism' (n. 15 above), pp. 169-243.

70. 8 Hen. VI c. 18 in S.R., II, 254-55; Rot. Parl., IV, 359: no. 60. Cf. Munro, Wool, Cloth, and Gold, pp. 84-92 and the sources cited in n. 82 below.

71. Cf. Munro, Wool, Cloth, and Gold, pp. 88-91; Munro, 'Bullionism' (n. 15 above), pp. 169-243; Postan, 'Credit' (n. 33 above), pp. 1-27; Power, 'Wool Trade' (n. 17 above), pp. 48-72; Rose-Marie Thielemans, Bourgogne et Angleterre: Relations politiques et économiques entre les Pays-Bas bourguignonne et l'Angleterre, 1435-1467 (Brussels, 1966), pp. 349-61.

72. Cf. Nicholas Posthumus, De geschiedenis van de Leidsche lakenindustrie, I: De middeleeuwen, veertiende tot zestiende eeuw (The Hague, 1908) and Posthumus, ed. Bronnen tot de geschiedenis van de Leidsche textielnijverheid, 1333-1795 (3 vols. The Hague, 1910-1939). Cf. also Hans Van Werveke, De koopman-ondernemer en de ondernemer in de Vlaamsche lakennijverheid van de middeleeuwen (Antwerp, 1946), with French résumé.

73. Munro, Wool, Cloth, and Gold, pp. 94-104; appendices pp. 198-201.

74. Raymond de Roover, Money, Banking, and Credit (n. 33 above), pp. 237-39, 338-41; de Roover, Gresham on Foreign Exchange (Cambridge, Mass., 1949), pp. 35-36, 82; Van der Wee, Antwerp Market (n. 43 above), 333-68, esp. 357-58; and most recently Van der Wee, 'Monetary, Credit, and Banking Systems', Cambridge Economic History, V (1977), 322-24.

75. Munro, Wool, Cloth, and Gold, pp. 134-35, 149-51; Spufford, Monetary Problems (n. 28 above), pp. 113-22.

76. Algemeen Rijksarchief van Belgiё, Rekenkamer, no. 18,105, citing a ducal ordinance of 15 October 1456 that raised the taille per marc (244.753 g) of courtes or double mites, at 12 grains fineness argent-le-roy (0.040 fine), from 216 to 240 coins, thus raising the traite of the silver marc from 36s.0d. groot to 40s.0d. groot, a debasement of 10%. But the debasement of courtes (and mites) did not take place until after 3 September 1457, when this account commenced.

77. Munro, Wool, Cloth, and Gold, pp. 150, 157-58, 193-95; Spufford, Monetary Problems (n. 28 above), pp. 118-22, 176-78.

78. Rot. Parl. VI, 108-09; no. 36; Craig, The Mint (n. 22 above); Munro, Wool, Cloth, and Gold, pp. 128-31.

79. Mayhew, 'Yorkist Recoinage' (n. 3 above), pp. 62-73; Craig, The Mint (n. 22 above), pp. 91-92, 412; Munro, Wool, Cloth, and Gold, pp. 155-62.

80. Spufford, Monetary Problems (n. 28 above), pp. 115-21.

81. Day, 'Bullion Famine' (n. 6 above), pp. 40-46.

82. Postan, 'Credit' (n. 33 above), pp. 7-10; Power, 'Wool Trade' (n. 17 above), pp. 79-90; Thielemans, Bourgogne et Angleterre (n. 71 above), pp. 56-61, 90-107, 149-212, 365-424; Terrence H. Lloyd, The English Wool Trade in the Middle Ages (Cambridge, 1977), pp. 257-87. Munro, Wool, Cloth, and Gold, chaps. 4-6. On Calais see also Spufford, Monetary Problems (n. 28 above), pp. 95-105.

83. By the Act of Retainer for the Calais Staple, Feb. 1473, permitting bills of exchange transactions at the Staple, any acts to the contrary notwithstanding. That act was reconfirmed in 1487, 1503, and 1515. Rot. Parl., VI, 60: no. 59; 395-97; no. 14; 525: no. 3. Formal renunciation of the Calais laws took place only with the Anglo-Burgundian treaty of 12 July 1478. Thomas Rymer, ed. Foedera, conventiones, et acta publica (2nd ed. 12 vols. London, 1727), XII, 77-86.

84. Munro, 'Wool-Price Schedules' (n. 49 above), (ca. 1499); Posthumus, Bronnen (n. 72 above), II, 294-5, no. 867 (1518); 297-9, no. 869; 316-17, no. 903 (1522: Leyden).

85. Goswin von der Ropp, ed. Hanserecesse, 1431-1476 (Second Series, 7 vols. Leipzig, 1876-92), I, 135, no. 192 (22 Oct. 1433). Cf. also the letter of the Flemish towns to the Hanse Diet, 20 Oct. in ibid. I, 133, no. 191.

86. See the sources cited in notes 43 and 64 above.

87. Van der Wee, Antwerp Market (n. 43 above), II, 61-73; H. L. Gray, 'English Foreign Trade from 1446 to 1482', Studies in English Trade (n. 13 above), pp. 1-38; Michael Postan, 'Economic and Political Relations of England and the Hanse, 1400-1475', ibid., pp. 150-53; Postan, 'Trade', C.E.H., II, 246-56; Munro, Wool, Cloth, and Gold, pp. 131-54.

88. See the sources cited in n. 87 above and also E. M. Carus-Wilson, 'The Iceland Trade' and 'The Overseas Trade of Bristol', Studies in English Trade (n. 13 above), pp. 155-246.

89. See E. R. Daenell, Die Blutezeit der deutschen Hanse (2 vols. Berlin, 1905), I, 397-440; II, 73-5, 114-16, 121-23, 140-66, 185-95, 235-68; Philippe Dollinger, La Hanse, XIIe-XVIIe siècles (Paris, 1964), pp. 309-10, 351-71; Posthumus, Leidsche lakenindustrie (n. 72 above), I, 238-57; Ammann, 'Tuchindustrie' (n. 63 above), pp. 49-52, 58-61. F. Ketner, Handel en scheepvaart van Amsterdam in de vijftiende eeuw (Leiden, 1946), pp. 95-129. On Dutch expansion into the Baltic see also T. S. Jansma, 'Philippe le Bon et la guerre hollando-wende (1438-1441)', Revue du Nord, XLII (1960), 5-18.

90. See the sources cited in notes 79 above, 92 below.

91. Munro, Wool, Cloth, and Gold, pp. 156 (graph VI), 168-70; appendices pp. 198-200, 202-04, 209-11.

92. Van der Wee, Antwerp Market (n. 43 above), II, 80-83. But this monetary policy evidently proved successful only with Duke Charles' subsequent debasements of 1467 and 1474. Munro, Wool, Cloth, and Gold, pp. 170, 199, 203-04. Cf. also the important article of J. A. Van Houtte, 'La genèse du grand marché international d'Anvers à la fin du moyen âge', Revue belge de philologie et d'histoire, XIX (1940), 87-126.

93. Carus-Wilson and Coleman, England's Export Trade (n. 13 above), pp. 95-111; Munro, 'Industrial Protectionism' (n. 49 above), pp. 245-51, 264-67; and sources cited in notes 87-88 above.

94. Dietrich Schäfer, ed. Hanserecesse, 1477-1530, III, 105, cited in Henri Pirenne, 'Une crise industrielle au XVI siècle: la draperie urbaine et la "nouvelle draperie" en Flandre', in Histoire économique de l'occident médiéval, ed. E. Coornaert (Paris, 1951), p. 625.

95. Cf. Emile Coornaert, 'Draperies rurales, draperies urbaines: l'evolution de l'industrie flamande au moyen âge et au XVI siècle', Revue belge de philologie et d'histoire, XXVIII (1950), 59-96; Coornaert, Un centre industriel d'autrefois: la draperie-sayetterie d'Hondschoote, XIVe-XVIIIe siècle (Paris, 1930), pp. 1-22, 189-254; and Pirenne, 'Crise industrielle' (n. 94 above), pp. 631-43. Originally published in 1905, Pirenne's article should be used with great care, because he has confused the nature and technology of the two types of draperies.

96. Cf. Coornaert, 'Draperies rurales', pp. 72-86, 90-95; Nicholas, Town and Countryside (n. 48 above), pp. 76-116, 203-231; Herman Van der Wee, 'Structural Changes and Specialization in the Industry of the Southern Netherlands, 1100-1600', Economic History Review, 2nd ser. XXVIII (1975), 207-15; Félicien Favresse, 'Lés debuts de la nouvelle draperie bruxelloise', Revue belge de philologie et d'histoire, XXVIII (1950), reprinted in Etudes sur les métiers bruxellois au moyen âge (Brussels, 1961), pp. 75-84.

97. Munro, 'Wool-Price Schedules' (n. 49 above).

98. Cf. Munro, Wool, Cloth, and Gold, pp. 1-9; Van der Wee, 'Structural Changes', pp. 205-11; Miskimin, Economy, (n. 2 above), pp. 86-105, 134-44; Herlihy, Pistoia (n. 21 above), pp. 55-120, 180-212; Lopez, 'Hard Times' (n. 35 above), pp. 19-32.

99. Henri De Sagher et al. eds. Recueil de documents relatifs à l'histoire de l'industrie drapière en Flandre, 2me partie (3 vols. Brussels, 1951-66), II, 85-97, 99-102, no. 242 (Diksmuide); 625-35, 649-50, no. 377 (Langemarck); III, 521, 564, no. 586:195 (Wervik); Coornaert, Hondschoote (n. 95 above), p. 191 n. 2 (Kortrijk). For bans on the use of any but fine English wools in the luxury draperies cf. O. Delepierre and M. F. Willems, eds. Collection des keuren ou statuts de tous les métiers de Bruges (Ghent, 1842), p. 42 (ca. 1380); Posthumus, Bronnen (n. 72 above), I, 20-21, no. 12 (Leiden, 1396); 74, no. 74:17 (1418); 132, no. 115 (1423); Stadsarchief te Leuven, no. 722, fo. 3r. (art. 9: 1442); Stadsarchief te Brussel, no. XVI: het wit Correctieboek, fo. 193r. (1444); Espinas and Pirenne, Recueil (n. 56 above), III, 633-38, no. 792 (Ypres, ca. 1390). See below notes 111-13.

100. Espinas and Pirenne, Recueil (n. 56 above), I, 49, no. 20 (Aardenburg, c. 1350); 159, no. 63 (Arras, 1367); 168, no. 66:5 (Arras, 1377); 377, no. 139:54 (Bruges, 1282); 400, no. 141:25 (Bruges, 1284); 456-7, no. 142:22 (Bruges, 1290); III, 476, no. 158:14 (Ypres, ca. 1280-1300); Michel Dubois, 'Textes et fragments relatifs à la draperie de Tournai au moyen âge', Revue du Nord, XXXII (1950), 147, no. 3 (early 14th century, Tournai), 160, no. 166 (1367). Nevertheless, some Spanish wools were imported into both Flanders and England ca. 1200-ca. 1300 evidently to be used in cheap saergen. Cf. Espinas and Pirenne, Recueil, I, 389,

no. 140:6 (Bruges, 1282); Gilliodts-Van Severen, Estaple de Bruges (n. 59 above), I, 19, no. 14 (1200); 106, no. 140 (Bruges, 1303); Gras, English Customs (n. 13 above), p. 269 (Sandwich, 1303), p. 363 (Southampton, 1308).

101. Robert Lopez, 'The Origin of the Merino Sheep', The Joshua Starr Memorial Volume (Jewish Social Studies no. V, New York, 1953), pp. 161-68; Jaime Vicens Vives, Economic History of Spain (3rd ed. Princeton, 1969), pp. 250-51.

102. Julius Klein, The Mesta: A Study in Spanish Economic History, 1273-1836 (Cambridge, Mass., 1920), pp. 3-8, 12-21, 27-30, 316-25, 607; Julia de L. Mann, The Cloth Industry in the West of England from 1640 to 1880 (Oxford, 1971), pp. xvi, 257-60, 266-67; H. B. Carter, His Majesty's Spanish Flocks: Sir Joseph Banks and the Merinos of George III (London, 1964), pp. 4, 6, 9, 11, 106-09, 413, 420-22, 469.

103. E. Rossini and M. F. Mazzaoui, 'Societa e tecnica nel medioevo: la produzione dei panni di lana a Verona nei secoli XIII-XIV-XV', Atti e memorie della Accademia di Agricoltura, Scienze, et Lettere di Verona, 6th ser. XXI (1969-70), 47; Federigo Melis, Aspetti della vita economica medievale: studi nell'archivo Datini di Prato, I (Siena, 1962), 488, no. 350 (Aug. 1390).

104. Rot. Parl. IV, 126: no. 16.

105. De Sagher, Recueil (n. 99 above), II, 276-80, no. 265.

106. Gilliodts-Van Severen, Archives de Bruges (n. 59 above), IV, 496-98, no. 970 (11 Oct. 1428).

107. François Morand, ed. Chronique de Jean le Fèvre de St. Remy, II (Paris, 1876), 378.

108. H. J. Smit, ed. Bronnen tot de geschiedenis van den handel met Engeland, Schotland, en Ierland, 1150-1485, II (The Hague, 1928), 698, no. 1126. Munro, Wool, Cloth, and Gold, pp. 114-26.

109. Thielemans, Bourgogne et Angleterre (n. 71 above), pp. 473-4, no. 8.

110. Cf. De Sagher, Recueil (n. 99 above), I, 99-496; III, 93-228.

111. De Sagher, Recueil, I, 36, no. 102; III, 2; 37, no. 396; 112-20, no. 420; 304-05, no. 275; 527, no. 581; 582-85, no. 587; 611-16, no. 597; K. Höhlbaum, ed. Hansisches Urkundenbuch, X (Leipzig, 1939), 639, no. 1050; von der Ropp, Hanserecesse (n. 85 above), IV, 312, no. 444:4; L. Gilliodts-Van Severen, ed. 'Les relations de la Hanse teutonique avec la ville de Bruges', Compte rendu des séances de la Commission Royale d'Histoire, 4th ser. VII (1879-80), 216, no. 15; 233, no. 18; Favresse, Métiers bruxellois (n. 96 above), pp. 59-84; Stadsarchief te Leuven, no. 722 (keuren).

112. See n. 99 above.

113. De Sagher, Recueil (n. 99 above), III, 520-21, no. 577; 527-31, nos. 581-82; 564, no. 586:195.

114. Ibid., III, 527, no. 581.

115. Sir George Warner, ed. The Libelle of Englyshe Polycye: A Poem on the Use of Sea Power (Oxford, 1926), p. 6. Cf. also the comment of Clement Armstrong, ca. 1535, that Spanish wools even then had to be mixed with English wools to produce cloths 'of durable weryng'. R. H. Tawney and Eileen Power, eds. Tudor Economic Documents (3 vols. London, 1924), III, 102.

116. De Sagher, Recueil (n. 99 above), I, 102-05, no. 36 (Oct. 1510).

117. Cf. M. G. Willemsen, ed. 'Le règlement général de la draperie malinoise de 1544', Bulletin du cercle archéologique de Malines, XX (1910), 1-115; M. J. Lameere and H. Simont, eds. Recueil des ordonnances des Pays Bas, 2me ser. 1506-1700 (Brussels, 1910), V, 272-3 (Ghent, 1546); Stadsarchief te Brussel, nos. 1435-37 (1497-1540). See n. 64, 72 above.

118. Coornaert, Hondschoote (n. 95 above), pp. 22-43, 236-54; Van der Wee, 'Structural Changes' (n. 96 above), pp. 211-18; Florence Edler, 'Le commerce d'exportation des sayes d'Hondschoote vers l'Italie d'après la correspondance d'une firme anversoise, entre 1538 et 1544', Revue du Nord, XXII (1936), 249-65; Munro, Wool, Cloth, and Gold, pp. 1-9, 180-85.

Table 1. Purchases of Cloth Seals by the Tôwn of Ypres, Sales of the Ghent Drapery Tax Farms, and Exports of English Wool and Cloths, in Five-Year Averages, 1335-39 to 1395-99

	Ypres	Ypres	Ypres	Ypres	Ypres	Ghent	England	England
Years	Seals for dyed cloths at tentering frame	Seals for 'Dueten' cloths	Seals for medley cloths at inspection perch ('Mellés')	Seals for blue cloths at inspection perch	Seals for other dyed cloths at the Cloth Hall	Drapery tax-farm sales in pounds groot	Wool exports in sacks of 364 lb	Cloth exports in 24 x 1.75 yds
1335-9	47,400[a]				14,300[a]	114.33	22,850	4,000[b]
1340-4	33,710	10,840			11,800	120.87	19,732	6,000[b]
1345-9	33,000	3,100			12,379	107.09	n.a.	n.a.
1350-4	37,610	5,270	7,090	3,220	7,470	112.48	30,204	1,621
1355-9	43,575	1,450	23,125	9,425	4,750	110.66	32,544	7,051
1360-4	53,662		26,963	7,132	4,256	99.95	30,183	11,168
1365-9	47,374		26,550	5,189	4,728	67.78	29,603	14,804
1370-4	33,826		37,550	2,050	3,347	49.36	24,081	12,790
1375-9	23,675		46,200	3,225	104	38.64	21,659	13,000[b]
1380-4	12,082		27,993	3,183	24	23.84	18,612	19,560[b]
1385-9	n.a.		n.a.	n.a.	n.a.	n.a.	17,412	25,900[b]
1390-4	n.a.		n.a.	n.a.	n.a.	n.a.	19,543	37,200[b]
1395-9	n.a.		n.a.	n.a.	n.a.	n.a.	17,546	40,660[b]

a. 1335-36 only.

b. estimated from available and extrapolated data.

Table 2. Outputs of the Mints of England (London, York, and Calais) and Flanders (Ghent, Bruges, Mechelen, Fauquemont) in Kilograms of Pure Metal and Constant Pounds Sterling of 1351-1411 Values, in Five-Year Averages, 1335-9 to 1395-9

	Flanders			England		
Years	Gold kg	Silver kg	Total in £ sterling	Gold kg	Silver kg	Total in £ sterling
1335-9	212.4	5,748.8	31,306.2		483.1	1,865.6
1340-4	660.8[a]	883.8[a]	31,741.5[a]	188.3	3,629.6	22,088.3
1345-9	118.4	4,886.3	23,946.5	606.0	3,112.1	37,996.4
1350-4	693.9	5,761.2	51,996.2	1,743.6	15,582.7	134,925.4
1355-9	2,947.7	7,839.6	156,636.2	1,774.9	6,401.1	100,806.2
1360-4	2,673.1	4,107.6	130,454.6	2,416.1	1,858.8	110,752.1
1365-9	2,084.9	9,232.0	125,027.1	1,827.7	283.3	79,444.2
1370-4	1,828.3	8,047.2	109,451.0	958.8	198.8	41,867.9
1375-9	931.3	2,250.5	48,611.6	253.2	510.6	12,826.9
1380-4	553.5	3,711.2	38,061.1	156.2	326.2	7,957.3
1385-9	450.3	1,369.9	24,595.4	471.6	187.8	20,943.5
1390-4	483.4	4,073.1	36,453.4	635.3	300.1	28,392.9
1395-9	320.2	5,940.4	36,669.3	444.3	167.8	19,692.0

a. 16 April to 10 October 1343 only.
1 kg gold = £42.86763 sterling; 1 kg silver = £3.861948.
Ratio 11.1:1 exactly.

Table 3. Kilograms of Pure Silver and Gold Struck in the Mints of the Burgundian Low Countries, in Five-Year Averages, from 1420-4 to 1495-9

Years	Flanders	Brabant	Holland	Namur & Hainaut	Total
Silver					
1420-4	12,910.5	818.8		153.4	13,882.7
1425-9	5,090.0	36.2		746.0	5,872.2
1430-4	4,812.9	1,043.3	709.6	1,100.0	7,675.7
1435-9	4,771.6	1,155.8	979.5		6,906.8
1440-4	226.7		85.4		312.0
1445-9	12.9				12.9
1450-4	15.1		1.5	25.8	42.5
1455-9	89.4	59.9	7.8	29.2	186.2
1460-4	-	-	-	-	-
1465-9	2,073.5	1,002.2	73.7	103.6	3,253.0
1470-4	5,117.9	2,289.1			7,407.1
1475-9	3,452.1	4,985.7			8,437.7
1480-4	2,853.7	3,256.6	682.9		6,793.2
1485-9	1,070.3	4,807.5	2,397.6		8,275.4
1490-4	950.5	1,561.4	382.1		2,894.0
1495-9	1,634.8	2,357.4		336.3	4,328.5
Gold					
1420-4	11.27	3.12			14.39
1425-9	391.11	4.32	243.38	271.55	910.36
1430-4	189.52	437.63	248.01	854.12	1,729.28
1435-9	361.58	339.61	61.73		762.93
1440-4	102.73		6.71		109.43
1445-9	23.04				23.04
1450-4	161.99	60.62	19.53	104.08	346.22
1455-9	316.69	260.68	39.15	110.54	727.06
1460-4	11.12	2.63			13.75
1465-9	153.24	46.02	3.43	7.00	209.68
1470-4	74.31	21.73			96.04
1475-9	280.64	297.04			577.69
1480-4	30.68	28.99	5.65		65.32
1485-9	2.07	89.04	31.27		122.37
1490-4	8.90	36.03[a]	1.52		46.45
1495-9	69.21	43.75			112.97

a. Of the total amount of fine gold struck in the quinquennium Mich. 1489 to Mich. 1494, 232.266 kg (= 46.452 kg x 5), 111.43 kg or 48% were struck at Mechelen from 1 Oct. to 24 Dec. 1489).

Table 4. Values in Current Pounds Groot Flemish of the Silver and Gold Mint Outputs of the Burgundian Low Countries, in Five-Year Averages, from 1420-4 to 1495-9

Years	Flanders	Brabant	Holland	Namur & Hainaut	Total
Silver					
1420-4	62,560.1	3,958.6		734.9	67,253.54
1425-9	26,747.8	197.7		3,843.7	30,789.19
1430-4	25,353.5	5,692.5	3,773.2	6,163.3	40,982.46
1435-9	24,457.2	5,924.3	5,077.5		35,458.98
1440-4	1,171.7		450.4		1,622.01
1445-9	76.7				76.67
1450-4	81.4		8.8	133.2	223.43
1455-9	539.3	329.6	44.6	151.7	1,065.20
1460-4	-	-	-	-	-
1465-9	12,473.7	6,011.5	436.8	613.1	19,535.13
1470-4	30,985.8	13,770.9			44,756.71
1475-9	24,026.0	35,896.9			59,922.82
1480-4	22,759.5	25,714.1	5,206.2		53,679.77
1485-9	10,052.1	56,516.3	26,820.5		93,388.90
1490-4	6,910.8	11,551.9	2,282.9		20.745.60
1495-9	13,751.1	19,876.9		2,859.2	36,487.21
Gold					
1420-4	532.9	159.4			692.29
1425-9	23,406.2	281.3	15,707.5	17,219.7	56,614.70
1430-4	10,585.0	28,342.6	16,199.9	59,709.1	114,836.55
1435-9	20,154.1	18,929.1	3,441.3		42,524.45
1440-4	5,905.6		373.9		6,279.57
1445-9	1,337.8				1,337.83
1450-4	9,927.8	3,715.4	1,197.1	6,378.5	21,218.74
1455-9	19,408.5	15,976.4	2,399.3	6,774.4	44,558.69
1460-4	681.4	161.0			842.41
1465-9	9,929.5	2,954.5	217.6	441.2	13,545.76
1470-4	4,832.4	1,413.1			6,245.43
1475-9	21,273.5	22,516.7			43,790.16
1480-4	2,776.3	2,528.0	474.2		5,778.47
1485-9	153.6	16,136.2	3,792.5		20,082.34
1490-4	596.3	5,030.8[a]	93.8		5,720.98
1495-9	6,490.4	4,044.2			10,534.59

a. Of the total value of gold struck in the quinquennium Mich. 1489 to Mich. 1494, £28,604.91 groot (= £5,720.98 x 5), £20,807.88 gr. or 72.7% (at highly inflated values) were struck at Mechelen from 1 Oct. to 24 Dec. 1489).

Table 5. Mint Outputs in the Burgundian Low Countries in Kilograms of Pure Metal and their Values in Current Pounds Groot: Consolidated Totals in Five-Year Averages from 1420-4 to 1495-9

Years	Gold kg	Silver kg	Gold £ groot	Silver £ groot	Total £ groot	Index 1420-4=100
1420-4	14.4	13,882.7	692.3	67,253.5	67,945.8	100.0
1425-9	910.4	5,872.2	56,614.7	30,789.2	87,403.9	128.6
1430-4	1,729.3	7,675.7	114,836.6	40,982.5	155,819.1	229.3
1435-9	762.9	6,906.8	42,524.5	35,459.0	77,983.5	114.8
1440-4	109.4	312.0	6,279.6	1,622.0	7,901.6	11.6
1445-9	23.0	12.9	1,337.8	76.7	1,414.5	2.1
1450-4	346.2	42.5	21,218.7	223.4	21,442.1	31.6
1455-9	727.1	186.2	44,558.7	1,065.2	45,623.9	67.2
1460-4	13.8	-	842.4	-	842.4	1.2
1465-9	209.7	3,253.0	13,545.8	19,535.1	33,080.9	48.7
1470-4	96.0	7,407.1	6,245.4	44,756.7	51,002.1	75.1
1475-9	577.7	8,437.7	43,790.2	59,922.8	103,713.0	152.6
1480-4	65.3	6,793.2	5,778.5	53,679.8	59,458.3	87.5
1485-9	122.4	8,275.4	20,082.3	93,388.9	113,471.2	167.0
1490-4[a]	46.5	2,894.0	5,721.0	20,745.6	26,466.6	39.0
1495-9	113.0	4,328.5	10,534.6	36,487.2	47,021.8	69.2

a. See notes to tables 3 and 4.

Table 6. Values in Current Pounds Groot Flemish of One Kilogram of Pure Gold and of Pure Silver, and their Ratios, as Struck in the Mints of the Burgundian Low Countries, in Five-Year Averages, from 1420-4 to 1495-9

Years	Gold kg in £ groot	Silver kg in £ groot	Gold index 1420-24=100	Silver index 1420-24=100	Gold to silver ratio	Ratio of Burgundian and English ratios
1420-4	48.102	4.844	100.0	100.0	9.93	0.966
1425-9	62.190	5.243	129.3	108.2	11.86	1.154
1430-4	66.407	5.339	138.1	110.2	12.44	1.210
1435-9	55.738	5.134	115.9	106.0	10.86	1.056
1440-4	57.382	5.199	119.3	107.3	11.04	1.074
1445-9	58.061	5.932[a]	120.7	[122.5]	[9.79]	[0.952]
1450-4	61.286	5.263	127.4	108.6	11.64	1.132
1455-9	61.286	5.720[b]	127.4	118.1	10.71	1.042
1460-4	61.286	-	127.4	-	-	-
1465-9	64.599	6.005	134.3	124.0	10.76	0.969
1470-4	65.027	6.042	135.2	124.7	10.76	0.969
1475-9	75.803	7.102[c]	157.6	146.6	10.67	0.961
1480-4	88.468	7.902[c]	183.9	163.1	11.20	1.009
1485-9	164.109	11.285	341.2	233.0	14.54	1.310
1490-4	123.156[d]	7.168	256.0	148.0	17.18[d]	1.548[d]
1495-9	93.254	8.430	193.9	174.0	11.06	0.996

a. No change in the silver standard; but 32% of the silver metal, with 41.3% of the value of the silver coinage struck, was in double mites (courtes), 'black money', whose traite per silver marc was so much higher to account for alloys and minting costs.

b. 10% debasement of mites and double mites.

c. Between 1478 and 1483 the Antwerp mint struck silver coins that were 12.5% 'weaker' than those struck at the Flemish mints.

d. The gold:silver values and ratios are misleading because the means are so strongly biased by the Mechelen gold output of 1 Oct.-24 Dec. 1489, as explained in Table 3 note a, Table 4 note a.

Table 7. Values in Pounds Groot Flemish of One Kilogram of Fine Gold: Free Market Rates at Antwerp and Official Burgundian Mint Rates, 1420-1499

Year	Market rates at Antwerp £ gr	Official rates £ gr	Market as % of official rates	Year	Market rates at Antwerp £ gr	Official rates £ gr	Market as % of official rates
1420	46.083	47.290	97.4	1440	61.455	55.738	110.3
1421	46.104	47.290	97.5	1441	61.455	55.738	110.3
1422	46.104	47.290	97.5	1442	61.455	55.738	110.3
1423	46.296	47.290	97.9	1443	58.976	58.061	101.6
1424	48.379	47.290	102.3	1444	60.255	58.061	103.8
1425	49.603	56.783	87.4	1445	60.255	58.061	103.8
1426	49.677	64.411	77.1	1446	60.255	58.061	103.8
1427	49.677	50.672	98.0	1447	61.455	58.061	105.8
1428	53.163	50.672	104.9	1448	61.455	58.061	105.8
1429	49.841	58.835	84.7	1449	61.455	58.061	105.8
1430	49.841	58.835	84.7	1450	61.455	58.061	105.8
1431	49.841	[67.032][a]		1451	62.563	58.061	107.8
1432	49.841	[73.113][a]		1452	62.563	58.061	107.8
1433	51.738	55.738[b]	92.8	1453	62.563	58.061	107.8
1434	56.870	55.738	102.0	1454	60.255	61.286	98.3
1435	56.779	55.738	101.9	1455	61.455	61.286	100.3
1436	57.870	55.738	103.8	1456	62.563	61.286	102.1
1437	58.976	55.738	105.8	1457	62.563	61.286	102.1
1438	58.976	55.738	105.8	1458	63.710	61.286	104.0
1439	60.255	55.738	108.1	1459	63.710	61.286	104.0

(Table contd.)

Table 7 (contd.)

Year	Market rates at Antwerp £ gr	Official rates £ gr	Market as % of official rates	Year	Market rates at Antwerp £ gr	Official rates £ gr	Market as % of official rates
1460	61.455	61.286	100.3	1480	82.672	83.607	98.9
1461	62.563	61.286	102.1	1481	83.921	83.607	100.4
1462	63.710	61.286	104.0	1482	89.606	92.897	96.5
1463	66.138	61.286	107.9	1483	91.979	92.897	99.0
1464	67.259	61.286	109.7	1484	95.785	[74.318][c]	
1465	68.418	61.286	111.6	1485	99.206	102.187	97.1
1466	69.618	63.478	109.7	1486	105.219	102.187	103.0
1467	70.862	65.028	109.0	1487	114.784	121.347	94.6
1468	70.862	65.028	109.0	1488	146.199	146.199	100.0
1469	70.862	65.028	109.0	1489	204.248	204.248	100.0
1470	71.963	65.028	110.7	1490	66.138	61.931	106.8
1471	71.963	65.028	110.7	1491	73.292	61.931	118.3
1472	73.099	66.576	109.8	1492	80.283	74.318	108.0
1473	73.099	66.576	109.8	1493	85.208	82.183	103.7
1474	74.272	74.318	99.9	1494	89.896	85.734	104.9
1475	74.272	74.318	99.9	1495	94.482	86.704	109.0
1476	75.483	74.318	101.6	1496	87.352	90.704	96.3
1477	80.283	83.607	96.0	1497	85.208	90.704	93.9
1478	80.283	83.607	96.0	1498	89.896	90.714	99.1
1479	81.460	83.607	97.4	1499	94.482	94.482	100.0

a. Namur mint; no gold struck in Flanders b. From the October 1433 monetary reform c. At the rebel Ghent mint

Table 8. Mint Outputs of England (London, Calais, York, Bristol) in Kilograms of Pure Metal and their Values in Current Pounds Sterling, in Five-Year Averages from 1420-4 to 1495-9

Years	Gold kg	Silver kg	Gold £ sterling	Silver £ sterling	Total £ sterling	Index 1420-4=100
1420-4	2,387.8	1,953.7	113,732.1	9,054.0	122,786.1	100.0
1425-9	832.9	6,318.3	39,670.3	29,281.0	68,951.2	56.2
1430-4	267.7	9,006.5	12,750.6	41,738.9	54,489.5	44.4
1435-9	133.6	1,715.1	6,365.2	7,948.4	14,313.7	11.7
1440-4	107.6	271.6	5,123.2	1,258.5	6,381.7	5.2
1445-9	50.7	229.7	2,414.8	1,064.6	3,479.4	2.8
1450-4	83.8	1,578.6	3,989.5	7,315.6	11,305.1	9.2
1455-9	24.3	1,142.3	1,159.6	5,294.0	6,453.6	5.3
1460-4	82.4	2,169.4	4,502.9	10,219.8	14,722.7	12.0
1465-9	1,625.8	6,610.3	104,541.5	38,293.1	142,834.6	116.3
1470-4	598.3	2,567.1	38,470.3	14,871.3	53,341.6	43.4
1475-9	433.1	1,243.8	27,851.3	7,204.9	35,056.3	28.6
1480-4	286.4	955.9	18,416.8	5,537.5	23,954.3	19.5
1485-9	129.3	896.9	8,313.9	5,195.4	13,509.4	11.0
1490-4	n.a.	n.a.	n.a.	n.a.	n.a.	n.a.
1495-9	291.8	2,034.2	18,761.0	11,783.9	30,545.0	24.9

Table 9. Chi-Square Contingency Tables of the Outputs of the English and Burgundian Mints, in Constant Pounds Sterling of 1411-64 Values, in Five Year-Averages, 1420-4 to 1495-9

England

Years	Gold coinages		Silver coinages		Total coinage
	Recorded	Expected	Recorded	Expected	
1420-4	113,732.14	81,142.97	9,053.98	41,643.11	122,786.12
1425-9	39,670.27	45,566.34	29,280.97	23,384.95	68,951.24
1430-4	12,750.59	36,009.29	41,738.93	18,480.21	54,489.52
1435-9	6,365.22	9,459.12	7,948.44	4,854.48	14,313.66
1440-4	5,123.16	4,217.33	1,258.50	2,164.36	6,381.66
1445-9	2,414.83	2,299.36	1,064.56	1,180.04	3,479.39
1450-4	3,989.50	7,470.95	7,315.61	3,834.14	11,305.11
1455-9	1,159.62	4,264.85	5,294.02	2,188.75	6,453.64
1460-4	3,924.63	9,237.60	10,053.84	4,740.80	13,978.47
1465-9	77,438.13	71,419.58	30,634.49	36,653.00	108,072.62
1470-4	28,496.54	26,693.97	11,897.04	13,699.52	40,393.58
1475-9	20,630.62	17,442.76	5,763.94	8,951.73	26,394.56
1480-4	13,642.10	11,938.29	4,422.99	6,126.81	18,065.09
1485-9	6,158.46	6,816.58	4,156.35	3,498.31	10,314.81
1490-4	n.a.	n.a.	n.a.	n.a.	n.a.
1495-9	13,897.07	15,413.76	9,427.14	7,910.44	23,324.21
Totals	349,392.75		179,310.65		528,703.50
	= 7,335.454 kg (x 5)*		= 38,691.761 kg (x 5)*		
	66.085%		33.915%		

Chi-square = 114,088.6544 (with 14 degrees of freedom)

C = 0.4212947

1 kg gold = £47.630697
1 kg silver = £4.63433806

*Total Gold = 36,677.27 kg

*Total Silver = 193,458.80 kg

Table 9 (contd.)

Low Countries

Years	Gold Coinages Recorded	Gold Coinages Expected	Silver Coinages Recorded	Silver Coinages Expected	Total coinage
1420-4	685.50	28,707.38	64,337.20	36,315.32	65,022.70
1425-9	43,360.89	31,158.60	27,213.86	39,416.15	70,574.75
1430-4	82,366.91	52,069.74	35,571.94	65,869.11	117,938.85
1435-9	36,338.94	30,175.31	32,008.65	38,172.27	68,347.59
1440-4	5,212.47	2,939.64	1,445.87	3,718.69	6,658.34
1445-9	1,097.51	510.99	59.89	646.41	1,157.40
1450-4	16,490.84	7,367.53	196.75	9,320.06	16,687.59
1455-9	34,630.33	15,670.23	863.02	19,823.11	35,493.35
1460-4	654.70	289.05	—	365.65	654.70
1465-9	9,987.68	11,065.34	15,075.52	13,997.85	25,063.20
1470-4	4,574.60	17,174.90	34,326.86	21,726.55	38,901.46
1475-9	27,515.59	29,412.07	39,103.25	37,206.76	66,618.84
1480-4	3,111.09	15,272.82	31,482.11	19,320.37	34,593.20
1485-9	5,828.66	19,505.33	39,351.24	24,674.57	44,179.90
1490-4	2,212.59	6,898.19	13,411.92	8,726.32	15,624.51
1495-9	5,380.69	11,231.90	20,059.76	14,208.54	25,440.45
Totals	279,448.99		353,507.84		632,956.83
	= 5,866.994 kg (x 5)*		= 76,280.091 kg (x 5)*		
	44.15%		55.85%		

Chi-square = 220,458.6019 (with 15 degrees of freedom)

C = 0.5082569

1 kg gold = £47.630697
1 kg silver = £4.6343381

*Total Gold = 29,334.97 kg *Total Silver = 381,400.45 kg

Table 10. A Comparison of Long-Term Averages of Mint Outputs of England (1235-1499), Flanders (1335-1419), and the Burgundian Low Countries (Flanders included, 1420-1499) in Kilograms of Pure Metal and Constant Pounds Sterling of 1351-1411 Values

Period of the Per Annum Mean	England			Flanders-Burgundian Low Countries		
	Gold kg	Silver kg	Total value in constant £ sterling	Gold kg	Silver kg	Total value in constant £ sterling
1235-1299		14,424.92	55,708.28			
1300-1399	573.80[a]	5,699.92	46,610.40			
1270-1369	427.83[b]	9,095.69	53,467.21			
1370-1469	581.19	1,726.19	31,580.64			
1335-1369	1,222.37[c]	4,478.66	69,696.89	1,455.07[d]	6,262.59[d]	86,561.14[d]
1335-1399	882.78[e]	2,541.68	47,658.36	1,108.12[f]	5,247.32[f]	67,767.38[f]
1370-1469	581.19	1,726.19	31,580.64	475.14	3,440.32	33,654.51
1400-1499	549.64	2,133.18	31,800.17	297.83	4,077.49	28,514.42

a. Average of 100 years; from striking of gold in Jan. 1344 to 1399 (56 years), annual average of 1,024.65 kg
b. Average of 100 years; for 1344-69 (26 years), annual average of 1,645.51 kg gold
c. Average of 35 years; for 1344-69, annual average as in b above
d. Quinquennium 1340-4 omitted, since account of Apr.-Oct. 1343 alone survives; if used to estimate average of 1340-4, the amounts would be: 1,341.61 kg gold, 5,494.20 kg silver; £78,872.60
e. Annual average of 1344-99= 1,024.65 kg gold.
f. If surviving account of Apr.-Oct. 1343 used to estimate average of 1340-4, overall average for 1335-1339 would be: 1,073.71 kg gold, 4,911.66 kg silver; £65,073.08

Constant pounds sterling: 1 kg gold = £42.8676271; 1 kg silver = £3.8619484

Table 11. Indices of Mint Output Values and of Prices in the Burgundian Low Countries and England, in Five-Year Averages, from 1420–4 to 1495–9, with the average of 1420–4 as base 100

	Burgundian Low Countries			England	
Years	Mint output index (current £ groot)	Van der Wee price index Flanders	Van der Wee price index Brabant	Phelps Brown & Hopkins price index	Mint output index (current £ sterling)
1420–4	100.0	100.0	100.0	100.0	100.0
1425–9	128.6	110.1	113.1	106.2	56.2
1430–4	229.3	109.1	118.9	114.5	44.4
1435–9	114.8	116.7	140.8	114.3	11.7
1440–4	11.6	99.9	121.7	102.8	5.2
1445–9	2.1	97.5	118.8	97.4	2.8
1450–4	31.6	89.3	108.8	101.4	9.2
1455–9	67.2	108.1	131.6	95.8	5.3
1460–4	1.2	89.5	109.0	100.0	12.0
1465–9	48.7	90.9	110.7	107.0	116.3
1470–4	75.1	92.3	112.4	99.6	43.4
1475–9	152.6	107.4	130.8	87.9	28.6
1480–4	87.5	145.4	177.0	129.8	19.5
1485–9	167.0	159.4	194.1	100.8	11.0
1490–4	39.0	134.7	164.0	106.2	n.a.
1495–9	69.2	108.0	131.5	95.2	24.9

Table 12. Textile Production and Trade in the Burgundian Low Countries: Number of Stall Rentals in the Ypres Cloth Halls; Drapery Tax Farm Sales in Ypres, Ghent, Mechelen and Leuven; and Exports of English Wools and Cloths, in Five Year Averages, 1400–4 to 1500–4

Years	Ypres Drapery stalls	Ypres Tax farm £ groot	Ghent Tax farm shill. gr.	Mechelen Tax farm £ groot	Leuven Tax farm Rijngulden	English Woolsack exports	English Cloth exports
1400–4	n.a.	n.a.	110.3	309.7	2,385	12,552	n.a.
1405–9	414.5	272.9	146.1	295.9	2,990	12,997	30,332
1410–4	406.0	267.7	137.5	310.2	2,518	12,684	27,516
1415–9	502.0	269.7	177.8	296.5	1,588	13,515	28,834
1420–4	423.0	266.1	156.9	382.8	1,126	13,401	36,395
1425–9	364.4	255.3	195.1	395.9	757	13,255	41,510
1430–4	320.0	236.2	153.1	305.0	570	7,508	40,860
1435–9	216.4	172.8	88.7	176.2	541	3,236	42,898
1440–4	187.2	174.3	82.6	221.1	417	9,759	56,944
1445–9	159.2	175.3	103.6	175.2	286	6,592	49,448
1450–4	109.0	154.1	75.1	165.4	344	7,769	37,380
1455–9	73.2	150.9	36.1	158.3	216	7,266	37,542
1460–4	61.8	103.0	25.0	168.3	193	5,315	30,934
1465–9	71.4	91.5	37.0	187.2	271	7,944	35,130
1470–4	73.6	82.5	54.0	215.3	263	7,575	35,725
1475–9	58.8	72.5	49.4	256.4	282	7,950	45,115
1480–4	21.8	65.6	34.4	254.3	328	7,160	55,184
1485–9	10.5	103.7	9.5	290.6	786	8,021	48,516
1490–4	-	100.3	3.0	234.9	672	5,734	56,797
1495–9	-	134.6	7.4	256.3	587	9,444	59,502
1500–4			12.6	264.2		7,028	78,590

Table 13. Textile Production and Trade in Flanders: Sales of Tax Farms for the Hondschoote Sayetterie, Kortrijk Linens, and Dendermonde Flax in livres parisis;* and Rentals of Stalls for Non-Woollen Textiles in the Ypres Cloth Halls, in Five-Year Averages, 1400-4 to 1505-9

Years	Hondschoote Sayetterie £ parisis	Kortrijk Linens £ parisis	Dendermonde Flax £ parisis	Ypres Stall rentals for non-woollens
1400-4	54.40	42.92	74.04	n.a.
1405-9	56.00	64.13	80.16	73.5
1410-4	90.40	92.00	93.96	45.5
1415-9	111.20	92.14	86.40	39.9
1420-4	141.60	96.80	102.96	43.5
1425-9	164.00	143.60	106.20	57.6
1430-4	170.00	198.31	n.a.	51.9
1435-9	n.a.	213.16	n.a.	42.0
1440-4	180.00	312.80	n.a.	42.4
1445-9	250.00	502.80	198.36	64.6
1450-4	329.60	304.80	131.76	69.0
1455-9	392.00	347.20	187.08	71.0
1460-4	392.00	426.60	207.96	63.4
1465-9	435.20	462.80	285.60	79.0
1470-4	456.00	371.60	320.88	82.8
1475-9	440.00	308.63	288.00	60.0
1480-4	400.00	260.80	248.40	69.8
1485-9	510.00	177.90	197.28	85.6
1490-4	n.a.	162.50	135.00	76.5
1495-9	368.00	164.60	191.76	78.8
1500-4	552.00			
1505-9	660.00			

* £12 parisis = £1 groot

Table 14. Prices of Woollen Cloths in the Burgundian Low Countries: Five-Year Averages in Pounds Groot Flemish, 1400-4 to 1495-9

Years	Ghent Dickedinnen	Ypres Fine dyed	Bruges Fine whites	Kortrijk Dyed 30 ells	Various Nouvelles Draperies	Neuve-Eglise 30 ells	Leuven Cloths made from non-English wools
1400-4	5.919			3.238	3.118		2.303
1405-9	5.922	5.419	4.500	3.421	3.263		2.544
1410-4	5.793	5.334	4.710	3.435	2.881		2.638
1415-9	5.935	5.517	4.720	3.424	2.646		2.618
1420-4	6.082	5.060	4.260	3.550	2.637		2.433
1425-9	6.063	5.359	4.500	3.917	2.700	1.935	2.729
1430-4	6.835	6.000	5.290	4.187	3.675	2.165	3.037
1435-9	7.281	6.468	5.333	3.750	3.750	2.083	2.710
1440-4	7.765		7.400	4.285	3.778	2.172	2.707
1445-9	7.925	7.694	7.300	4.038	3.380	2.263	2.511
1450-4	6.950	7.583	8.000	4.000	3.594	2.316	2.228
1455-9	7.702	7.907	8.000		3.306	2.037	2.208
1460-4	8.000	7.510			3.075	2.428	2.305
1465-9	8.100	7.671			3.125	2.002	2.359
1470-4	8.642	7.773				1.771	2.350
1475-9	8.875	7.667				1.900	2.453
1480-4	10.348	10.190				2.250	2.830
1485-9	14.893	11.487					
1490-4	16.233	12.233					
1495-9	14.667	13.411					3.382

Table 15. Indices of Cloth Prices and of Van der Wee's "Composite Unit of Consumables"[a] in the Burgundian Low Countries, in Five-Year Averages, 1400 to 1495-9 (1420-4 = 100)

Years	Van der Wee price index	Ghent Dickedinnen	Ypres Fine dyed	Bruges Fine white	Kortrijk 30 ells (dyed)	Various Nouvelles Draperies	Leuven Cloths of non-English wools
1400-4	92.0	97.3			91.2	118.2	94.7
1405-9	97.4	97.4	107.1	105.6	96.4	123.7	104.6
1410-4	91.0	95.2	105.4	110.6	96.8	109.3	108.4
1415-9	102.1	97.6	109.0	110.8	96.5	100.3	107.6
1420-4	100.0	100.0	100.0	100.0	100.0	100.0	100.0
1425-9	110.1	99.7	105.9	105.6	110.3	102.4	112.2
1430-4	109.1	112.4	118.6	124.2	117.9	139.4	124.8
1435-9	116.7	119.7	127.8	125.2	105.6	142.2	111.4
1440-4	99.9	127.7		173.7	120.7	143.3	111.3
1445-9	97.5	130.3	152.1	171.4	113.7	128.2	103.2
1450-4	89.3	114.3	149.9	187.8	112.7	136.3	91.6
1455-9	108.1	126.6	156.3	187.8		125.4	90.8
1460-4	89.5	131.5	148.4			116.6	94.7
1465-9	90.9	133.2	151.6			118.5	97.0
1470-4	92.3	142.1	153.6				96.6
1475-9	107.4	145.9	151.5				100.8
1480-4	145.4	170.1	201.4				116.3
1485-9	159.4	244.9	227.0				
1490-4	134.7	266.9	241.8				139.0
1495-9	108.0	241.2	265.0				

a. converted to Flemish groots

Table 16. Domestic Prices of Better Quality English Wools, Values of English Cloths Exported from London and Southampton, Sales Prices of Ghent Dickedinnen Cloths, Expressed in Pounds Sterling, with Price-Relatives, in Five-Year Averages, 1400-4 to 1495-9

Year	Prices in Pounds Sterling			Price-Relatives: 1420-4 = 100			
	English wool sack of 364 lb	English cloth 24x1.75 yds	Ghent cloth	Phelps Brown index	English wool	English cloth	Ghent cloth
1400-4	5.572	1.666	5.647	115.1	108.5	69.4	96.8
1405-9	6.057		5.650	104.4	117.9		96.9
1410-4	6.236		7.206	110.3	121.4		123.5
1415-9	4.652		6.872	114.7	90.6		117.8
1420-4	5.136	2.402	5.833	100.0	100.0	100.0	100.0
1425-9	4.859	2.001	5.675	106.2	94.6	83.3	97.3
1430-4	5.546	2.464	5.874	114.5	108.0	102.6	100.7
1435-9	5.550	2.729	6.597	114.3	108.1	113.6	113.1
1440-4	5.204	2.295	7.035	102.8	101.3	95.5	120.6
1445-9	5.610	2.731	7.180	97.4	109.2	113.7	123.1
1450-4	4.514	2.037	6.297	101.4	87.9	84.8	108.0
1455-9	4.132	2.062	6.978	95.8	80.5	85.8	119.6
1460-4	4.394	2.215	7.248	100.0	85.6	92.2	124.3
1465-9	5.906	1.866	8.388	107.0	115.0	77.7	143.8
1470-4	5.285	2.096	8.340	99.6	102.9	87.3	143.0
1475-9	6.143[a]	2.382	7.535	87.9	119.6	99.2	129.2
1480-4	7.779	2.723	7.272	129.8	151.5	113.4	124.7
1485-9	8.671[b]	2.905	7.366	100.8	168.8	120.9	126.3
1490-4	5.742	2.494	11.422	106.2	111.8	103.8	195.8
1495-9	5.308	2.802	9.833	95.2	103.3	116.7	168.6

a. 1478 only; b. 1485 only.

Table 17. Correlations of the Value of the Burgundian Low Countries' Mint Outputs in Pounds Groot Flemish with the Van der Wee Price Index (Flemish groots), Lagged by One Year, 1420-1499

Statistic	1420-1499	1435-1463	1435-1479	1435-1499
N	71	22	36	56
d.f.	69	20	34	54
r	0.26774	0.56838	0.44165	0.40128
r^2	0.07169	0.32305	0.19505	0.16103
Critical Level				
5%	0.23352	0.42280	0.32918	0.26327
1%	0.30383	0.53687	0.42388	0.34155
t-statistic	2.30833	3.08940	2.87031	3.21939
Sign. Level	2.39831%	0.57821%	0.70059%	0.21756%
Regression				
a	171.4221	159.4891	156.9738	166.0143
b	+0.000218	+0.000310	+0.000238	+0.000416
Mean of X	63,421.872	35,274.541	47,639.442	52,626.950
s.d. of X	51,106.472	47,904.148	45,145.609	44,460.404
Mean of Y	185.223	170.427	168.314	187.905
s.d. of Y	41.535	36.135	24.872	46.087

N = number of pairs of mint output values and Van der Wee price indices, lagged by one year, correlated. Only years with mint outputs were correlated: 1420-47, 1454-62, and 1466-99.

d.f. = degrees of freedom

r = correlation coefficient

r^2 = coefficient of determination

a = Y-intercept

b = slope

X = value of Burgundian mint outputs in pounds groot Flemish

Y = Van der Wee price index, lagged one year

Critical level: minimum value of r that is significant and not the result of the sampling distribution (standard error) of r, allowing 1% and 5% possibility of error

Table 18. Correlations of Van der Wee's Price Index (in Flemish groots) with the Values of One Kilogram of Pure Silver and Gold Coined, in Pounds Groot: Five-Year Averages, 1420-4 to 1495-9

Statistic	XY Silver and Price Index	ZY Gold and Price Index	XZ Silver and Gold
N	16	16	16
d.f.	14	14	14
r	0.76476	0.82093	0.91901
r^2	0.58486	0.67392	0.84458
Critical Level			
5%	0.49740	0.49740	0.49740
1%	0.62267	0.62267	0.62267
t-statistic	4.44108	5.37907	8.72215
Sign. Level	0.05589%	0.00972%	0.00005%
Regression			
a	51.05135	67.75014	2.46293
b	9.24187	0.55905	0.05178
Means of X and Z	6.367	75.385	75.385
s.d. of X and Z	1.689	29.971	29.971
Means of Y and X	109.894	109.894	6.367
s.d. of Y and X	20.410	20.410	1.689

X = value of 1 kg pure silver coined, in Flemish pounds groot

Y = Van der Wee Price Index, in Flemish groots

Z = value of 1 kg pure gold coined, in Flemish pounds groot

N = pairs of quinquennial means correlated (XY, ZY, XZ)

SOURCES FOR THE TABLES

Note that all tables, except Table 7, employ a Michaelmas financial year, ending on 29 September. Table 7 uses a regular calendar year.

1. Table 1: The Ypres and Ghent draperies; English wool and cloth exports, 1335-99.

(a) Ypres: Georges Espinas and Henri Pirenne, eds. Receuil de documents relatifs à l'histoire de l'industrie drapière en Flandre, 1er partie, (4 vols. Brussels, 1906-20), III, 809-34, no. 910.

(b) Ghent: Ibid., II, 624-25.

(c) England: Eleanora Carus-Wilson and Olive Coleman, England's Export Trade, 1275-1547 (Oxford, 1963), pp. 45-54, 75-87; E. M. Carus-Wilson, "Trends in the Export of English Woollens in the Fourteenth Century", Medieval Merchant Venturers: Collected Studies (London, 1954), pp. xviii (and graph facing), 239-64.

2. Table 2: Flemish and English Mint Outputs, 1335-99.

(a) Flanders: (i) 1335-1384: Victor Gaillard, ed. Recherches sur les monnaies des comtes de Flandre, II: Sous les règnes de Louis de Crécy et de Louis de Mâle (Ghent, 1856); Hans Van Werveke, De muntslag in Vlaanderen onder Lodewijk van Mâle (Mededelingen van de koninklijke Vlaamse Academie voor Wetenschappen, Letteren, en Schone Kunsten van België, Klasse der Letteren, no. XI:5, Brussels, 1949). Not included are some Mechelen accounts recently discovered by Prof. Wim Blockmans; but I have made extrapolations for some of the missing accounts. (ii) 1384-1399: Algemeen Rijksarchief (België) [hereafter ARA], Rekenkamer, nos. 48, 976-77 (Mechelen); Comptes en rouleaux, nos. 2142-43, 2145-46 (Mechelen); nos. 824-26 (Ghent), nos. 776-87 (Bruges); nos. 2586-87 (Fauquemont). Cf. John H. Munro, Wool, Cloth, and Gold: The Struggle for Bullion in Anglo-Burgundian Trade, 1340-1478 (Brussels and Toronto, 1973), pp. 187-97.

(b) England: C. G. Crump and C. Johnson, "Tables of Bullion Coined Under Edward I, II, and III", The Numismatic Chronicle, 4th ser. XIII (1913), 200-45; C. G. Brooke and E. Stokes, "Tables of Bullion Coined from 1377 to 1550", The Numismatic Chronicle, 5th ser. IX (1929), 27-69; Terence H. Lloyd, The English Wool Trade in the Middle Ages (Cambridge, 1977), p. 241, table 15: 'Gold minted at Calais, 1363-1404'.

3. Tables 3 to 6: Burgundian Mint Outputs, 1420-1499.

(a) Ghent: ARA, Comptes en Rouleaux no. 831; Acquits de Lille nos. 936-37; Rekenkamer, nos. 580, and 18,195-200; Archives départementales du Nord (Lille) [hereafter ADN], Série B.1606, fo. 32v-3r.

(b) Bruges: ADN, nos. 19,960 and 19,312; Série B. no. 1606; ARA, Rekenkamer, nos. 18,103-124; Acquits de Lille no. 1512.

(c) Mechelen: ARA, Acquits de Lille, no. 1512; Rekenkamer no. 18,242.

(d) Leuven: ARA, Rekenkamer, nos. 18,067-072.

(e) Brussels: ARA, Rekenkamer, nos. 17,986-989.

(f) Antwerp: ARA, Rekenkamer, nos. 17,880-882.

(g) Holland: Dordrecht, Zevenbergen, The Hague: Algemeen Rijksarchief van der Nederlanden, Rekeningen van de grafelijkiedsrekenkamer, nos. 4937: I-XVIII; P. O. Van der Chijs, De munten der voormalige graafschappen Holland en Zeeland (Haarlem, 1858), corrected by Peter Spufford, Monetary Problems and Policies in the Burgundian Netherlands, 1433-1496 (Leiden, 1970), pp. 184-85.

(h) Valenciennes: ADN, B.17,651; Serie B.31; 19,975/19,402; ARA, Acquits de Lille, nos. 937, 1512; Spufford, Monetary Problems, p. 184 (for 1455-56).

(i) Namur: ARA, Rekenkamer, nos. 18,203-204.
Cf. Munro, Wool, Cloth, and Gold, pp. 187-97 (for accounts up to 1480).

4. Table 7: Burgundian Gold Values, 1420-1499 (calendar years)

Herman Van der Wee, The Growth of the Antwerp Market and the European Economy, Fourteenth to Sixteenth Centuries (3 vols. The Hague, 1963), I, 123-33; and the mint account sources cited for Tables 3-6.

5. Table 8: English Mint Outputs, 1420-1499

G. C. Brooke and E. Stokes, "Tables of Bullion Coined from 1377 to 1550", The Numismatic Chronicle, 5th ser. IX (1929), 27-69; F. A. Walters, "Supplementary Notes on the Coinage of Henry VI", The Numismatic Chronicle, 4th ser. XI (1911), 171-72; Public Record Office (LTR) E. 364/59, 61-3, 65-66, 69, 72; and (KR) E.101/192-93 (for Calais); and Calendars of the Patent Rolls, 1422-1429, pp. 337-38, 502; CPR 1429-36, pp. 256-57, 259 (for Calais). Statistics for the Tower Mint have been corrected for the years 1432, 1433 by information in Sir John Craig, The Mint: A History of the London Mint from A.D. 287 to 1948 (Cambridge, 1953), pp. 408, 412.

6. Tables 9-10: Chi-Square Contingency Tables and Long Term Averages of English, Flemish, and Burgundian Mint Outputs. See the sources cited for Tables 2-6 and 8.

7. Table 11: English and Burgundian Mint Outputs and Price Indices

(a) England: E. H. Phelps Brown and Sheila V. Hopkins, "Seven Centuries of the Prices of Consumables, Compared with Builders' Wage-Rates", Economica, new series, XXIII (1956), reprinted in E. M.Carus-Wilson, ed. Essays in Economic History, II (London, 1962), 194.

(b) The Low Countries (Brabant): Herman Van der Wee, "Prijzen en lonen als ontwikkelingsvariabelen: Een vergelijkend onderzoek tussen Engeland en de zuidelijke Nederlanden, 1400-1700", Hulde aan Charles Verlinden (1976), pp. 413-47. See also the sources for mint outputs cited for tables 3-6 and 8.

8. Table 12: Textile Production and Trade in the Low Countries, 1400-99.

(a) Ypres: ARA, Rekenkamer, nos. 38,635-722 (municipal accounts).

(b) Ghent: Stadsarchief te Gent, Stadsrekeningen, Reeks 400:11-38.

(c) Mechelen: Stadsarchief te Mechelen, Stadsrekeningen nos. 76-190; ARA, Rekenkamer, nos. 41, 219-272 (municipal accounts).

(d) Leuven: Stadsarchief te Leuven, Stadsrekeningen, nos. 5006-124.

(e) England: Carus-Wilson and Coleman, England's Export Trade, pp. 55-72, 87-115.

9. Table 13: Textile Production and Trade in the Low Countries, 1400-1499

(a) Hondschoote: Emile Coornaert, Un centre industriel d'autrefois: la draperie-sayetterie d'Hondschoote, XIVe-XVIIIe siècles (Paris, 1930), appendix, pp. 485-91.

(b) Kortrijk (Courtrai): ARA, Rekenkamer, nos. 33,153-243 (municipal accounts).

(c) Dendermonde: ARA, Rekenkamer, nos. 37,981-056 (municipal accounts).

(d) Ypres: ARA, Rekenkamer, nos. 38,635-722 (municipal accounts).

10. Tables 14 and 15: Flemish and Brabantine Cloth Prices, 1400-1499

(a) Ghent: Stadsarchief te Gent, Stadsrekeningen, Reeks 400:11-34.

(b) Ypres: ARA, Rekenkamer, nos. 38,635-722.

(c) Bruges: Stadsarchief te Brugge, Stadsrekeningen 1400-1499; and ARA, Rekenkamer, nos. 32,461-549 (municipal accounts).

(d) Kortrijk, Neuve-Eglise (Nieuwkerk), and Other Nouvelles Draperies: Wervik, Roeselare, Commines, Menen, Messines, Niepkerk, Montreuil, Hesdin, Lille, Armentières, and Diest (Brabant): prices recorded at Bruges and the Franc de Bruges (Brugse Vrij), in ARA, Rekenkamer, nos. 32,461-536 (Bruges municipal accounts), nos. 42,521-563 (accounts of the Franc); Stadsarchief te Brugge, Stadsrekeningen 1400-1485.

(e) Leuven: Stadsarchief te Leuven, Stadsrekeningen, nos. 5006-124.

(f) Van der Wee price index: see sources for table 11.

11. Table 16: Prices of English Wools, English Cloths, Ghent Cloths

(a) English wools: T. H. Lloyd, The Movement of Wool Prices in Medieval England (Cambridge, 1973), pp. 40-44, cols. 3-5, 10-13: wools from Berkshire and Berkshire and Wiltshire Downs, Hampshire (Winchester), Worcestershire, Cotswolds, Chilterns, Northeast Oxfordshire, and North Buckinghamshire.

(b) English cloths: Public Record Office, K.R. Exchequer Accounts Various, Particular Customs Accounts, E.122/76/13, 74/11, 77/11, 77/4, 73/23, 73/25, 194/14-18, 78/7, 79/5 (London); E.122/139/4, 139/7-8, 141/4, 141/21-2, 209/1, 141/25, 140/62, 141/29, 141/31, 141/33, 141/35-36, 209/8, 141/38, 142/8, 142/10, 143/1, 142/11-12 (Southampton); L.T.R. Enrolled Customs, E.356/19-24, for export prices at London and Southampton.

(c) Ghent Cloths: see sources for tables 14 and 15.

(d) Price Indices: see sources for table 11.

12. Tables 17 and 18: Correlations

See the sources for tables 3-8 and 11.

LA POLITIQUE MONÉTAIRE EN FLANDRE DES DUCS DE BOURGOGNE DE LA MAISON DE VALOIS, 1384-1430.[1]

Pierre Cockshaw

J'ai souhaité, dans cette communication, soulever un seul problème: dans quelle mesure, entre 1384 et 1430, le duc de Bourgogne en qualité de comte de Flandre puis de Namur, de régent de Hainaut et de Hollande et enfin de duc de Brabant a-t-il tenté d'élaborer, de réaliser, de diriger une politique monétaire cohérente, dans quelle mesure a-t-il été aidé, guidé et conseillé par l'administration, les Etats, les Villes ou les marchands.

La thèse volontariste, la croyance à une "politique des monnaies" a été défendue par H. Laurent dans La loi de Gresham au moyen âge, puis suivie par H. Van Werveke dans De Vlaamse Munthervorming avant d'être adoptée par Marc Bloch. Pour ceux-ci, les dévaluations flamandes entre 1386 et 1390 étaient sciemment provoquées par le duc Philippe le Hardi dans le but de créer des difficultés économiques au duché de Brabant et de le rendre ainsi plus docile à la Flandre.

Au contraire, je n'ai trouvé dans les décisions prises par les ducs Philippe le Hardi, Jean sans Peur et Philippe le Bon qu'incohérence et incompréhension des phénomènes monétaires.

Quelques exemples serviront à illustrer mon propos:

1. Depuis août 1388, le duc Philippe le Hardi avait décidé la frappe en Flandre, de nobles d'or imités du noble anglais. Peu après, il avait accordé, à la demande des membres de Flandre, la libre circulation du noble anglais en Flandre à la condition "que ce feust a tel pris comme les nostres". Le noble anglais, monnaie internationale, étant plus apprécié sur le marché, vit son cours haussé par rapport au noble flamand. Le duc réagit le 6 octobre 1397 en interdisant le cours des nobles anglais en Flandre. L'argument principal était que les nobles flamands étant "aussi bons et de aussi bon or et poix et alloy ou meilleur comme sont lesdiz nobles d'Engleterre", mais dépréciés de fait, ces pièces étaient exportées comme billon et vendues à la monnaie de Calais. Mais cette interdiction posait des problèmes commerciaux graves et presqu'immédiatement les Membres de Flandre, les députés de Bruges, Gand, Ypres et du Franc demandèrent la levée de cette mesure. En vain!
   Ils revinrent à la charge de multiples fois avant de voir le duc, le 31 juillet 1400, accepter enfin la libre circulation du noble anglais. Mais ce qui est frappant, c'est que les arguments avancés pour autoriser son cours sont les mêmes que ceux utilisés pour décider de son interdiction: les marchands flamands ont besoin de nobles anglais pour leurs achats de laine. La circulation de ces pièces étant interdite en Flandre, ils

doivent en acheter à Calais et "tout l'or que l'en peut forgier en noz monnoies a Bruges s'en va hors de nostredit pays et est en grande partie porté audit lieu de Calais".
Mais il y a mieux encore que cette volte-face. Car la raison principale de l'interdiction des nobles anglais n'est pas à chercher dans des raisons monétaires ou commerciales mais dans l'orgueil et la vanité blessée. C'est que le roi d'Angleterre s'est permis d'interdire le cours des nobles flamands en Angleterre alors pourtant que le poids et l'aloi de ces pièces est bon. Ainsi le roi anglais se permet de porter atteinte à l'un des attributs essentiels de la souveraineté, le droit de frapper monnaie. C'est là plus que ce qu'un duc de Bourgogne fils, frère et oncle de rois peut tolérer.

2. Le duc Jean sans Peur décidait, par son ordonnance de décembre 1416 au si mélancolique préambule, de dévaluer ses monnaies d'or et d'argent. Il y était obligé, rappelait-il, par les dévaluations des monnaies françaises et anglaises et les émissions des mauvaises monnaies hollandaises et liégeoises. Mais en même temps qu'il dévaluait les monnaies d'or en poids et d'argent en aloi, il augmentait dans des proportions incroyables son propre seigneuriage. Comme si le duc Jean avait espéré, à la faveur de la crise monétaire et de la dévaluation, s'assurer une source de revenus énormes et renflouer ainsi le déficit des finances ducales. C'est à une réaction rapide et décidée des villes que l'on doit de voir cette mesure rapportée et de prendre des mesures plus conformes aux intérêts du pays.

3. Le duc Philippe le Bon enfin frappe, en qualité de comte de Flandre, de la monnaie relativement bonne, bien meilleure en tous cas que celle frappée dans les états voisins de la Flandre; mais le même Philippe, en qualité de comte de Namur, fait forger de la mauvaise monnaie, imitée, d'un poids et d'un aloi toujours inférieur. Voilà un prince qui volontairement, et dans le but d'augmenter ses revenus, frappe de la mauvaise monnaie destinée à inonder les états voisins et donc la Flandre, à chasser la bonne monnaie et à lui permettre, parce que sa monnaie est mauvaise, de percevoir de plantureux bénéfices. Cette méthode lui permettait, bien sûr, de s'assurer d'importantes rentrées d'argent et de ne pas devoir quémander des aides aux Etats de Flandre, toujours désireux de limiter les pouvoirs des princes. Mais à quel prix?

Rien, en conclusion, ne vient confirmer la thèse défendue par H. Laurent, H. Van Werveke ou M. Bloch.

Au contraire, les ducs paraissent éprouver la même incompréhension que celle qu'avouait Gilles Li Muisis, à comprendre les phénomènes monétaires: "En monnoie est li cose moult obscure, Elle vont haut et bas, se ne set on que foire, Quand on quide wagnier, on troeve le contraire".

Mais que penser de ceux qui les entouraient, et devaient les conseiller? C'est un chancelier que la correspondance de la Chambre des Comptes nous révèle ingénu en problèmes monétaires; ce sont des conseillers que les rapports nous révèlent désemparés. Au contraire, les seuls avis compétents qui parviennent aux ducs ont pour origine la chambre des comptes, le personnel monétaire et les Membres de Flandre. C'est-à-dire de ceux-là même dont Marc Bloch avait cru pouvoir remarquer[2] qu'ils concevaient la politique de l'Etat "sous les couleurs de celle qu'ils considéraient comme la plus profitable pour eux-mêmes" !

NOTES

1) On ne trouvera ici que le résumé de ma communication. Je prépare, en effet, une étude plus détaillée consacrée à la politique monétaire en Flandre des ducs de Bourgogne entre 1384 et 1433, ouvrage qui sera accompagné de la publication d'ordonnances monétaires et de comptes de la monnaie.

2) Annales, 1953, p. 157.

THE FLEMISH MONETARY POLICY OF THE DUKES OF BURGUNDY OF THE HOUSE OF VALOIS, 1384-1430[1]

Pierre Cockshaw

I hope in this paper to take up a single problem: to what extent, between 1384 and 1430, did the duke of Burgundy as count of Flanders, and then of Namur, as regent of Hainaut and of Holland, and finally as duke of Brabant, attempt to develop, achieve and direct a coherent monetary policy, and how far was he helped, guided and advised by the administration, the Estates, the towns and the merchants?

The 'voluntarist' thesis, the belief in a firm monetary policy has been defended by H. Laurent in La Loi de Gresham au moyen age, followed by H. Van Werveke in De Vlaemse Munthervorming before being adopted by Marc Bloch. For these scholars, the Flemish devaluations between 1386 and 1390 were consciously instigated by duke Philippe le Hardi with the intention of creating economic difficulties in the duchy of Brabant and thus rendering Brabant more amenable to Flanders.

In contrast, I have found only incoherence and misunderstanding of monetary phenomena in the decisions taken by the dukes Philippe le Hardi, Jean sans Peur and Philippe le Bon.

Some examples will serve to illustrate my thesis:

1. From August 1388, duke Philippe le Hardi had decided to strike in Flanders gold nobles imitating the English noble. Soon afterwards, at the request of the Members of Flanders, he granted free circulation of the English noble on condition 'that it would pass at such a price as our own.' But the English noble, an international currency, being more in demand on the market, saw its rate rise in relation to the Flemish noble. The duke reacted on 6 October 1397 by prohibiting the flow of English nobles into Flanders. The principal argument was that the Flemish nobles were 'as good, and of as good gold and weight and alloy, if not better than the said nobles of England,' but they were less valued and were exported as bullion and sold to the mint of Calais.

But this prohibition posed several commercial problems and almost immediately the Members of Flanders, the deputies of Bruges, Ghent, Ypres, and le Franc demanded the lifting of this measure. In vain.

They returned to their complaint many times before seeing the duke finally accept the free circulation of the English noble on 31 July, 1400. But what is striking is that the arguments advanced to authorise the circulation of the noble are the same as those used to justify its prohibition: the Flemish merchants needed English nobles for their wool purchases. The circulation of these pieces being prohibited in Flanders, they were obliged to buy them in Calais and 'all the gold which can be struck in our mints at Bruges leaves our own said country and is in great part carried to the said place of Calais.'

But there are still better examples than this volte-face. For the principal reason for the prohibition of English nobles is not to be looked for in monetary or commercial theory but in pride and wounded vanity. It is because the king of England took the liberty of prohibiting the circulation of Flemish nobles in England even though the weight and alloy of these pieces was good. Thus the English king allowed himself to sully one of the essential attributes of Burgundian sovereignty, the right to strike coin. That was more than a duke of Burgundy—son, brother and uncle of kings—could tolerate.

2. Duke Jean sans Peur decided by his ordinance of December 1416, in an extremely melancholy preamble, to devalue his gold and silver coinage. He had been obliged to do this, he recalled, by the devaluation of French and English money and the issues of bad money from Holland and Liege. But at the same time as he devalued his gold coin in weight and his silver in alloy he increased his own seignorage an incredible amount. Thus Duke Jean had hoped by means of the monetary crisis and the devaluation to provide himself with an enormous source of revenue and thus retrieve the deficit in the ducal finances. It was only as a result of rapid and decisive action by the towns that this measure was rescinded and action more in line with the interests of the country taken.

3. Duke Philippe le Bon, as count of Flanders, eventually struck relatively good money, much better at any rate than the issues of Flanders' neighbour states. But Philippe himself as count of Namur, had bad, imitative money struck at an altogether inferior weight and alloy. Here is a prince who voluntarily, in order to increase his revenues, strikes bad money intended to inundate neighbouring states, including Flanders, to drive out good money and to allow him, because the money is base, to collect plentiful profits. Certainly this method permitted him to acquire an important income of silver, without having to seek the help of the Estates of Flanders who always sought to limit the power of princes. But at what price?

In conclusion, nothing can confirm the thesis defended by H. Laurent, H. Van Werveke or M. Bloch. On the contrary, the dukes seem to demonstrate the same lack of understanding of monetary phenomena as Gilles Li Muisis who asserted: 'Money is a difficult thing, Coins go high and low, When one looks for a gain, one finds the reverse.'

But what are we to think of those who surrounded and had to advise the dukes? There is a chancellor, revealed by the correspondence of the Chambres des Comptes as ingenuous in monetary problems; there are the advisers revealed by the reports to be helpless. By contrast the only competent advice which reached the dukes originated with the Chambre des Comptes, the mint personnel and the Members of Flanders. That is to say the very people of whom Marc Bloch remarked[2] that they saw the policies of the state 'in the light of what they considered most profitable for themselves.'

NOTES

1. This is only a résumé of the paper read at the Symposium. My more detailed study of monetary policy in Flanders under the dukes of Burgundy between 1382 and 1433 which will include the publication of monetary ordonnances and mint accounts is in preparation.

2. Annales, 1953, p. 157.

CALAIS AND ITS MINT: PART ONE

Peter Spufford

In this first part I am concerned with the broad historical outline of the role played by the mint of Calais in the fourteenth and fifteenth centuries.[1] In the second part Peter Woodhead is much more concerned with the detail of the coins and their issue. It is intended that the two parts be read together as a complementary whole. The reader will, however, observe differences in emphasis and opinion between the two parts.

It is in many ways paradoxical to include Calais and its mint in a symposium on 'Coinage and Economic Development in the Low Countries', for although Calais lay geographically within the Low Countries (in the county of Boulogne), it was an essentially English town, for long the Staple for English wool. Similarly its mint was almost exclusively concerned in the production of English coin, for circulation in England. Unlike the mint of the king of France at Tournai, it did not strike large quantities of coins of Low Countries types for circulation in the Low Countries.

The mint at Calais was open for the production of English coin over two distinct periods of time.[2] The first account for English coin from the Calais mint begins on 20 February 1363, and the last firm date for this period of its operation is the account ending on 30 March 1403. It is, however, possible that it went on working for a further year.[3] In this first period the Calais mint primarily struck English gold nobles. The first mint account of the second period begins on 20 July 1422,[4] and the last payment of seignorage from the mint was made for the year 1439-40. Again there is a lack of clarity about a precise end date for the mint's operations. It was probably open, but inactive, for one or possibly two more years before being finally closed.[5] In this second period the Calais mint primarily struck English silver groats and half-groats.

It was by no means a negligible mint. At its busiest, around 1365, and again around 1430, its production of coin greatly exceeded that of the London mint, and, in the latter period, also of the mint of Flanders at Ghent.

Thus, for an initial period of forty years, and then again for a second period of twenty years, a major European mint operated in a town in which next to nothing had ever been minted before, and where there was to be no mint afterwards. Put as bluntly as this, it is quite apparent that the Calais mint was an artificial creation.

Its creator was Edward III and it was part of the package involved in transferring the English wool staple from Bruges to Calais in 1363. In 1363, Calais had already been in English hands for sixteen years, since it had been captured in 1347, after a protracted siege, following the Crécy campaign in the previous year. Calais had already become an English town to a certain extent, with not only an English garrison, but also a strong colony of English burgesses. It was an ideal port for Englishmen wishing to go to the continent, whether Edward III himself at the head of an English army in 1359, or English merchants with wool or cloth to sell in the Low Countries. From 1353 to 1359 the English cloth staple had already been fixed there during a period of strained Anglo-Flemish relations.

When peace with France was at last agreed in 1360 Edward III found himself in possession of vast lands in France, all of which, except Calais, could be made to pay for themselves. Calais, however, even with a reduced peacetime garrison, looked as if it was going to be a perpetual drain on Edward's finances. He could hardly abandon it. It was too useful, and besides had cost too much effort to acquire. However, if the still lucrative and highly taxed wool trade between England and Flanders could be made to pass through Calais, it would make the town financially independent of the Crown.[6] The chanelling of the wool trade through Calais, as well as solving the problem of how to pay the garrison, also provided a solution to a dispute that had troubled the English wool trade for the previous forty years—whether it should be regulated in England, or on the continent. Should the exporters of English wool be compelled to take it to a single continental staple, whilst free to make their way thither as they liked; or should sellers be compelled to take the wool to one of a number of regional staples inside England ? Since Calais was both English, and on the continent, it had the merit of partially satisfying the advocates of a continental staple, and those of home staples. 'Partially' because the advocates of home staples were not immediately entirely convinced that Calais was in England, and from 1365 to 1369 a compromise was therefore adopted involving both home staples and a Calais staple. As a 'continental' staple Calais, in the second half of the fourteenth century, thus took over one of the functions that Bruges had normally performed in the first half of the century. It was, however, an artificial division of functions, for Bruges still remained the real market for English wool, and Calais was, in some sense, no more than a compulsory outport to it, connected to it by the road through Gravelines and by such coasting vessels as could enter the Zwin.

When there had been a continental staple, an obligation had rested on the exporters of English wool to convert any money or bullion that they brought back with them into English coin on their return to England. When there had been home staples, the obligation fell on the buyers to convert their purchase money into English coin before buying the wool. Either way round the regulations were designed to ensure that only English coin circulated in England. At the time that the Staple was moved to Calais in 1363 these regulations were by and large effective. If the Durham hoard and the Beaumont hoard from Cumberland, both deposited about this date, are reliable indicators, and they may not be, being so very far to the north of England, English coin formed no less than ninety-nine per cent of the silver in circulation. Continental sterlings had sunk to a mere one per cent of the currency.[7]

In the thirteenth and the first half of the fourteenth century the largest quantities of foreign coin and bullion were exchanged at the royal exchanges in London and at Canterbury, which was conveniently situated at the point where the roads converged from Sandwich and the other English Channel ports. It was then minted at the mints associated with these exchanges. No other mints than those at London and Canterbury had access to such a quantity of foreign metal, and no other mints produced English coin in significant quantities. The production figures printed by Crump and Johnson show that the quantity minted at Canterbury shrank from 1318 to 1329, in parallel with that at London. There was usually more minted at Canterbury, sometimes less.[8] This decline in minting corresponded to the deterioration in England's balance of trade down to 1322-36, when the country became a net exporter of precious metal.[9] It is no wonder that Canterbury, previously the key mint for the import of precious metal should have suffered. Moreover because of the opening of the Hundred Years War the recovery of wool exports during the 1330s failed to bring in any extra bullion to the English mints, which remained in a state of near idleness. The earnings of the wool trade were almost wholely diverted to be spent abroad on behalf of the king from 1336 to at least 1343, and probably until after the end of the expensive Calais campaign in 1347.[10] The last known account of the Canterbury mint comes to an end in December 1346 after more than two decades of virtual inactivity. There seems to have been some sort of plan to open a replacement mint at Calais a few months later, immediately after its capture by the English, but nothing seems to have come of this.[11] It was not yet an opportune moment, and when in the 1350s there were sometimes once again positive balances of payments, the enormous quantities of coin struck were all produced at the London mint. It was however still a decade of uncertainty, when funds were repeatedly diverted from the wool trade, and money was sent abroad for military purposes, as it was, for instance, to finance the expeditions of 1357 and 1359. It was not until the peace of 1360 that 'normality' was restored, for the first time in forty years. It was in this new peace time situation that the decision was made to remove the staple to Calais. Such a decision made it necessary to re-examine whether the current provision of exchanges and mints was adequate. Instead of the longer crossing from London to Bruges, the short channel crossing to Calais from Sandwich now looked particularly attractive, and there was no longer any exchange or mint at Canterbury to intercept foreign coin or bullion which might enter England this way. The removal of the Staple to Calais was no sudden move under pressure of circumstances. It had been planned from at least May 1361 and premises had been built before the move took place in February 1363.[12] At the same time the abortive plans for an English mint at Calais were revived, but in very different and much more opportune circumstances. There was now a positive balance of trade, much of it about to be compelled to pass through Calais, and there was no longer the likelihood of it being dissipated by military expenditure. It is little wonder that in the 1360s the newly opened Calais mint rapidly took the place that the Canterbury mint had occupied at the beginning of the century as the principal funnel through which England's positive balance of payments was transformed into English coin.

There was some ambiguity about who should supply this new mint with bullion. Was it to be the English shippers of wool, as it had been when the staple had been held on the continent? Or was it to be the foreign buyers, as when the staple had been held in England? Initially the obligation was laid on the Staplers. It took the same form as that imposed on their predecessors in 1340, that they bring two marks of bullion to the mint for every sack of wool that they had shipped. This was soon extended to an obligation that all foreign coins brought to the staple were to be reminted, and that only English money was to be current in Calais.[13] This effectively transferred the obligation to the buyers, and it was later made explicit that buyers exchange their bullion or foreign coin for English coin, before purchasing wool. This satisfied the exporters, who had long complained that in Flanders they had been paid in foreign coin that was overvalued in English terms.[14]

Because in the fourteenth century the wool was only partially paid for in ready money it is quite impossible to establish any direct relationship between the scale of minting at Calais, and the scale of export of wool through Calais. The rest of the payment for the wool was made in bills payable at Bruges and so became immediately involved with England's overall balance of payments. It would not be proper to re-open this debate. It was thoroughly discussed two years ago by T. H. Lloyd at the symposium on Edwardian Monetary Affairs. He then concluded that, in the early 1360s, when the Calais mint was opened:

> 'English exports were earning more than £300,000 a year overseas and that no more than half of this, possibly less than half, was required to pay for the import of commodities. The balance was available for overseas expenditure by the crown or by private persons, or for repatriation in the form of specie'.[15]

He went on to suggest that this positive balance was greatly diminished, if not actually reversed, in the following years, particularly by the enormous costs of twenty years of unsuccessful defensive war from 1369 onwards. However, he ended by saying that, in the last years of the century England once more had a favourable balance of trade.[16]

No-one has yet attempted to draw up a balance of the payments leaving or entering England either in the two difficult opening decades of the fifteenth century, or in the two rather more affluent decades that followed. However, Professor Gray many years ago produced a tentative balance for the middle of the fifteenth century. He felt that this showed that in the 1440s, even after the Calais mint had closed, England still had a positive balance of payments.[17] This is a view that has more recently been endorsed by Mme. Desmed-Thielemans.[18]

In those periods in which England did have a positive general balance of payments, gold or silver necessarily came into England. Since the Staplers' wool was England's largest single export, unbalanced by any import on their part, a large proportion of any overall favourable balance came through their hands. The mint at Calais, however much it may have been an artificial creation of Edward III, thus came to be on the route by which continental gold or silver reached England.

Professor Munro's major work has demonstrated very clearly why at different times one metal should be preferred for payment at particular periods rather than the other. He has shown why, for example, the favourable balance coming into England from the mid 1420s to 1440 should be paid in silver, whilst that of the late 1380s and the 1390s had been paid in gold.[19] This correlates very neatly with the preponderance of silver, and of gold, respectively, struck at Calais at exactly these periods, as Mr. Woodhead explains in more detail.[20]

Extension of Professor Munro's principles backwards in time similarly explains why the balances of the 1360s were also largely paid in gold. Once again this correlates with the preponderance of gold in the early issues of the Calais mint at that time. Before the large-scale penetration of gold into north-western Europe in the 1330s, all earlier favourable balances, such as those which passed through the Canterbury mint, were, of necessity, paid in silver.

It is possible to illustrate from English hoard evidence how in large measure the coins struck at Calais did actually come into England. Of 130 'Treaty' and 'post-Treaty' nobles deposited in the 1370s in the East Raynham hoard, thirty-five had been minted at the Calais mint, nearly thirty per cent of the total. A rather higher proportion of Calais pieces was to be found among the nobles of the same period in the Bredgar hoard, deposited a decade later.[21] The surviving accounts suggest that the 'Treaty' and 'post-Treaty' nobles struck in the Calais mint formed just over 40% of the total coinage of such nobles.[22] The proportion of Calais nobles in these hoards although lower, is not appreciably lower than the mint proportion. It would need many more hoards to be able to guess how high the proportion of Calais nobles entering England was, but these two hoards are, nevertheless, suggestive.

Not only did the genuine Calais nobles largely circulate in England, but, from 1388 onwards, they were supplemented by the imitative Flemish nobles struck for Philip the Bold at the Ghent mint at the request of the échevins of Ghent.[23] In Lloyd's opinion English wool was undoubtedly sold to Flemings at Calais for these nobles, rather than for newly acquired Calais nobles as the English law required.[24] The Flemish nobles accompanied the Calais ones into England. They appear in English hoards of the 1390s, were proclaimed against in 1392, and formed the subject of a parliamentary petition in 1401,[25] but were largely removed from circulation, along with the English nobles that they had imitated, by the recoinage of 1412.[26]

The Holwell hoard, from Leicestershire, probably buried in the 1420s, provides an example of the circulation of Calais coin in midland England during the period when the Calais mint was primarily minting silver. In this hoard there were 277 Calais groats of Henry VI, as against 59 London groats and 2 York groats; and 56 Calais half-groats of Henry VI, as against 8 London half-groats.[27]

A certain number of silver coins of Calais have been found in hoards in the Low Countries, but I would like to suggest that in many cases they did not come directly into circulation from Calais, but by way of England. English silver coins were not to be found in hoards deposited in the Burgundian Netherlands in the 1420s and 1430s when the Calais mint was open.[28] On the other hand, 86 English silver coins were found in the hoards deposited at Venraij, Flushing and Zandvoorde in the 1480s, more than forty years later. 42 of these had been minted at Calais.[29] I would tentatively suggest that they had gone from Calais to England when they were newly minted, and remained there until after 1466 when the comparative advantages offered by the differing gold: silver ratios in England and the Burgundian Netherlands were reversed.[30] After 1466 merchants certainly attempted to bring English silver coin into the Burgundian Netherlands. Between 1466 and 1469 English groats, or stoters as they were called in the accounts, were the coins most frequently seized in

Flanders by those attempting to enforce the currency regulations against prohibited pieces.[31]

This, however, is the posthumous history of the Calais mint. It was crippled by the siege of Calais in 1436 which temporarily brought trade to a total standstill, and suffocated from 1439 onwards by Philip the Good's deliberate prohibition of the export of any bullion to Calais,[32] backed up by the intimidating activities of his officials who seized illicit bullion from travellers at Gravelines on their road to Calais. Bullion seizures continued until at least April 1442, which implies that at that date merchants were still seeking to carry bullion to Calais, although there is no positive evidence of the operation of the mint after 1439/40.[33]

Although this brings my general narrative to a close, there remain a number of particular questions which seem important to discuss. Why did the Calais mint close in or about 1404? Why, having closed, did it re-open in 1422? and Why, having again closed, in or around 1440, did it not similarly re-open once more in the 1460s?

Professor Munro has characterised the competition for bullion between English and Low Country mints in the twenty years before 1404 as the 'War of the Gold "Nobles" '. He concluded that, surprisingly, it was Philip the Bold, the Burgundian ruler of Flanders, who won this war, despite the bias in favour of silver in the bullion prices offered at his mints.[34] Mr. Lloyd has taken up Professor Munro's notion of mint competition for limited supplies of bullion, and with additional evidence of the production of the Calais mint, which Professor Munro was unable to find,[35] concluded that on the contrary, it was the English who 'won the war', as indeed they should have done, in view of the bias in favour of gold in the bullion prices offered in the English mints. On his figures the London and Calais mints between them struck approximately 36,000 Troyes Marcs of gold into nobles between 1384 and 1402, whilst the combined mints of the Burgundian Netherlands only struck about 22,000 marcs of gold in the same period, much of it also into nobles. In this same period of time the mints of the Burgundian Netherlands struck approximately twenty-two times as much silver as their English counterparts.[36]

This fits much more with natural expectations arising out of the relative mint-ratios which so strongly favoured gold in England and silver in the Low Countries. Even though the Low Countries mints did not produce more gold than the English ones, it is still surprising that they produced as much as they did. However it is quite clear that it was produced in the Low Countries for circulation in England. No evidence has been found that the exodus of his newly minted Flemish nobles caused Duke Philip any concern before 1397.[37]

Was there in fact really a war at all? or rather was it not a war against an increasing scarcity of precious metals in Europe, rather than a war between two 'countries' for control of the diminishing stock of gold. Professor Munro brought out the 'great scarcity of money' that afflicted both England and Flanders.[38] This brought about the drastic decline of the minting in Flanders of silver, its preferred metal, from 1397, and in London and Calais of gold, their preferred metal, from 1399. The 'great scarcity' became so severe in 1402 that the Flemish mints had to close for lack of bullion, and the Calais mint essentially had to close for the same reason in the next year or two. It was not that the Burgundians had brought about the closure of the Calais mint by a successful 'guerre monétaire', it was rather that the English and the Burgundians alike were the common victims of a general bullion famine. In a very recent panoramic survey, Dr. Day has not only beautifully documented what many historians have for some time suspected, that there was a general European bullion famine in the later middle ages, but has also pinpointed its timing to the last years of the fourteenth century, and the first years of the fifteenth century.[39] He has shown that not only were the mints of Flanders and Calais closing in 1402, but that almost all the mints of France had already closed by that date, and that even in the silver producing island of Sardinia the mints were also closed. Even in Florence, Europe's most important banking centre, no silver could be found for minting. He attributes this famine to the radical decline in the production of European silver mines, and the interruption in the gold trade across the Sahara, combined with the continuation on a large scale of the export of precious metals to the Levant.

Dr. Day concludes that, in Europe in general, the worst of his crisis was over by about 1415-20. This fits with the particular circumstances of Calais. There was some silver again in Flanders as early as 1410-12, but it did not last, and minting really only got under way again in 1420. In England there was a general recoinage in 1412. In the next two years most of the stock of gold in England passed through the process of re-minting,[40] but then the earlier negligible level of minting was resumed. It was only in 1418 that a genuine growth in the production of coin at the London mint began. All this time the Calais mint remained closed. The Calais mint was nominally included in the arrangements for the recoinage of 1412, but nothing came of it, since there was no large stock of old nobles on hand there in need of recoining. However, by 1420 there was not only more precious metal about in Flanders and England, but peace was also restored in that year, so that such funds as were being generated by the stagnant wool trade were no longer diverted to finance Henry V's war efforts. Peace also highlighted the problem of paying the garrison at Calais in exactly the same way as it had done after the peace of 1360. Indeed the garrison threatened to mutiny unless paid. The statute to re-establish the Calais mint was part of the response to this problem, just as it had been sixty years before, and now that there was bullion about once more it was possible for the mint to reopen in 1422.

The particular circumstances of Calais in the late 1430s brought the activity of its mint to a close rather earlier than other European mints, but the second, and more severe, bullion famine of the following years brought practically every other European mint to a standstill as well.

After being closed for eight and seventeen years respectively the Flemish and Brabançon mints at Bruges and Malines re-opened in 1454 to recoin the gold circulating in the Burgundian Netherlands. One aspiration expressed in a Commons' petition of that year about the management of the Calais staple was that 'money should be coined in the King's mint there, and from thence be carried and spread in the realm to pay the growers of wool ... the lack whereof was greatly hurtful to the commonwealth.'[41] Just as Calais had been unable to share in the English recoinage of 1412, so it was now again unable to share in this Burgundian recoinage of 1454. In a recoinage a 'national' mint primarily depended on the amount of coin currently circulating in the whole country, but the Calais mint was never in this position. Instead it had to draw its supplies of precious metal from the flow from the Netherlands to England, and for this 1454 was no more propitious than 1412. Even though the heavy government expenditure on the war in France had come to an end the previous year, the English balance of payments still seems to have been in a deplorable state and growing worse. From around 1446 English overseas trade had been suffering from violent fluctuations. There was a dramatic and continuing shrinkage not only in the immediately relevant wool exports of the Staplers, but also in cloth exports and in the shipping of goods paying poundage.[42] The Calais mint could not re-open, and the mints at Bruges and Malines closed again once the recoinage was over. The second European bullion famine grew worse still, until by the early 1460s there was not only an almost total lack of silver and gold, but also a considerable shortage of black money as well.[43]

The combination of new discoveries, technical improvements and the injection of south German capital into mining brought about the opening up of new silver mines in central Europe from the mid-1460s and the re-opening of others that had earlier been abandoned. Silver once more began to be mined in considerable quantities and became available for minting. There was a very sudden end to the bullion famine and the mints of western Europe were able to re-open. Why did the Calais mint not share in this general revival? Anglo-Burgundian trade was reviving at the same time and the conditions look ripe for the re-opening of the Calais mint, but it did not happen. The combined reforms of the coinages of England by Edward IV and of the Low Countries by Philip the Good and Charles the Rash between 1464 and 1467 meant that the relationships between gold and silver in England and the Low Countries swung back again to favour gold in England and silver in the Low Countries. Any balance in favour of England was therefore likely to be paid in gold, and in favour of the Low Countries in silver. Both seemed to have happened. English silver groats have been found in subsequent hoards in the Low Countries, and others were confiscated by ducal officials on their way into Flanders.[44] Since the Calais mint was not opened to convert them into English money the gold coins from the Low Countries were not intercepted, but entered England and have been found in at least one English hoard, despite all the traditional prohibitions against the circulation of foreign coin in England. In the Fishpool hoard, from Nottinghamshire, deposited at about the time of Edward IV's monetary reforms, there were 166 Burgundian pieces among a total of 1237 gold coins. Only four of these were nobles and half-nobles that had entered the country in the late fourteenth century and escaped the recoinage of 1412. All the remainder had come into the country much more recently. There were 135 gold Lions, the most recent Burgundian coins, part of the recoinage for which the mints of the Low Countries had been temporarily re-opened in the mid-1450s, and 27 gold Riders, struck mostly in the 1430s, before the bullion famine had closed the Burgundian mints.[45] The new Burgundian gold pieces struck after the monetary reform of 1466, the florins of St. Andrew, also circulated in England, to such an extent that it became worth while to forge them. The confession of John Stafford of Middlewich in Cheshire, when arraigned before the Lord Mayor of York, is most interesting in this respect.

> 'John Stafford...there confessed and shewed how he was abiding and inhabited within the maner of Wynfeld, in Derbyshire, belonging to therle of Shrewsbury, late decessid, in which maner the said John did find certain conyng yrens...bering the print of the Duch coigne callid Saint Andrew, with the which yrens he hath coigned and set the prynts of the said irins opon laton gilted by the space of a yere or moo, and thoght to have uttered theme to suche as he might, and over that he confessid that he had coigned hertofore in Derbyshire, wherupon he was indited, for the which he did purchesse a speciall chartour undre the Kings brood seal of England'[46]

It is not at all clear when the forgery began. If his testimony is not itself a fabrication, he had found dies made by, and presumably already used by, an earlier forger, before he started his own counterfeiting. I have not yet tracked down the indictment that brought his first spell of illicit coining to an end, but the subsequent pardon was enrolled in the Patent Rolls on 1 September 1473. His second experiment with forgery came to an end on 17 December 1484 when he was arrested in York with a hundred pieces of coined laton on him, 'which he thoght to have gilted and utterd within this Citie, and othre places, in the grete disseit and hurt of the Kings people'. If his own confession is not false, he had taken up forgery again only in the previous year. The implication is that enough florins of St. Andrew had reached Derbyshire by the early 1470s, if not earlier, for it to be worth forging them, and that sufficient still remained in circulation in York ten years later for it to be worthwhile to try again. Unfortunately no sizable hoard of gold coins, buried in the 1470s or 1480s, has yet been found in England. It is therefore not possible to guess at how large a proportion of the gold coin then circulating in England was made up of florins of St. Andrew. One stray example was found at Wiston in Suffolk in 1854.[47]

Had there been a mint at Calais it is much less probable that such a quantity of lions and riders as were found in the Fishpool hoard, or of the florins of St. Andrews that tempted John Stafford to forge them, would have come into circulation, in England. It would have been possible to mint gold again in Calais in the late 1460s. It remains a puzzle why it was not done. At some point the decision must have been taken to abandon the traditional English policy of insisting that all foreign coin be reminted and not permitted to circulate in England. Fourteen years ago I probably wrongly suggested that this radical decision was made in 1469, in the negotiations leading up to the monetary convention of that year, which permitted the free circulation of English coin in the Low Countries, and of Burgundian coin in England.[48] Commercial discussions, with or without a monetary content, had lasted on and off for two years,[49] but even before this the lions and riders found in the Fishpool hoard had been permitted to come into England, and to circulate here. It seems that the 1469 convention did not mark the beginning of the circulation of Burgundian coin in England, but merely its regularisation.[50] Although the political reversals of 1469-71 prevented any formal ratification of the 1469 agreements, they seem to have been effective. One corollary was the abrogation of the Calais bullion ordinances by Edward IV in 1473, after his restoration to the English throne with Burgundian aid. The Staplers were no longer to be bound to exact the whole, or even a large part, of the price of the wool that they sold, in ready money, paid at Calais. This dismantling both of the obligation to transform Burgundian coin into English, and to pay over large quantities of ready money at Calais removed the necessity of reopening the Calais mint.

It still remained nominally in existence until the sixteenth century, and its mastership was held in plurality with that of the Tower mint. It is just possible that an extremely brief and minor revival of minting at Calais may have taken place in 1539,[51] but the real possibility of reopening it as a major mint was not in the 1530s, but in the 1460s, and was deliberately turned down. The Cely Papers show very clearly the pattern of what happened instead. Staplers nominally received half of the payment for the sales of their wool in cash. However, only a part of this half was paid over in actual coin at Calais, the remainder was to be paid at Bruges against short term bills. The other half was also paid at Bruges, but against longer term bills. The larger part of the Staplers' receipts were therefore not in cash at all, and the export of wool was no longer England's major export. The great revival, and indeed expansion, of English exports from the 1460s was led by cloth, not wool, as in the past. Yet, even if cash played a minor part in the sales of the Staplers, and their sales no longer played the major role that they had done, there was still some flow of cash into England through Calais. In the absence of a mint at Calais the Celys' notes of 'Redey money by me', as jotted down in Calais in the late 1470s and the 1480s could no longer consist of details of newly minted English coin. Instead they listed a great variety of coin from the Netherlands and beyond, in which English money played a negligible part.[52] From 1479 their correspondence shows them sending Burgundian silver double patards into England, for by then the relative values set on gold and silver in the two countries again favoured the sending of silver from the Low Countries into England. Letters of 1479, 1481, 1482 and 1484 show them sending home sums of £10, £12, £23 and even £40 or £50 in what they called 'carolus', 'carowlles', 'carolles', 'carlys', 'carlyche' or 'carleche' groats—the double patards struck by the late duke, Charles. At the beginning, in 1479, they were not well received, but by 1481 they were particularly sought for and were used by Richard Cely for making wool purchases in the Cotswolds. Double patards went on circulating in England until the 1530s, and hoards from the 1480s and the 1490s suggest that Burgundian double patards may have then formed as much as a fifth of the silver coin circulating in England.[53]

The silver double patards shipped from Calais into England in the 1480s were only the latest in a long line of coins which had flowed into the country whenever the overall balance of payments had been in England's favour. They had been preceded in the 1450s and 1460s by gold lions and florins of St. Andrew, in the 1420s by English groats minted in Calais, in the 1390s by Flemish nobles, in the twenty years before that by English nobles minted in Calais, and even before that by large quantities of unknown coins reminted into English pennies at Canterbury after their arrival in England.

NOTES

1. I am indebted to my colleague Dr. Robin Studd for reading my part of this paper in draft.

2. It had earlier struck a very limited amount of coin for Edward III as king of France, see below p. 185 and S. E. Rigold, 'Une trouvaille dans un puits à la cathédrale d'York', Bulletin de la Société Française de Numismatique, xxxiii (1978), 394-6.

3. T. H. Lloyd, The English Wool Trade in the Middle Ages, (Cambridge, 1977), p. 245, [henceforth Wool Trade].

4. John H. Munro, Wool, Cloth and Gold. The Struggle for Bullion in Anglo-Burgundian Trade 1340-1478 (Brussels/Toronto, 1973), pp. 188-93.

5. Peter Spufford, Monetary Problems and Policies in the Burgundian Netherlands 1433-1496 (Leiden, 1970) [henceforth Monetary Problems and Policies].

6. I am indebted to Lloyd's Wool Trade for this interpretation of the move of the staple to Calais, as well as for a great deal of the background to this paper.

7. J. D. A. Thompson, Inventory of British Coin Hoards A.D. 600-1500 (London, 1956). Hoards numbered 149 and 38.

8. C. G. Crump and C. Johnson, 'Tables of Bullion coined under Edward I, II and III', Numismatic Chronicle, 4th ser., xiii (1913), 200-245.

9. T. H. Lloyd, 'Overseas Trade and the English Money Supply in the Fourteenth Century', Edwardian Monetary Affairs (1279-1344), ed. N. J. Mayhew, British Archaeological Reports, 36 (Oxford, 1977), 103-8 [henceforth 'Trade and Money Supply'].

10. Idem, pp. 108-110.

11. See below p 184.

12. Lloyd, Wool Trade, p. 210.

13. John H. Munro, op.cit., p. 39.

14. Lloyd, Wool Trade, p. 240.

15. Lloyd, 'Trade and Money Supply', p. 115.

16. Ibid., pp. 116-121.

17. H. L. Gray, 'English Foreign Trade from 1446 to 1482', Studies in English Trade in the Fifteenth Century, ed. E. Power and M. M. Postan (London, 1933), pp. 10-20.

18. M-R. Thielemans, Bourgogne et Angleterre 1435-1467 (Brussels, 1966), pp. 362-4.

19. Munro, op.cit. This is a major theme of the book, but see especially Graphs III and IV, pp. 71 and 97, and Graph I, p. 48.

20. See below, pp. 187-8.

21. Thompson, op.cit., hoards numbered 151/157 and 57.

22. Crump and Johnson, art. cit.

23. Munro, op.cit., p. 47.

24. Lloyd, Wool Trade, p. 244.

25. Peter Spufford, 'Continental Coins in Late Medieval England', British Numismatic Journal, xxxii (1964), pp. 129-132.

26. For example only 4 of the 63 nobles in the Horsted Keynes hoard, from Sussex, of around 1430, antedated the recoinage, and none of these was Flemish. Thompson, op.cit., hoard no. 194.

27. Thompson, op.cit., hoard no. 192.

28. This is not really surprising in view of the proportional values then set on gold and silver by the English and Burgundian mints. Whilst silver from Flanders was feeding the Calais mint in the 1420s, gold nobles from England were circulating in Flanders. Complaints of the loss of English gold to Flanders were made in parliament in 1423 and 1429 and a significant number of English nobles have been found in Burgundian coin hoards from this period. Spufford, Monetary Problems and Policies, pp. 58-9.

29. Jaarboek voor Munt- en Penningkunde, xlv (1958), 155-161; Tijdschrift ...voor Munt- en Penningkunde, viii (1900), 215-232; Revue Belge de Numismatique, lxiv (1908), 254ff.

30. Munro, op.cit., particularly Graph VI, p. 156.

31. Spufford, Monetary Problems and Policies, pp. 121-2.

32. This was in part a counter-measure to the English requirement, under the ill-conceived Bullion Ordinances of 1429 and 1433, that all the traditional elements of credit be eliminated from payments for the Staplers' wool and 'the hool paiement be made in hand'. Munro, op.cit., p. 84ff.

33. Spufford, op.cit., pp. 98-104; and Munro, op.cit., p. 191, who printed the production figures for the Calais mint that I failed to find. They are reproduced below, pp. 192-8, and show how rapidly minting declined in the 1430s.

34. Munro, op.cit., pp. 43-63.

35. Both Professor Munro's production figures for the Calais mint, and those of Mr. Lloyd, are reprinted in Appendix I (below pp. 192-8), together with the long known figures originally printed by Crump and Johnson.

36. Lloyd, Wool Trade, p. 246, and 'Trade and Money Supply', p. 119.

37. Munro, op.cit., p. 52, and also above p. 163 for evidence recently found by M. Cockshaw.

38. Munro, op.cit., pp. 48 and 58-61.

39. John Day, 'The Great Bullion Famine of the Fifteenth Century', Past and Present, lxxix (1978), 3-54. Professor Munro discusses this monetary contraction in greater detail above, pp. 95-161, particularly in its long term consequences.

40. The recoinage was intended to take in both gold and silver. However a great deal of the silver coin in circulation was too worn and light to make it worth while for its owners to have it reminted. It therefore continued in circulation, as the Attenborough (c. 1420) and Terrington (c. 1425) hoards bear witness. Marion M. Archibald, 'The Attenborough, Notts., 1966 Hoard', British Numismatic Journal, xxxviii (1969), 50-83.

41. Rotuli Parliamentorum, v, 276.

42. H. L. Gray, 'English Foreign Trade from 1446 to 1482', Studies in English Trade in the Fifteenth Century, ed. E. Power and M. M. Postan (London, 1933), pp. 20-38.

43. See Chapter 11 of my forthcoming book on money and its use in mediaeval Europe.

44. See above, pp. 175-6 and notes 29-31.

45. Marion M. Archibald, 'Fishpool, Blidworth (Notts.), 1966 Hoard', Numismatic Chronicle, 7th ser., vii (1967), 135-145.

46. York Civic Records, ed. Angelo Raine. Yorkshire Archaeological Society, Record Series, xcviii (1939), 106-8.

47. Archaeologia, xlvi (1881), 270, note 1. I am indebted to Dr. Michael Metcalf for this reference.

48. Peter Spufford, 'Burgundian Double Patards in Late Medieval England', British Numismatic Journal, xxxiii (1964), 111-114.

49. Munro, op.cit., pp. 171-176. Professor Munro's description of the 1469 convention and mine are complementary. They were written independently and both need to be read to gain a full impression of it.

50. Marion Archibald, art.cit., p. 139.

51. T. F. Reddaway, 'The English Royal Mint at Calais', British Numismatic Journal, xxxiv (1965), 124-5. C. E. Challis, The Tudor Coinage (Manchester, 1978), p. 6, describes the evidence of actual minting at Calais as very slender indeed. He points out, however (p. 9), that the idea of minting at Calais was still in the air in 1545.

52. There are a number of such lists of 'Redey Money by me' among the unpublished part of the Cely Papers. They were not included in Mrs. Alison Hanham's edition, since she confined herself to the letters. I quoted one such list, of c. 1478 (Public Record Office, London, C.47/37/15/14) in my Monetary Problems and Policies, p. 67.

53. Spufford, art.cit., pp. 114-117.

CALAIS AND ITS MINT: PART TWO

P. Woodhead

In the preceding pages Peter Spufford has brought out the main points in the economic history of Calais as an English mint town situated on the mainland of Europe. When I was asked by the organisers of the symposium to write a complementary paper on the administrative history of the Calais mint itself and on its numismatic history and significance, I readily agreed for both are well known and it seemed just a question of summarising the evidence largely scattered through a good many volumes of periodical literature. In the event I have been led into studies that are nowhere near complete, nor can be completed in the immediate future. My revised present purpose is therefore to write a short note drawing together the most salient facts that are known about the Calais mint and its coins, pointing the way to where more detailed accounts are presently available and, more important, highlighting where further work and research is certainly necessary.

Perhaps the most important fact, which is seldom recognised, is that there are three main periods to consider. The first, lasting only a very short time from 1347, may be termed the 'French period'. The second, or 'English period' commences in 1363 and lasts to about 1440. The third, or 'Unknown period' refers to 1539.

A. THE FRENCH PERIOD

Previous histories of the Calais mint have all recited the records relating to its opening in 1347 and passed straight on, for no coins were known.[1] Now that at least two specimens are known to survive from this first period, it needs briefly to be looked at again.

Calais fell to Edward III on 3 August 1347. Only two months later, on 20 October 1347, he granted to William de Salop the office of keeper of the dies or assayer there.[2] Four months later still, a further order dated 6 February 1348 provided that the moneyers should make 'white' money (i.e. of good silver, not billon) as made in England and of the same weight and alloy as English coins.[3] No coins of English type are known that can be attributed to this period, and it is quite likely that none were ever struck. The plan to operate a mint at Calais was apparently not abandoned, however, for a writ was sent on 28 May 1349 to the Captain of Calais ordering him to strike coin to suit local needs as he deemed necessary.[4] Moreover, a year later, on 5 May 1350, an indenture between the king and the merchants of Calais testified that the king had ordered money to be struck 'of gold and silver, white and black, agreeing in stamp, weight, alloy and all other things with the money of France.'[5] It must be acknowledged that this entry was cancelled on the roll because it was surrendered and testimony given that nothing was done thereon,[6] but that statement could be ambiguous.

Was nothing done about striking coins of French type or perhaps was it that the merchants did not fulfill their part of the bargain and so became unentitled to receive the benefits due to them under the agreement? There are now known coins of Calais closely copying the doubles tournois issued by Philip VI of France in 1348-49.[7] Two specimens are recorded. The first is in poor condition, so much so that three distinguished French numismatists in the last century not only read it incorrectly but also differently from each other.[8] A second specimen recently discovered is in even worse condition, but from the pair it is now clear that the obverse legend is an abbreviation of Edwardus Dei Gratia Angliæ et Franciæ Rex, with Moneta Calesis on the reverse.[9]

While these are the only coins that can presently unequivocably be put to this first period of the Calais mint, there are some other possible candidates. One was reported to have the reverse legend as Moneta Calesie, but must be regarded with reserve.[10] At this time coins in the name of King Edward were struck in profusion in his duchy of Aquitaine, both copying and adapting French regal coinage types.[11] Some of these do not specify that they are of Aquitaine and could possibly have been struck in Calais (it was not the French custom at this period to specify the name of the mint on the coins). Coins unknown to Hewlett, including an écu d'or, are published by Lafaurie as being possibly of Calais.[12]

B. THE ENGLISH PERIOD

The wool staple continued at Bruges until the autumn of 1362,[13] but Parliament discussed the project of making Calais the sole centre of the English wool trade, and on 1 March 1363 the full staple was established there.[14] Henry de Brisele's indenture as master of the Calais mint was dated the same day.[15] His actual appointment was a little earlier, for by a writ dated 20 February 1363 he was discharged from the custody of the Devon mines by reason of the fact that he had been appointed mint master at Calais:[16] the mint accounts at Calais run from this earlier date.[17] Although the mastership of the mint was a crown appointment, the warden of the exchange and the assayer were to be appointed by the mayor and aldermen of Calais with the assent of the governor and treasurer of the town.[18] No record of these latter appointments in 1363 appears to survive, but an exchange was certainly set up, for Adam de Saint Ive, who farmed the exchange in England, on 10 December 1363 was allowed a reduction in his payments because an exchange at Calais had been instituted— and was still being held— shortly after his terms had been agreed on 3 March of the same year.[19] The staff and workers of the Calais mint were granted the same rights and privileges as those in London,[20] and the terms of Henry de Brisele's indenture in respect of the coins he was to strike were identical to those of the master of the London mint.[21]

If, as Spufford happily phrases it, medieval men 'were not entirely convinced that Calais was in England',[22] so too numismatists in the last century, on both sides of the Channel, tended to regard the English type coins of Calais as French and quite separate from the emissions of the undoubted English mints. But the terms of the mint indentures continued to be identical. Dies were supplied from London to Calais. After a few years it became the custom for the same man to hold in plurality the posts of master at both London and Calais, with one to be executed by deputy. Effectively Calais became a branch of the London mint. Progress in the classification of the coins only became possible when it was realised that neither London nor Calais could adequately be studied without constant reference to the other. Indeed, the attribution of the gold coins to their mint of striking only became possible when that was done.

In the early years of this century F. A. Walters published a brilliant series of articles classifying the coins of the later Plantagenet kings, [23] which for the first time brought order to the series. Although in many respects now superseded, they still have a considerable value for every student. A generation later L. A. Lawrence, G. C. Brooke and C. A. Whitton subjected the coins of these kings to minute examination and it is their classifications which are in their essentials used today,[24] together with C. E. Blunt's discerning study of the heavy coins of Henry IV.[25] Much of the work of Lawrence, Brooke and Whitton was concerned in attempts to establish separate distinguishing marks for each three-month period of the pyx trials. More recently W. J. Potter has re-examined virtually all the classifications, and pointed out that in places they had overstrained the evidence in what had been an unnecessary exercise: the mint indentures did not require separate marks for each pyx period, but only for each mint master.[26] Potter's consequent emendations were, however, still constrained to distinguish the emissionsof each king, and relied on Ruding[27] for dates of mint output whereas corrected figures had long been in print.[28] The ambition of virtually all numismatists in all countries and series, to attempt to allocate every individual coin to a particular ruler is seen now to be an unreal goal, for the medieval mind did not work in that way.[29] Still less is it practicable in cases where successive rulers had the same name: with three Henries in succession there was no constraint on the mint officials to mark the change of ruler in any way at all.

Our present system of classifying the coins of Edward III through to Henry VI, although undoubtedly correct in its essentials, requires a complete reappraisal in its minutiæ. A new approach to this has been demonstrated by Miss M. M. Archibald's penetrating remarks which clearly show that study of the sequential use of individual punches is of fundamental importance.[30] The new technique is currently being used to good effect for an earlier coinage,[31] but still awaits a dedicated student to apply it to the later Plantagenets.

The administrative history of the mint and exchange cannot yet be adequately written. Published documents are more extensive than when Walker was writing,[32] but there is overwhelming mass of documentation surviving from the period which will probably never be printed. I, like most numismatists, am not technically equipped to search the bulky rolls and other records. Some fruitful sources are clear: one of the most urgent desiderata is the availability of full transcripts of the mint accounts themselves, which have been quarried by several historians for particular information but which still have much to offer. At this time we cannot certainly compile a complete list of the masters of the Calais mint, and the other officials there are in utter confusion.[33]

The special character of the mint at Calais is evidenced by it striking only gold coin for long periods, and in its last years, by striking enormous quantities of silver and no gold at all. The reason for these fluctuations are political at times, economic at others and usually a combination of both. The recent works of J. H. Munro and T. H. Lloyd discuss these factors in great detail[34] and in the same works they also publish their discoveries of fresh mint output data—which are of vital importance to the numismatist.

Which brings me to perhaps the most important point of this note—and the purpose of the Symposium. Cooperation between historians and numismatists is essential to a full understanding of the administrative history and of the coinage of the Calais mint. Each can provide a service to the other in the understanding of what happened, and why. Neither can produce a definitive study without the aid of the other. The following paragraphs sketch only the broad outlines.

From the mint accounts it is seen that silver coinage was struck only between February 1363 and April 1365, and did not reappear until the next century. It follows that all these coins are of the so-called 'Treaty' issues.[35] Gold coins, however, which had commenced at the same time continued to be struck up to and beyond the resumption of hostilities with France in 1369. The abrogation of the treaty of Bretigny evidently did not lead to an immediate cessation of trade, for gold continued to be brought to the mint at a substantial rate until 1374. This is the more surprising as the staple was removed from Calais in June 1369, and at the same time a ban imposed on direct denizen exports. The staple was returned to Calais in August 1370, however, and Lloyd suggests that the English merchants largely held back their wool in the expectation that the restrictions would soon be lifted:[37] the mint account for the period covers the long period from August 1368 to October 1370 and could well conceal in its totals a temporary drop followed by a recovery. From 1371 tensions grew with Flanders over its right to trade with France, Flemish ships were seized, Flemish citizens were arrested in England and English citizens arrested in Flanders.[38] Because of these difficulties licences were granted to merchants to avoid Calais from 1371, and these continued in 1372 and 1373.[39] It is probable that heavy fines had to be paid to obtain those licences,[40] and the mint accounts of gold purchases are certainly suggestive that, in spite of the difficulties, a large volume of wool still passed through Calais until the beginning of 1374. Thereafter the mint accounts show a much diminished level of activity, dropping away to a figure of £90 face value in the two and a half years ended 7 January 1384, and nothing at all in the next three years. There was a sudden revival of activity in 1387, and output continued thereafter at a modest, but significant, level for the remainder of Richard II's reign.

A factor which undoubtedly had an effect on mint output in the 1390s was the imitation of English gold nobles in Flanders. Complaints were made in England about the introduction of Flemish nobles by Calais merchants, which were said to be worth only 6s.6d. (instead of 6s.8d.) and that three or four were found in every £5 of money (i.e. in 15 nobles).[41] Clearly, if the regulations requiring foreign coin to be taken to the king's mint were not rigorously enforced, there was a profit to be made by introducing the Flemish imitations into England. It has been suggested that the low output of English mints (including Calais) at a time of strong export trade is accounted for by this fact.[42]

On his accession Henry IV reintroduced the regulations for taking gold to Calais instead of the Tower mint in London,[43] and the mint account at Calais for August 1399 to September 1401 shows a sharp increase which may be attributable to this. It soon dropped away again, and after March 1403 the mint was inoperative, not to reopen until 1422, although new appointments of mint masters at London continued to recite that they were also masters of the mints at Calais.[44]

1420 saw for a time the end of conflict in France. The Anglo-Burgundian treaty of Troyes was signed and the king of France recognised Henry V as heir to the French throne. In May 1421 the staple petitioned Parliament for the re-opening of the Calais mint on the grounds that the Treasurer and Victualler of Calais refused to receive payments unless they were in English nobles.[45] At that Parliament it was ordained that a mint should be had within Calais[46] and this was included in the general confirmation of all the statutes concerning money made at the December Parliament of the same year.[47] On 16 May 1422 dies for coining the three denominations of gold and five of silver were issued to the Calais mint.[48] Work on the new coins must have begun very soon after, for the first deliveries of new coin took place on 20 July 1422.[49] Most of the throughput was gold in the first half of the following decade, though there was a reduced output until 1431, when gold production apparently ceased. Silver coin was also struck from 1422, but in only moderate amounts until the reduction in gold virtually coincided with a great increase in the amount of silver. This activity continued through to the early 1430s but then quickly declined. The last traced mint account, in the year ended Michaelmas 1440, is for less than £600 face value. This appears to have been the last issue of the Calais mint. No doubt the final collapse was a reflection of the transfer of the duke of Burgundy's alliance to the king of France, the renewal of hostilities and the reversal of English interests in France.

C. THE UNKNOWN PERIOD

Although the output of coin from the Calais mint came to an end in about 1440, mint and exchange officials still continued to be appointed for over another century. Whether these were sinecures or empty titles is not clear, but is certainly a warning that at other periods in time an appointment does not necessarily mean activity. Recently T. F. Reddaway has, however, drawn to our attention that coin dies were apparently used in the Calais mint in 1539.[50] No coins are known that were struck there at that time.

NOTES

This paper has been entirely rewritten from that delivered at the Symposium. I would like to thank Mr. J. D. Brand who kindly drew some source material to my attention, and has been good enough to read through more than one draft and make valuable suggestions. The remaining imperfections are, of course, my own.

1. The principal general accounts devoted to the mint of Calais are: R. Rudings, Annals of the Coinage 3rd ed. (1840). II. 254-57. L. Deschamps de Pas, 'Etude sur les monnaies de Calais', RBN 39 (1883), 175-224; J. Bailhache 'L'atelier monétaire anglais de Calais (1347-1487)', RN 4e serie 20 (1916), 214-38, and reprinted in translation as 'The English Mint of Calais (1347-

1487)', _Num. Circ_. XXV (1917), 529-48 and XXVI (1918), 37-41; and A. S. Walker, 'The Calais Mint, A.D. 1347-1470', _BNJ_ XVI (1921-22), 77-112.

2. Rymer's _Foedera_ (Record edition), 3i, 140.

3. _Ibid_. 150. William de Salop is here described as 'custos monete'.

4. _Foedera_, 3i, 185.

5. _CCR_, 1349-54, 224.

6. _Ibid_.

7. J. Lafaurie, _Les monnaies des rois de France_, I (1951), 45, type 275.

8. The three readings, are conveniently brought together in F. Poey d'Avant, _Monnaies féodales de France_, III (1862), 379.

9. S. E. Rigold, 'Une trouvaille dans un puits à la cathédrale d'York', _B.S.F.N._ 1978, 394-96.

10. B. Fillon, _Collection J. Rousseau_ (1860), 117, and E. Caron, _Monnaies féodales francaises_, (1882), 378. The coin was apparently not in the Rousseau collection; it was not engraved, and it seems to have been only conjecture on Caron's part that attributed it to an imitation of the last type of _double_ of Philip VI (Lafaurie, _op.cit_., type 272) which was continued as the first type of John II (Lafaurie 329). Fillon gave the reverse reading as _Villa Calesie_—exactly the same as his misreading of the known type mentioned above—and in the absence of any known specimens today one must wonder whether both sides of the coin were misread. Fillon's other allusion to doubles of Calais apparently related to coins which are normally attributed to Aquitaine.

11. See L. M. Hewlett, _Anglo-Gallic Coins_ (1920).

12. Lafaurie, _op.cit_., types 289-291.

13. T. H. Lloyd, _The English Wool Trade in the Middle Ages_ (1977), 210.

14. _Foedera_, 3ii, 690-92.

15. _CCR_ 1360-64, 535-36.

16. _CPR_ 1361-64, 313.

17. See Appendix 1.

18. _Foedera_, 3ii, 692.

19. _CCR_ 1360-64, 495; for the original grant, _CCR_ 1360-64, 516. Walker, _op.cit_., misdated from the same entries the opening of the exchange to 1362.

20. _Foedera_, 3ii, 693.

21. _CCR_ 1360-64, 535-36.

22. See above, p. 172.

23. F. A. Walters, 'Some Remarks on the last Silver Coinage of Edward III', _NC_ 1902, 176-83; 'The Silver Coinage of the Reign of Henry VI', _NC_ 1902,

224-66; 'The Gold Coinage of the Reign of Henry VI', NC 1903, 286-310; 'The Coinage of Richard II', NC 1904, 326-52; 'The Coinage of Henry IV', NC 1905, 247-306; 'The Coinage of Henry V', NC 1906, 172-218; 'An Unpublished Half-groat Probably Attributable to the Heavy Coinage of Henry IV', NC 1907, 120; 'Groats from a Presumed Find in London, NC 1907, 427-33; 'A Find of English Silver Coins in Hampshire', NC 1908, 311-18; 'The Stamford Find and Supplementary Notes on the Coinage of Henry VI', NC 1911, 153-75; and see also the Sale Catalogues of his collections in 1913 and 1932.

24. L. A. Lawrence, 'The Coinage of Edward III from 1351', in NC 1926, 417-67; 1929, 106-68; 1932, 96-174; and 1933, 15-79: his earlier work, 'The Coinage of Henry IV', NC 1905, 83-99 is also of use. G. C. Brooke, 'A Find of Nobles at Horsted Keynes, Sussex', NC 1929, 285-95; 'Privy Marks in the Reign of Henry V', NC 1930, 44-87; 'A Find of Nobles at Borth (Cardiganshire)', NC 1931, 53-61; and English Coins (1932); not forgetting 'A Find of Nobles of Edward III at East Raynham, Norfolk', NC 1911, 291-330. C. A. Whitton, 'A Note on the East Raynham Hoard', BNJ XXII (1934-37), 187-88; 'The Heavy Coinage of Henry VI', BNJ XXIII (1938-41), 59-90, 206-67 and 399-437; 'Some Aspects of English Currency in the Later Middle Ages', BNJ XXIV (1941-44), 36-46; 'A Note on the Post-Treaty Nobles of Edward III', BNJ XXIV (1941-44), 110-12; 'The Heavy Coinage of Henry VI—Addenda and Corrigenda', BNJ XXIV (1941-44), 118-19.

25. C. E. Blunt, 'The Heavy Gold Coinage of Henry IV', BNJ XXIV (1941-44), 22-27; 'Unrecorded Heavy Nobles of Henry IV and Some Remarks on that Issue', BNJ XXXVI (1967), 106-13.

26. W. J. W. Potter, 'The Heavy Groats of Henry VI', BNJ XXVIII (1955-57), 299-311; 'The Silver Coinages of Richard II, Henry IV and Henry V', BNJ XXIX (1958-59), 334-52, and XXX (1960-61), 124-150; 'The Silver Coinage of Edward III from 1351', NC 1960, 137-81, and 1962, 203-24; 'The Gold Coinages of Edward III', NC 1963, 107-28, and 1964, 305-18. Several other scholars have, of course, written on this period.

27. R. Ruding, *op.cit*. 451-2.

28. CPR 1422-29, 337-40 and 519-20 and CPR 1429-36, 256-57 and 258-59.

29. Nor, for that matter, does the modern mint official normally change the name on coins immediately on a change of monarch.

30. See, for example, BNJ XXXVIII (1969), 51, and NC 1967, 135-36.

31. On the coinages of Edwards I and II, for example.

32. Principally the Calendars of Close Rolls for the later part of the period, and the Fine Rolls. No previous writers on the Calais mint appear to have made use of the Summary Calendars of the French Rolls for Henry V and Henry VI which were published as appendices to the Reports of the Deputy Keeper of the Public Records: Henry V in the *44th Annual Report* (1883), 543-638, and Henry VI in the *48th Annual Report* (1887), 217-450.

33. A list of the known masters of the Calais mint is given at Appendix III. There probably are some gaps in the records of the fourteenth century. A note of the masters in the reign of Edward III was given by D. Greaves 'Calais under Edward III' G. Unwin (ed.) Finance and Trade Under Edward III (1918), 350. Masters of the London mint have been discussed by T. F. Reddaway, 'The King's Mint and Exchange in London 1343-1543', English Historical Review LXXXII (1967), 1-23. From 1394 all masters at London were also masters at Calais.

34. J. H. Munro, Wool, Cloth, and Gold: The Struggle for Bullion in Anglo-Burgundian Trade, 1340-1478 (1973). T. H. Lloyd, The English Wool Trade in the Middle Ages (1977) and 'Overseas Trade and the English Money Supply in the Fourteenth Century', in N. J. Mayhew (ed.) Edwardian Monetary Affairs (1279-1344), (1977). I am indebted to both these gentlemen for further information.

35. The gold and large silver coins of Edward III are normally divided into three main groups: 'Pre-Treaty' for those issued prior to the treaty of Bretigny; 'Treaty' for those issued in the period of peace when the title of King of France was dropped by Edward from his coins; and 'Post-Treaty' for those issued after Edward resumed the French title in 1369.

36. Lloyd, The English Wool Trade..., 217.

37. Ibid., 217.

38. Ibid., 218-19.

39. Ibid., 219-20.

40. Ibid., 220.

41. Rolls of Parliament, iii, 470. Dr. Spufford has pointed out that the Flemish nobles were in fact worth only 1 d. less than the English: P. Spufford, 'Continental Coins in Late Medieval Europe', BNJ XXXII (1963), 127-139, particularly p. 130. See also Munro, op.cit., 60.

42. Munro, op.cit., 53-54.

43. Rolls of Parliament, iii, 470.

44. Reddaway, op.cit.

45. Rolls of Parliament, iv, 146.

46. Statutes of the Realm II (1816), 207.

47. Ibid. 210.

48. Proceedings and Ordinances of the Privy Council, ii, 332.

49. CPR 1422-29, 337-40.

50. T. F. Reddaway, 'The English Royal Mint at Calais', BNJ XXXIV (1965), 124-25.

APPENDIX I: Consolidated List of Calais Mint Output from Various Sources

Gold Period of Account		Gold purchased Tower pounds[1]	Equivalent value in coin[2]	Months in period of account[3]	Average Monthly Rate Tower pounds	 Value in coin
20.2.1363	10.4.64	3,529	52,929	13	257	3,849
10.4.64	13.4.65	683	10,248	12	57	854
13.4.65	13.4.66	6,387	95,805	12	532	7,984
13.4.66	20.3.68	7,597	113,960	23¼	327	4,902
20.3.68	27.8.68	607	9,100	5¼	116	1,743
27.8.68	26.10.70	3,462	51,922	26	133	1,997
26.10.70	16.10.71	1,031	15,465	11½	90	1,345
16.10.71	4.11.73	4,672	70,084	24½	191	2,861
4.11.73	16.6.74	609	9,128	7½	82	1,218
16.6.74	4.11.74	124	1,854	4½	28	413
4.11.74	14.7.75	110	1,653	8½	13	194
14.7.75	4.11.75	98	1,469	3½	28	420
4.11.75	15.5.81	1,985	29,769	66½	30	448
15.5.81	7.1.84	6	90	31¾	0.19	2.83
17.1.1387	28.2.88		32,537	13½		2,410
28.2.88	17.1.90	Account missing		22½		
17.1.90	17.1.93		6,618	36		184
17.1.93	17.1.94		22,184	12		1,056
17.1.94	17.10.95		19,680	21		937
17.10.95	18.10.97		10,564	24		440
18.10.97	25.8.99		363	22¼		16
25.8.99	29.9.1401		12,745	25¼		505

(contd.)

APPENDIX I: Consolidated List of Calais Mint Output from Various Sources

Gold		Average Rate Across Michaelmas to Michaelmas Periods[4]				
Period		No. of months	Purchases	Value in Coin	Annual Total	
20.2.1363	29.9.63	7¼	1,861	27,908	27,908	not a full year
30.9.63		6½	1,668	25,021		
	29.9.64	5½	313	4,697	29,718	
30.9.64		6½	370	5,551		
	29.9.65	5½	2,927	43,911	49,462	
30.9.65		6½	3,460	51,894		
	29.9.66	5½	1,797	26,958	78,852	
30.9.66	29.9.67	12	3,921	58,818	58,818	
30.9.67		5¾	1,879	28,184		
		5¼	607	9,100		
	29.9.68	1	133	1,997	39,281	
30.9.68	29.9.69	12	1,598	23,964	23,964	
30.9.69	29.9.70	12	1,598	23,964	23,964	
30.9.70		1	133	1,997		
	29.9.71	11	986	14,793	16,790	
30.9.71		½	45	672		
	29.9.72	11½	2,193	32,897	33,569	
30.9.72	29.9.73	12	2,288	34,326	34,326	
30.9.73		1	191	2,861		
		7½	609	9,128		
	29.9.77	3½	96	1,442	13,431	
30.9.74		1	28	412		
		8½	110	1,653		
	29.9.75	2½	70	1,049	3,114	

(contd.)

APPENDIX I (contd.)

Average Rate Across Michaelmas to Michaelmas Periods[4]

Period		No. of months	Purchases	Value in Coin	Annual Total	
30.9.75		1	28	420		
	29.9.76	11	329	4,924	5,344	
30.9.76	29.9.77	12	358	5,372	5,372	
30.9.77	29.9.78	12	358	5,372	5,372	
30.9.78	29.9.79	12	358	5,372	5,372	
30.9.79	29.9.80	12	358	5,372	5,372	
30.9.80		$7\frac{1}{2}$	224	3,357		
	29.9.81	$4\frac{1}{2}$	1	13	3,370	
30.9.81	29.9.82	12	2	34	34	
30.9.82	29.9.83	12	2	34	34	
30.9.83	7.1.84	$3\frac{1}{4}$	1	9	9	
17.1.87	29.9.87	$8\frac{1}{2}$		20,486	20,486	not a full year
30.9.87		5		12,051		
	29.9.88	7		account missing	12,051	not a full year
30.9.88	29.9.89	12		account missing	-	not a full year
30.9.89		$3\frac{1}{2}$		account missing	-	not a full year
	29.9.90	$8\frac{1}{2}$		1,563	1,563	not a full year
30.9.90	29.9.91	12		2,206	2,206	
30.9.91	29.9.92	12		2,206	2,206	
30.9.92		$3\frac{1}{2}$		643		
	29.9.93	$8\frac{1}{2}$		15,714	16,357	
30.9.93		$3\frac{1}{2}$		6,470		
	29.9.94	$8\frac{1}{2}$		7,965	14,435	

(contd.)

Appendix I (contd.)

Gold Period of Account		Gold purchased Tower pounds[1]	Equivalent value in coin[2]	Months in period of account[3]	Average Monthly Rate: Tower pounds	Average Monthly Rate: Value in coin
29.9.01	30.3.03		2,597	18		144
The figures below are derived from the Pyx trials[5]						
Period[6] ending	Period ending					
20.7.22	30.1.24	3,636	60,612	19	191	3,190
24.2.24	24.12.27	2,135	35,590	46	46	774
20.5.28	2.8.31	361	6,018	$38\frac{1}{2}$	9	156
Totals from 7.1422		6,132	102,220			
Silver						
20.2.63	10.4.64	2,678	3,348	13	195	243
10.4.64	13.4.65	390	488	12	33	41
The figures below are derived from the Pyx trials[5]						
Period[6] ending	Period ending					
20.7.22	18.9.22	959	1,439	say, 3	320	480
31.10.22	28.9.23	4,720	7,080	12	393	590
22.10.23	30.1.24	1,501	2,252	4	375	563
25.2.24	31.1.28	67,745	101,618	48	1,411	2,117
20.2.28	3.8.31	89,660	134,491	42	2,135	3,202
31.10.31	30.9.32	26,183	39,274	14	1,870	2,805
Sub-total from 7.1422		190,768	286,154			
The figures below appear in NC (1911), p. 173.						
10.2.36	30.3.36	1,770	2655.00	$1\frac{1}{2}$		
--39	--40	390	585	?		

APPENDIX I (contd.)

Gold

Silver

Average Rate Across Michaelmas to Michaelmas Periods[4]

Period		No. of months	Purchases	Value in Coin	Annual Total	
30.9.94	29.9.95	12		11,246	11,246	
30.9.95		½		469		
	29.9.96	11½		5,062	5,531	
30.9.96	29.9.97	12		5,282	5,282	
30.9.97		½		220		
	29.9.98	11½		188	408	
30.9.98		10¾		175		
	29.9.99	1¼		631	806	
30.9.99	29.9.1400	12		6,057	6,057	
30.9.1400	29.9.01	12		6,057	6,057	
30.9.01	29.9.02	12		1,731	1,731	
30.9.02	30.3.03	6		866	866	not a full year
The figures below are not derived from the Pyx report						
Approx.						
1.7.22	29.9.22	3	460	7,662		
30.9.22	29.9.23	12	2,360	39,336		
30.9.23	29.9.24	12	1,373	22,889		
30.9.24	29.9.25	12	883	14,723		
30.9.25	29.9.26	12	491	8,191		
30.9.26	29.9.27	12	272	4,539		
30.9.27	29.9.28	12	134	2,230		
30.9.28	29.9.29	12	104	1,727		
30.9.29	29.9.30	12	115	1,920		
30.9.30	29.9.31	12	121	2,020		
Totals from 7.1422			6,313	105,237		

(contd.)

APPENDIX I (contd.)

Silver

Average Rate Across Michaelmas to Michaelmas Periods[4]

Period		No. of months	Purchases	Value in Coin	Annual Total	
20.2.63	29.9.63	$7\frac{1}{4}$	1,412	1,765	1,765	not a full year
30.9.63		$6\frac{1}{2}$	1,268	1,583		
	29.9.64	$5\frac{1}{2}$	179	224	1,807	
30.9.64	13.4.65	$6\frac{1}{2}$	211	264	2,071	not a full year
The figures below are not derived from the Pyx report figures[4]						
about						
1.7.22	29.9.22	3	959	1,439		
30.9.22	29.9.23	12	4,722	7,083		
30.9.23	29.9.24	12	14,003	21,005		
30.9.24	29.9.25	12	18,466	27,699		
30.9.25	29.9.26	12	15,599	23,398		
30.9.26	29.9.27	12	14,250	21,375		
30.9.27	29.9.28	12	17,454	26,181		
30.9.28	29.9.29	12	23,870	35,805		
30.9.29	29.9.30	12	26,525	39,787		
30.9.30	29.9.31	12	30,684	46,026		
30.9.31	29.9.32	12	29,866	44,799		
Sub-totals from 7.1422			196,398	294,597		
30.9.32	29.9.33	12	27,351	41,025		
30.9.33	29.9.34	12	18.091	27,136		
30.9.34	29.9.35	12	13,195	19,793		
30.9.35	29.9.36	12	6,479	9,718		
30.9.38	29.9.39	12	390	585		

NOTES TO APPENDIX I

1. Figures up to 7.1.1384 are derived from Crump and Johnson 'Tables of Bullion Coined under Edward I, II and III' NC 1913, 234-5 (for Calais they included all the amounts they had found for Richard II, as well). Amounts are given here to the nearest whole Tower pound.

2. Coinage equivalents up to 7.1.1384 are calculated from Crump and Johnson's bullion purchased figures. Thereafter they are copied from Lloyd, The English Wool Trade, 271. Amounts given here are in pounds sterling to the nearest whole pound.

3. Calculated to the nearest quarter month.

4. Up to 1403 derived from the figures on p. 192 and 195. After 1422 calculated from Munro Wool, Cloth and Gold 191, 193, 196. It must be emphasized that the presentation of production figures on a 12 month basis, while perhaps convenient for their use by historians, can be misleading for numismatists. This is very well illustrated by the entry in the gold table for the period 15.5.81 to 7.1.84. During that period coin to the value of £90 was struck and in all probability this amount represents one brief burst of activity. It is most unlikely that it was spread evenly over a period of 31 3/4 months as the averaging out process suggests.

5. CPR 1422-29, 337-40 and 519-20; CPR 1429-36, 254-7 and 258-9.

6. The pyx report describes the opening of the 'schinches' into which the samples had been placed and from this it can be seen that a 'schinche' was sealed up approximately every month. Thus the first period ending 20.7.22 implies a start some 4 or 5 weeks earlier. The period ending 24.2.24 would have started after the period ending 30.1.24. There may, however, possibly be a gap in the records in the early months of 1328.

APPENDIX I

SUMMARY OF CONDITIONS RELATING TO THE COINAGE OF GOLD AND SILVER AT LONDON AND CALAIS, 1362

1. Gold

1.1 Gold was struck at 23 ct $3\frac{1}{2}$ grains fine (= 99.48% fine)

1.2 For each Tower pound of gold of correct fineness (worth £15.0.0 in coin) the mint makes:

		£ s. d.
4 oz.	15 nobles of 6s. 8d.	5. 0. 0
6 oz.	45 half nobles of 3s. 4d.	7. 10. 0
2 oz.	30 quarter nobles of 1s. 8d.	2. 10. 0
12 oz.		15. 0. 0

1.3 For each Tower pound of gold brought to the mint:

a. The King receives as seignorage	3. 6
b. The Master receives for production costs	1. 6
c. is issued	14. 15. 0
	£15. 0. 0

2. Silver

2.1 Silver was struck at 11 oz. 2 dwt. fine (= 92.5% fine)

2.2 For each Tower pound of silver of correct fineness (worth £1.5.0 in coin) the mint makes:[2]

3 oz. = 18 groats of 4d	6. 3
4 oz. = 50 half groats of 2d	8. 4
4 oz. = 100 pence	8. 4
1 oz. = 50 half pence	2. 1
12 oz.	£1. 5. 0

2.3 For each Tower pound of silver brought to the mint:

a. The King receives as seignorage	3
b. The Master receives for production costs	7
c. is issued	£1. 4. 2
	1. 5. 0

---

1. CCR, 1360-64, 293-96 and 535.

2. In addition the Calais mint was to coin a further £100 weight per year into farthings (CCR 1360-64, 535). However, no Calais farthings of the 1363-65 coinage are known.

APPENDIX III

SUMMARY OF CONDITIONS RELATING TO THE COINAGE GOLD AND SILVER AT CALAIS, 1422[3]

1. Gold

1.1 Gold was struck at 23 ct $3\frac{1}{2}$ grains fine (=99.48% fine)

1.2 For each Tower pound of gold of correct fineness (worth £16. 13. 4 in coin) the mint makes:

	£ s. d.
8 oz. = 33 1/3 nobles of 6s. 8d =	11. 2. 2 2/3
3 ox. = 25 half nobles of 3s. 4d. =	4. 3. 4
1 oz. = $16\frac{1}{2}$ quarter nobles of 1s. 8d.	1. 7. 9 1/3
12 oz.	£16. 13. 4

1.3 For each Tower pound of gold brought to the mint:

a. the King received as seignorage	3. 6
b. the Master receives for production costs	1. 6
c. is issued	16. 8. 4
	£16. 13. 4

2. Silver

2.1 Silver was struck at 11 oz. 2 dwt fine (= 92.5% fine).

2.2 For each Tower pound of silver of correct fineness (worth £1. 10. 0 in coin) the mint makes:

4 oz. = 30 groats of 4d	10. 0
2 oz. = 30 half groats of 2d	5. 0
3 oz. = 90 pence	7. 6
2 oz. = 120 half pence	5. 0
1 oz. = 120 farthings	2. 6
12 oz.	£1. 10. 0

2.3 For each Tower pound of silver brought to the exchange:

a. the King receives as seignorage	3
b. the Master receives for production costs	9
c. is issued	1. 9. 0
	£1. 10. 0

3. CCR 1419-22, 230-35 and CCR 1422-29, 59-62.

APPENDIX IV

MASTERS OF THE MINT AT CALAIS

	Date of Appointment	Date of Indenture	Other references
Ienry de Brisele	20.2.1363	1.3.1363	
Walter de Barde*	1.4.1364		
Thomas Kyng	1.7.1365		Assay ordered 20.1.1366
Walter de Barde*	25.10.1366		1.7.1367
Bardet de Malepilys	16.5.1371	20.5.1371	
Walter de Barde* (his deputy at Calais was Nanfer Molakyn)			18.12.1393 29.1.1394
John Wildeman*	9.10.1394	9.10.1394	
Nanfre Molakyn*	9.7.1395	9.7.1395	
Walter Merwe*	14.11.1399	1.7.1402	
Richard Garner*	22.2.1409 24.7.1409		
		1412	Imprisoned March 1413
Louis John*	1 and 8.4.1413	14.4.1413 26.7.1421	
Bartholomew Goldbeter*	13.2.1422	13.3.1422	
alias Leman	1.10.1422	16.2.1423	died 1431
William Rus*		8.9.1431	
John Paddesley*		10.7.1434	
Robert Manfelde*		13.12.1445	
	16.12.1451	16.12.1451	

* Also Master of the mint at London.

COINS AND ACCOUNTS IN THE EASTERN NETHERLANDS

H. Enno van Gelder

Introduction

The late medieval monetary history of the County of Holland as well as of Flanders and Brabant, the territories that were eventually united into the Burgundian state of Philip the Good of Burgundy, is relatively well known.

By contrast, developments in the eastern territories of the present Kingdom of the Netherlands, mainly the Bishopric of Utrecht and the Duchy of Guelders, have hardly been investigated. The classification of the extensive coin series in our trays is hampered by an almost complete lack of pertinent archival material: only a handful of scattered ordinances regulating these coinages have been preserved. As a consequence the order of the successive issues remains obscure; neither the exact names of the coins nor their intrinsic and nominal values are known, and we are still far from understanding the monetary policy and its impact on circulation.

It seems, however, that a contribution towards a better understanding of the coinages of the late XIVth and early XVth centuries can be made by utilizing the numerous references to money occurring in the accounts of municipal and other official administrations. Fortunately, extensive and continuous series of such accounts have survived for both Guelders and Utrecht and in recent years many of them have been made available in print, as historians realize the importance of this kind of source for many types of research.

A somewhat discouraging complication which makes these accounts less easy of access is the medieval accounting practice of expressing all amounts of money paid or received in pounds, which are certainly firmly connected with the gold and silver coins actually passed in transactions, but are related to them in a rather intricate way. Therefore, some introductory explanations are necessary of the accounting systems in use in Guelders and Utrecht, before the results of the study of these accounts can be used to explain the nature of the actual coins they are referring to.

As long as the circulation was virtually restricted to one denomination, the silver penny, the notation of larger numbers of pence in pounds and shillings or simply multiples of 240 and 12 pence was quite satisfactory. During the XIVth century, however, two fundamental changes in the coinage, the replacement of the single penny by multiples, of which the *groot* soon became the dominating element in the coinage, and the general, but chronologically as well as geographically extremely uneven debasement of these large silver coins, required drastic adaptations of the traditional system of book-keeping.

The substitution of the penny by the *groot* (plural form: *groten*) as the fundamental unit of the coinage can find its expression in the accounts in three ways. The most simple manner is to choose the *groot* as the unit of the pound-shilling-pence system and write a sum of 240 *groten* as 1 pound *groten*, and 12 *groten* as 1 shilling *groten*. This system was widely used in the western Netherlands where it resulted into the so-called Flemish pound of 240 *groten* (or 6 guilders) surviving until the XVIIIth century, but is hardly ever found in the documents of the territories here under discussion.

It was much more usual there to adhere to former customs and to write 16 pence for 1 *groot*, as practiced in an earlier phase when both denominations circulated side by side and a *groot* represented the same value as 16 pence. This practice continued long after the small pence had disappeared from actual use. Accordingly an amount of 15 *groten* was written as 1 pound (15 x 16 = 240) and the other way round, the pound could be said to consist of 15 *groten*. Of course this definition of the pound could only be used when payments were based on a groot of 16 pence, as in the Arnhem and Zutphen accounts of about 1380. Elsewhere, coins with different values dominated; in the city of Utrecht for instance, the basic coin was the *wit* of 30 pence and therefore an amount of 8 *witten* was written as 1 pound, or in other words, accounts were being kept in pounds of 8 *witten*.

Less usual, but not unknown, is a third kind of adaptation. Sometimes the practical complications of maintaining the traditional pound-shilling-pence notation led accountants to relinquish it altogether and to write down sums of money directly in the actual coins in circulation. From 1392 onwards the municipal accounts of Deventer are kept in (Utrecht) silver plakken and (Guelders) gold *gulden*, evidently the coins dominating then, with a constant relation of 1 gulden = 16 *plakken*. Systems of this kind remained, however, relatively unusual.

Especially the latter kind of accounting could not fail to break down as soon as debasement of either the gold or the silver coin or of both of them changed the relation of their respective values. Within a few years at Deventer the actual gold *gulden* came to fetch a higher number of silver *plakken*. Nevertheless, the once established custom of writing a sum of 16 plakken as 1 *gulden* persisted, with the result that the reader of the accounts has to be aware of a dual meaning of the word *gulden*: it can either be the accounting device for writing down an amount of 16 *plakken*, or the name of the actual coin worth for instance 20 *plakken* and written down in the language of the account as 1 *gulden* 4 *plakken*.

It is more difficult to visualize the effects of the debasement of the silver coins on the notations in pound-shilling-pence systems, especially because all kinds of obligations implying the payment of certain amounts of silver coins used to be formulated in pounds etc. After each debasement the discharging of an obligation of say 1 pound by the payment of 15 *groten* meant a loss to the recipient, as he received coins of less metal content than he had expected to get. The simple remedy was to require for the pound due to him, instead of 15 good old *groten*, 18 of the new ones of lesser quality. In terms of accounting practice this meant that a pound (of 15 *groten* as they should be, but were not any longer) was computed at 18 *groten* (as they actually were available in circulation). Stipulations like "the pound computed at 18 *groten*" are as a matter of common occurrence in contracts of various kinds.

In some cases, as in the municipal accounts of Zutphen, adaptation of the current value of the pound to the debasement of the silver money, took place regularly: the heading of each account mentions the value of the pound for the current administrative year. Elsewhere, the practice was much more desultory and adaptation of the pound was made only at irregular intervals. Other administrations did not manipulate the basic unit of their accounts at all: in those cases the pound remained always the same multiple of the silver coin and its metal value dwindled to a mere fraction of what it once represented. Of course, other means, outside the sphere of book-keeping, were found to compensate for the disastrous effects of debasement.

In any case, these adaptations lead to the result that the forms of writing down single items and totals of the accounts are extremely confusing for the modern reader. The same payment may be noted in a quite different wording in accounts of neighbouring towns; the same gold coins may be accounted for by widely divergent notations in pounds and shillings (tables 1 and 2).

Table 1. Different notations for 1 Rhine gulden in 1402

Arnhem	5 £ parva moneta	value 75 Guelders groten
Zutphen	2 £ 7 s. 5 d.	
Deventer	1 gulden 19 plakken	value 43 Overijssel plakken
Utrecht (chapter)	6 £ 7 s. 6 d.	value 51 Utrecht witten
Utrecht (city)	3 £ 8 s. 2 d.	

Table 2. Notations for 1 Rhine gulden in different kinds of money of account

	Zutphen	Utrecht (chapter)	Deventer
	pounds of a changing number of groten	pound of a fixed number of witten	guldens of a fixed number of plakken
1390	2 £ 10 s.	4 £ 7 s. 6 d.	-
1400	2 £ 1 s.	6 £ 4 s. 6 d.	1 gulden 17½ plak
1410	2 £ 4 s. 2 d.	6 £ 17 s. 6 d.	1 gulden 20 plak
1420	2 £ 3 s. 6 d.	8 £ 5 s.	2 gulden 12 plak
1430	2 £ 8 s.	15 £	4 gulden 4 plak

Although these adaptations of the value of the accounting pounds in terms of current silver coins were undoubtedly caused by the concern to maintain the value of the pound, there is not any reason to assume that the authorities responsible ever succeeded in linking the value of their pounds correctly to quantities of precious metal. Therefore, even the most regularly adjusted pounds cannot be used as a measure for the depreciation of the current coins nor as a basis for reconstructing the history of the issues. Sums expressed in pounds should not only be converted to amounts of actual coins—which is possible as soon as the value of the pound assumed in a document is known—but it is also necessary to look for a common denominator outside the local coinage systems.

This may be found in the international gold coins circulating in the Netherlands, which were not affected by the monetary measures of the local authorities. For the XIVth century the gold ecu of France serves this purpose very well, but during the period under discussion the still frequent references to these ecus as good old schild must be viewed with suspicion, and it is clear that there were hardly any actual ecus in circulation and the word, in most cases, seems rather to have been used in a conventional sense. It is certainly safer to rely on references to the Rhine gulden, currently produced in large quantities by the four Electors on the Rhine and circulating abundantly in the eastern Netherlands.

Rhine guldens are mentioned in almost every account and it is possible, after converting the values given in pounds or gulden of account into silver groten, to construe tables of yearly rates of the Rhine gulden in terms of the local silver money. In this way a fairly accurate measure can be found for the rate of debasement of the silver coins put into circulation in Guelders and Utrecht which can serve as a compensation for the almost complete lack of direct evidence concerning these coinages. In the same way figures for the relation between the locally produced gold coins and both the Rhine gulden and the silver coins may be found, although these are less complete. The available evidence is provisionally presented below both in tables for selected years (Tables 3-4) and in simplified graphs. For the sake of accuracy a proviso should be added. The slight lowering of the alloy of the gulden of the Electors, especially in the years 1409-1419, could not be taken into account; this seems, however, an unimportant distortion in view of the many times stronger debasement of the local gold and silver coins.

Coins: Guelders (ca. 1390-1445)

The development of the coinage of the Dukes of Guelders can be checked against the continuous and parallel series of data provided by the municipal accounts of the towns of Arnhem and Zutphen from about 1390 onwards.

During the last decade of the XIVth century, the latter part of the reign of Duke William I (1371-1402), the valuations to be found in these accounts show several significant changes. The value of the Rhine gulden expressed in silver groten rises continually and by 1402 had reached 200% of its 1390 quotation. In the same texts a new Guelders gulden is mentioned with a fixed value of 31½ silver groot. At the same time the value of the pound used in the Zutphen accounts rises progressively from 15 to 31 silver groten, whereas in Arnhem side by side with a light pound of the fixed value of 15 groten a heavy pound is used which climbs from 15 to 24 groten.

All this seems to imply that the intrinsic value of both the silver groot and the Wilhelmus-gulden struck by the Duke decreased at approximately the same pace to about 50% of their former level. This debasement is also referred to in numerous complaints about the increasingly bad quality of Guelders coins emanating from the authorities in Holland and Utrecht. Moreover, it is in accordance with the evidence of the coins of the period themselves. The striking of the silver groten, introduced in 1390, ceased within a few years and they were replaced by double groten of visibly lower alloy; the alloy of the gold Wilhelmus-gulden, clearly distinguished from the Rhine gulden by its

Table 3. Rates in groten of some gold coins from the municipal accounts of Zutphen

	Rhine gulden	Guelders gulden	Arnhem gulden	Value of pound
1390	(35)	(32)		15
1395		31½		20½
1400	(68)	31½		26
1405	81	45		34
1410	100	54		46
1415	132	64	(128)	62
1420	200	100	176	100
1425	260		200	114
1430	336		224	140
1435	432		240	184
1440	608		328	272
1445	800		432	320

All figures have been reduced to groten; in fact, they are quoted in copperts= 4 groten from about 1410, in kromstaarten of 16 groten from about 1430.

type, was lowered according to a money-changers' note preserved by chance from 20 to less than 14 carats. This confirmation of the conclusions drawn from the municipal accounts by independent scraps of evidence gives some confidence that for later periods, where other types of evidence are hardly available, these accounts may be used as a main source for the reconstruction of monetary politics.

For the next reign of Reinald IV (1402-1423), only a single monetary regulation has survived and it dated from the very first months of his reign. The Duke had decided to put an end to the inflationary issues of the previous reign and ordered to strike a gold gulden of the full value of the Rhine gulden as well as silver coins of 4 groten, which, by the way, were to have only twice the silver content of the single groot of 1390. However, both the surviving coins of Reinald IV and the accounts of the period clearly show that the stabilizing of the Guelders money at the 1402 level was not achieved at all. Although new gold guldens were struck which exactly reproduced the type of the latest gulden issued by the Rhenish Electors in 1399, these evidently did not maintain the intrinsic value of their prototypes: within a few years the municipal accounts are differentiating between true Rhine gulden and Arnhem Rhine gulden, assigning to the latter an increasingly lower value in silver groten; later on they even have to distinguish a new Arnhem Rhine gulden as less valuable than the older ones. Again the alloy of the gold coins struck in the name of Duke Reinald in the Arnhem mint must have been decreased from time to time in the same way as during the reign of Duke William. The new silver coins of 4 groten, which are called coppert in Zutphen, blenk in Arnhem and meeuw in Nijmegen, were struck abundantly. But the silver content prescribed in 1402 was not maintained either: analysis of preserved specimens has given a

I ZUTPHEN: value of gold coins in groten

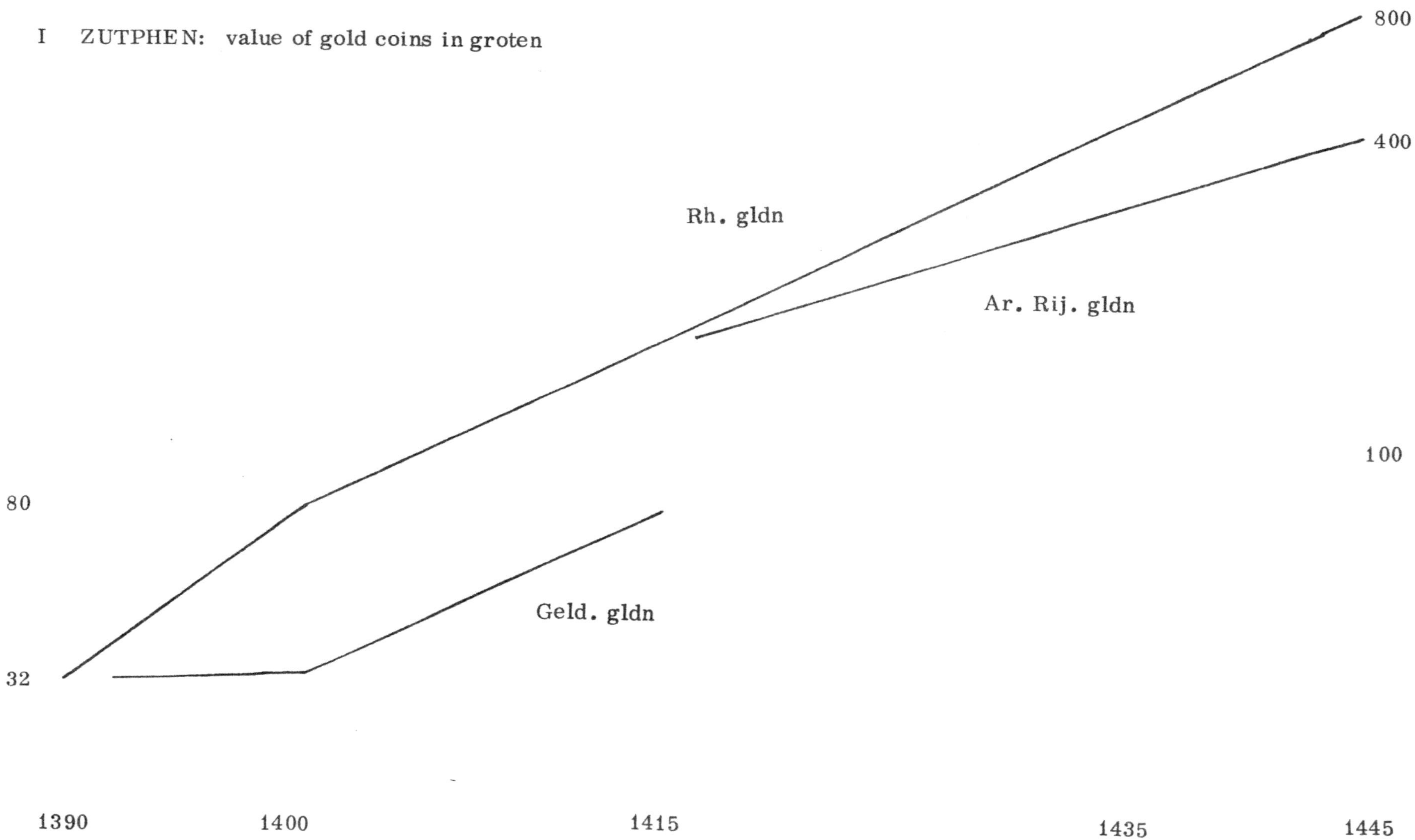

much lower alloy than expected and, moreover, the valuation of Guelders silver money in terms of the *Rhine gulden* in the municipal accounts continues to decrease virtually at the same pace as during the former reign. Towards the end of the reign the number of groten equivalent to a *Rhine gulden* is doubled again, that is to say the intrinsic value of the silver coins is gradually lowered to about 50%. The introduction of a new type somewhere in the 1410s, according to the Zutphen accounts issued at a nominal value of 6 *groten*, was only a further step in the process of debasement of the coinage.

For the long reign of Duke Arnold (1423-1473) regulations concerning the coinage are completely lacking. On the other hand a bewildering variety of types both of gold *gulden* and of silver coins has survived. From hoard evidence it appears that most of these types were put into circulation during the first 20 years of the reign. The striking of gold *guldens* of exactly the same type as the debased Arnhem *gulden* of Duke Reinald, but of a still lower gold content, must have been extremely abundant; not only do they seem to have dominated the circulation within the Duchy, but they were also widely used in the neighbouring territories where they remained, under the name of *Arnhem gulden*, *Arnoldus gulden*, *Arendsgulden*, the most frequently mentioned single gold coin for more than half a century. On the other hand, the several issues of silver coins, which must have succeeded each other at remarkably short intervals, have left hardly any traces in the accounts of either the Guelders towns or the neighbouring territories. It is clear especially from the Zutphen accounts that the recent ducal silver coins with presumably frequent changes of silver content and nominal value did no longer provide a workable basis for monetary transactions. About 1430 the Zutphen pound as unit of accounting is no longer defined in terms of Guelders silver money as it invariably used to be for several decades, but in terms of foreign silver coins. After a short period of hesitation the Zutphen pound is usually defined as a multiple of the *kromstaart*, the silver coin which Duke Philip of Burgundy as Count of Flanders struck in such enormous quantities from about 1425 onwards that for a few years it dominated most hoards in Guelders as well as elsewhere.

However, the preponderance of the references to *kromstaarten* in the accounts continues much longer than the effective circulation of the Flanders coins of this name, which were replaced from 1434 onwards by the new uniform coinage of the Burgundian Netherlands. Indeed, a few years later the Zutphen accounts distinguish unambiguously between the kromstaart as unit of account with a fixed value of 16 *groten* money of account on the one hand and the real Flanders *kromstaart* valued at 24 *groten* in 1444 and more in later years. The explanation must be that at this moment two different coins were called *kromstaart*: the Flemish silver piece and a local coin which could serve as a basis for the Zutphen accounting system. The latter can only be a silver coin struck by Duke Arnold which must at first have been at least nominally equivalent to the Flemish prototype, but as a result of further debasement became gradually distinct from it. As a matter of fact, one of the early silver coins struck in the name of Arnold shows a type clearly derived from the Flemish *kromstaart* and may be identified as the Guelders *kromstaart* introduced some time before 1435 and leading a separate existence from its homonymous prototype. In fact, the temporary linking of the Guelders silver coinage to that of Flanders did not succeed in stabilizing the Guelders money. The continually rising quotations of the Rhine gulden in terms of Guelders groten prove that the rate of debasement caused by both the large issues of gold Arnoldus gulden and of silver coins of presumably changing nominal values remained the same.

From the interpretation of the monetary references in the municipal accounts it appears that, notwithstanding the obvious similarity of the gold coins of the Dukes Reinald IV and Arnold and the unchanging weight of about 3 grams of the silver coins, the Guelders coinage of this period was characterized by a continuous deterioration which halved the intrinsic value of Guelders money once in every generation.

Coins: Utrecht (ca. 1390-1445)

The secular territories of the Bishops of Utrecht consisted of two parts separated by the Duchy of Guelders. Their connection in institutional and economic as well as monetary respects was rather loose. During the period under discussion the episcopal coins were struck almost exclusively in the eastern part, Overijssel, which for purposes of monetary history can be regarded almost as an independent territory. Here, the very extensive and complete series of municipal accounts of Deventer are as useful a source as those of Zutphen and Arnhem for Guelders.

Table 4. Rates in plakken of some gold coins from the municipal accounts of Deventer

	Rhine gulden	Guelders gulden	Arnhem gulden	Value of pound
1390	20			
1395	24	20		16
1400	41½	23		24
1405				24
1410	44			24
1415	51		49	24
1420	60		52	24
1425	75		56	24
1430	100		60	24
1435	120		60	
1440	122		60	
1445	128		60	

All figures have been reduced to plakken; towards the end of the period they are usually quoted in kromstaarten of about 4 plakken.

The dominant coin of the reign of Bishop Floris (1378-1393) was the silver plak of 2 groten. It formed the basis of the Deventer accounting unit, the pound of 10 plakken, replaced since 1392 by a gulden of account of 16 plakken. From references to the value of the Rhine gulden and of the frequently cited Guelders gulden it appears that in the 1390s the value of the money of Overijssel and that

II DEVENTER: value of gold coins in plakken

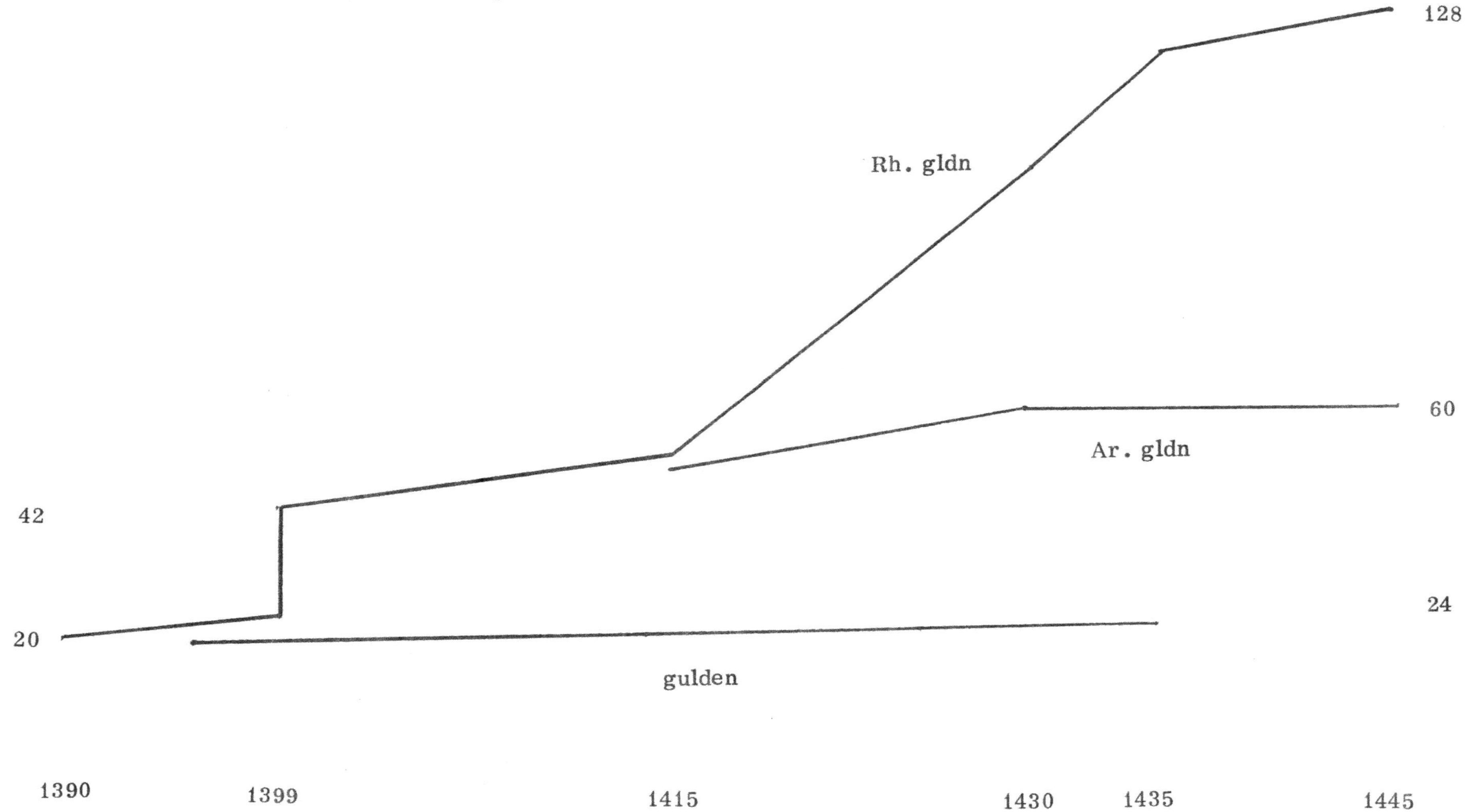

of Guelders was, notwithstanding the different manner of bookkeeping, essentially the same.

Early in the next reign, that of Bishop Frederick (1393-1423), however, they begin to diverge. Within a few years he introduced a new silver coin of the nominal value of 2 plakken, which continued to be struck almost to the end of his long reign. The intrinsic value of these new coins must have been appreciably less than twice that of the former single plak. Already in 1399 the Deventer as well as the Zwolle accounts show a change in the unit of account: the gulden is no longer reckoned at 16, but at 24 plakken, that is to say 12 new double plakken were considered to be equal to 16 old plakken. Although the accounting unit was maintained without change for the remainder of the reign, the steady rising of the quotations for Rhine gulden show that the quality of the silver coins deteriorated further, although their types remained unchanged. The rate of debasement, however, was much less than in neighbouring Guelders: during the first quarter of the XVth century it fell only about 25%, against 50% in Guelders. Moreover, the silver coinage was not accompanied by an abundant striking of gold coins. On the contrary, the Deventer accounts hardly ever mention Utrecht gold coins, but very frequently the steadily debasing Arnhem gulden. It appears that the policy of the Deventer mint was less aimed at enhancing the volume of coinage with a view to a large income from seignoriage than the Arnhem establishment.

After the death of Bishop Frederick the see of Utrecht was disputed by two rival claimants for some years. Bishop Rudolf (1423-1454), whose base was Overijssel, was eventually successful, but the schism certainly was an additional cause for monetary confusion. In the same way as in Guelders the local silver coins lost their usefulness as a basis for accounting purposes and for a decade the Deventer gulden of account was preferably defined in terms of the Flemish kromstaart. Only when Rudolf after some years was firmly established, did his rather voluminous issues of new coins, both in gold and silver, restore the equilibrium. His gold so-called postulaatguldens are often mentioned in the Deventer accounts after almost half a century of predominance of Guelders gold; his new silver coins of 4 plakken provide the basis for the unit of account. After 1437 the Deventer pound is defined as equal to four of these new coins instead of 16 plakken. At the same time, it appears that this coin (its specific name is not transmitted in the sources) had the same value as the Flemish kromstaart. Within a few years the latter name was applied to both coins indiscriminately and it remained in use for more than a century. However, unlike the development in Guelders, a dichotomy between the original Flanders kromstaart and the further debased local kromstaart did not occur here, as the Deventer coins did not deteriorate further and maintained a higher value than their Guelders namesakes.

As stated above, the monetary development in the western part of the Bishopric, centered around the city of Utrecht, was quite distinct from that in Overijssel. Unfortunately, the sources are much scarcer. A number of accounts of the municipal administration of Utrecht are available, but they do not form a continuous series; neither are the accounts of the Cathedral chapter sufficiently complete for this period. Moreover, the coins themselves are not a great help, as for most of the time coinage ceased altogether at the western episcopal mints.

III Value of Rhine gulden in three territories

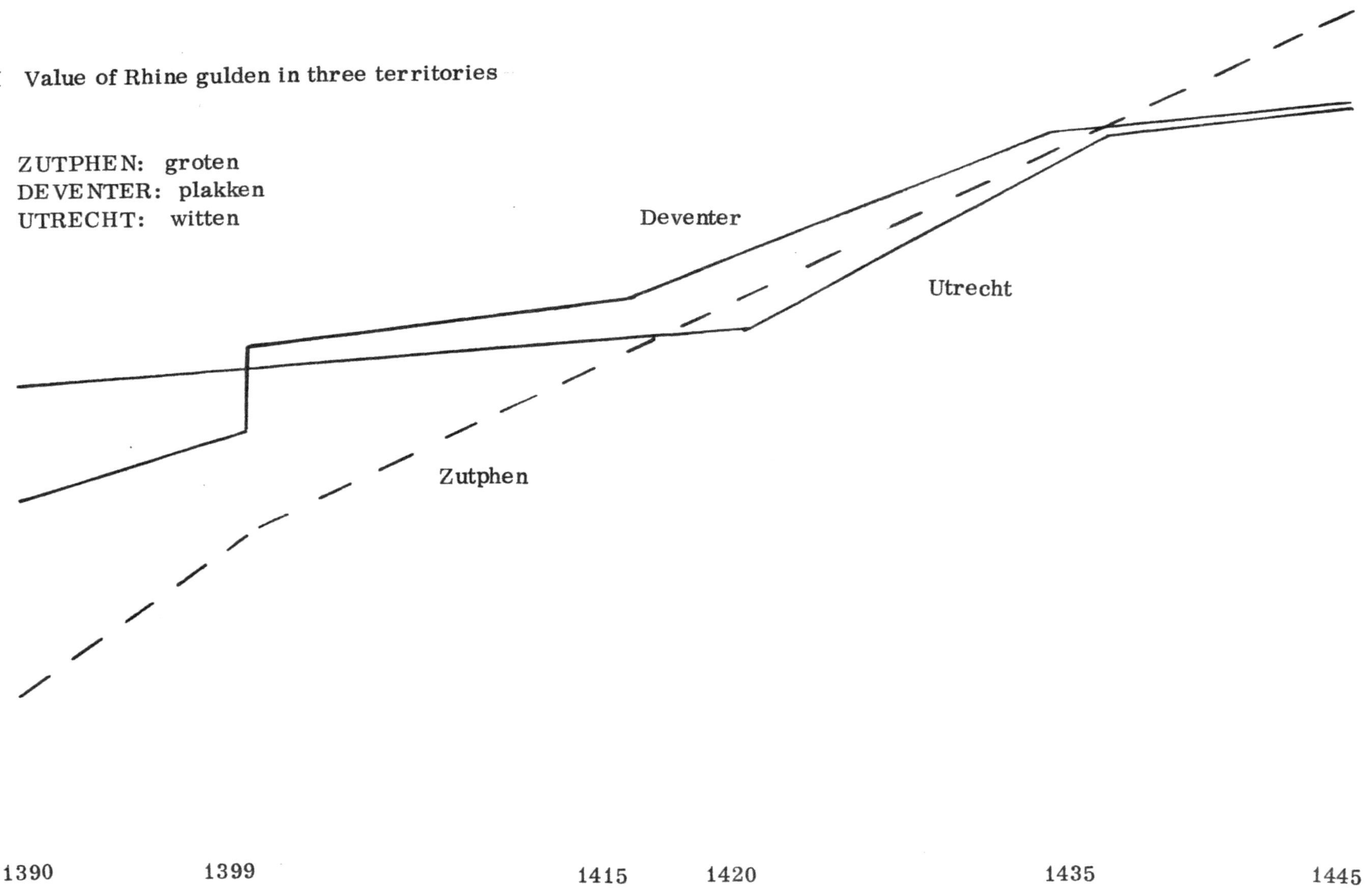

From the fragmentary accounts it is clear that the basis of the different accounting systems of both clerical and municipal administration was a silver coin called *wit* (plural: *witten*). In origin this was undoubtedly the silver *groot* of the Counts of Holland whose territories encirled Utrecht and its countryside. During the first quarter of the XVth century the values of foreign gold coins expressed in Utrecht *witten* show only a slight decline, less pronounced still than in Overijssel and not very different from the rate of decline which can be deduced for Holland itself from the official valuations published by the Counts. Taking into account the absence of any local coinage, one must conclude that Holland money must have dominated the circulation in Utrecht and that the episcopal issues from Overijssel had hardly any impact on this part of his territories.

Only in the very last years of Bishop Frederic, and more pronouncedly during the schism following his death and the sole reign of Rudolf, did matters change fundamentally. The incorporation of Holland into the Burgundian state and the subsequent introduction of a revaluated Burgundian coinage, does not seem to have affected the Utrecht territory. On the contrary, the restricted coin issues as well as the steep decline of the value of the Utrecht monies of account point to a new orientation, a severance of the connections with now Burgundian Holland and an assimilation to the eastern neighbours. The *wit* looses its position as a basic coin and is replaced by the *kromstaart*, now equal to 6 witten. The values attributed in the Utrecht accounts to the *Rhine gulden* and other foreign coins prove that the *kromstaart* used here was the same as the Flanders and Deventer *kromstaart*, used in Overijssel.

Bibliography

Printed editions of accounts:

De stadsrekeningen van Arnhem, ed. W. Jappe Alberts, 3 volumes (1352-1420), Groningen 1967-1971.

De stadsrekeningen van Zutphen, ed. R. Wartena, 3 volumes (1364/5-1445/6) Zutphen 1977.

De cameraarsrekeningen van Deventer, ed. J. J. van Doorninck e.a., 7 volumes (1337-1393), Deventer 1887-1914.

De cameraarsrekeningen van Deventer, ed. J. J. van Doorninck e.a., 7 volumes (1337-1393), Deventer 1887-1914.

De stadsrekeningen van Deventer, ed. G. M. de Meyer, 4 volumes (1394-1424), Groningen 1968-1976.

Bronnen tot de bouwgeschiedenis van den Dom te Utrecht, ed. N. B. Tenhaeff; W. Jappe Alberts, 3 volumes (1395-1528/9), 's-Gravenhage 1946-1976.

Some papers on money of account:

F. Ketner and N. B. Tenhaeff, Bijdrage tot de kennis van de Utrechtsche rekenmunten, *Tijdschrift voor Geschiedenis* 49, 1934, pp. 445-476.

N. W. Posthumus, *Nederlandse prijsgeschiedenis*, Vol. II, Leiden 1964, pp. xli-xlix and 12-30.

G. M. de Meyer, in _De stadsrekeningen van Deventer_, Vol. I, Groningen 1968, pp. xliii-lvi.

R. Wartena, Het Zutphens pond en de val van de groot, _Ondernemende Geschiedenis_, 's-Gravenhage 1977, pp. 33-49.

D. E. H. de Boer, _Graaf en grafiek_, Leiden 1978, pp. 169-190.

Principal coins referred to in the text:

Guelders (P. O. van der Chijs, _De munten der graven en hertogen van Gelderland_, Haarlem 1852).

William I	Guelders gulden, Wilhelmusgulden	vdC	6, 1
	single groot (ca. 1390)		7, 12 and 13
	double groot (ca. 1396)		8, 4
Reinald IV	Arnhem (Rhine) gulden, Reinaldus gulden		8, 3
	four groten (from 1402)		9, 7 and 8
	six groten (ca. 1417)		9, 14
Arnold	Arnhem gulden, Arnoldgulden		10, 3
	Guelders kromstaart		10, 13

Overijssel (P. O. van der Chijs, _De munten der bisschoppen van Utrecht_, Haarlem 1859).

Floris	single plak	vdC	12, 5
Frederick	double plak		13, 6; 14, 14
Rudolf	postulaatgulden, Rudolfgulden		15, 1
	four plakken		15, 3

www.ingramcontent.com/pod-product-compliance
Lightning Source LLC
LaVergne TN
LVHW071207210926
848482LV00015B/739